Peace Building in Northern Ireland, Israel and South Africa

Transition, Transformation and Reconciliation

Colin Knox
Professor of Public Policy
University of Ulster
Jordanstown
Northern Ireland

and

Pádraic Quirk
Community Relations Unit
Office of the First Minister and Deputy First Minister
Belfast
Northern Ireland

Published by PALGRAVE MACMILLAN
Houndmills, Basingstoke, Hampshire RG21 6XS and
175 Fifth Avenue, New York, N.Y. 10010
Companies and representatives throughout the world

PALGRAVE MACMILLAN is the global academic imprint of the Palgrave
Macmillan division of St. Martin's Press, LLC and of Palgrave Macmillan Ltd.
Macmillan® is a registered trademark in the United States, United Kingdom
and other countries. Palgrave is a registered trademark in the European
Union and other countries.

Outside North America
ISBN 0–333–68189–4

In North America
ISBN 0–312–23410–4

This book is printed on paper suitable for recycling and
made from fully managed and sustained forest sources.

A catalogue record for this book is available from the British Library.

Library of Congress Catalog Card Number: 00–023765

Transferred to digital printing 2003

Printed and bound in Great Britain by
Antony Rowe Ltd, Chippenham and Eastbourne

To Jenny and Ryan

Contents

Series Editors' Foreword

Peace Building in Northern Ireland, Israel and South Africa by Colin Knox and Pádraic Quirk

This new book on 'peace building' is one of a series of books on ethnic and intercommunity conflict. The phrase 'peace building' is itself an indication of the present, cautiously and relatively optimistic state of affairs in relation to some aspects and some examples of ethnic conflict. The three case-studies presented in the book, that is South Africa, Israel and Northern Ireland, are obvious (and common) choices in relation to such an idea as 'peace building' because in each of the three the process of change has reached a level of sophistication within which peace can at least be contemplated. The notion, however, that any of these three conflicts are solved is, the authors argue, premature and begs a great many questions.

The book is original and insightful in the way in which it combined macro and micro approaches to the study of the evolution of 'peace contexts' in each of the three regions. This approach is based on a hierarchical understanding of how peace is constructed by politicians, and the construction of a model of change, proposed by Lederach. However, in the working out of the detail and the reality the work adds body and complexity to abstract terms such as transition and transformation. The differences in emphases, and in maturity of development in relation to particular issues (such as separation and integration) are carefully thought through.

Although there already exists a considerable literature on each of these three conflicts; and an emergent comparative literature in relation both to these and other conflicts, this book represents a considerable practical and theoretical advance on much of what is available. It makes an important contribution to thinking about the universality of conflict and wide range of social transitions and transformations necessary to produce new functional societies, and their complex interactions and interrelationships.

Seamus Dunn
Valerie Morgan

Acknowledgements

The authors wish to acknowledge the invaluable insights provided by the many people who gave willingly of their time to be interviewed for the research in this book. Our interest in this area was initially stimulated through working with colleagues in the Centre for Study of Conflict. We thank in particular Professor Seamus Dunn and Professor John Darby for their moral and intellectual support.

1
The Comparative Context for Peace Building

Introduction

It may appear facile to suggest comparisons exist between three countries so obviously different in their social, geo-political and economic characteristics as Northern Ireland, Israel and South Africa. One obvious similarity is that all three countries are, to a greater or lesser extent, 'coming out of conflict' and, as a consequence, merit academic enquiry to uncover common characteristics which could promote peace building policy learning both within and between Northern Ireland, Israel and South Africa and, more generally, in other conflict zones. There are, however, different views on the validity of this approach. Giliomee (1990: 1–2), for example, argues that there is an abundance of individual studies about the three countries and a public perception that a common thread runs through the 'troubles' in Ulster, the 'unrest' in South Africa and the 'intifada' in the occupied territories, but 'with notable exceptions, scholars have been curiously reluctant to embark on systematic comparisons which aim at drawing conclusions by viewing South Africa, Northern Ireland and Israel together'. Cedric Thornberry (1998: 12), former Assistant Secretary-General of the United Nations, on the other hand, argues that whilst analogy can be helpful, one must beware of drawing close parallels between situations. 'This is why I am sometimes a little sceptical about some academic work in the field of conflict resolution. However well-intentioned, it can get a bit far from reality through failing to focus on what is unique in every situation'.

The theoretical basis for comparing these three countries is, however, best made by Walker Connor (1990). He begins by suggesting that the *conventional* treatments of Israel, Northern Ireland and South Africa

1

have, in fact, nothing in common. Northern Ireland, for example, has been described as a religious struggle between Catholics and Protestants, South Africa as a racial confrontation between blacks and whites, and Israel as an inter-ethnic conflict between Jews and Palestinians. In fact, he asserts, what is significant for comparative purposes is that all three cases are predicated upon fundamental differences over national identity or *ethno-national* dimensions. An ethnic group has been defined by Cashmore (1995: 102) as 'a group possessing some degree of coherence and solidarity composed of people who are, at least latently, aware of having common origins and interests'. Once the consciousness of being part of an ethnic group is created then distinct languages, religious beliefs and political institutions become part of that ethnicity. The fundamental conflicts therefore in all three countries is, according to Connor, between ethnic groups over national identity. This is substantiated in each of the three case-study countries. Oliver Tambo was unambiguous about the position of the ANC: 'this is not a civil rights struggle at all ... our struggle is basically, essentially, fundamentally a national liberation struggle'. Nusseibeh makes the same point about the Palestinian situation: 'the Palestinian struggle is not a civil rights struggle. It has always been a national struggle, and the movement that represents it is a national movement. The majority of the Palestinian population who created and been active in the Palestinian resistance are people who have been nationally and territorially dispossessed' (both cited in Giliomee, 1990). In the same vein, McGarry and O'Leary (1995) argue that the conflict in Northern Ireland is ethno-national:

> a systematic quarrel between the political organisations of two communities who want their state to be ruled by their nation, or who want what they perceive as 'their' state to protect their nation. Ethnic communities are perceived kinship groups. Their members share history and common culture, and in specific situations such communities are prone to competition and antagonistic conflict, especially when such conflict has a national character ... Explosive national conflicts arise between politically mobilised ethnic communities. Territory, sovereignty and national esteem are their media. Land, power, and recognition are their bloody issues. Northern Ireland has been the site of such ethno-conflict.
>
> (McGarry and O'Leary, 1995: 354–5)

There is, therefore, some validity in making such a comparison based upon the ethno-national roots of the conflicts. The comparative task of analysing peace building is, however, an ambitious one. The premise, for example, that all three countries have now 'solved' or, at the very least, are emerging from their conflicts and are actively involved in a peace building process is, of course, questionable. There can be no doubt that significant and positive developments towards the resolution of conflict have taken place in Northern Ireland, Israel and South Africa but a fragility exists which should caution against claims that either individually or collectively all three areas provide the basis of a generic model for peace building. We consider, in turn, recent events in all three countries to appreciate their tenuous grasp on peace and the potential for civil unrest or a return to political violence.

Northern Ireland: the Belfast Agreement

In Northern Ireland there is a cautious optimism following the Good Friday Agreement (10 April 1998) and its subsequent endorsement in a 'peace referendum' by its electorate (71.2 per cent) and voters in the Irish Republic (94 per cent). The former Secretary of State for Northern Ireland, Mo Mowlam, described it in the House of Commons as follows:

> The Agreement reached on Good Friday could be a significant turning point in the history of Northern Ireland. It could herald in a new era of peaceful coexistence and constructive co-operation. But let's have no illusions. It will take a long time to repair the physical and emotional damage of the past and bring about a sense of reconciliation and partnership.
>
> (Northern Ireland Secretary of State's statement
> to the House of Commons: 20 April 1998)

In the Agreement the British and Irish Governments formally resolved their historical differences through the general and mutual acceptance of the principle of consent – Northern Ireland is part of the United Kingdom, and will remain so, as long as a majority wishes. If the people of Northern Ireland were formally to consent to the establishment of a United Ireland, the government of the day would bring forward proposals, in consultation with the Irish Government, to give effect to that wish. The Irish Government has amended the Irish Constitution to bring it into line with this understanding, and the necessary changes have been made to Northern Ireland constitutional legislation (articles 2 and 3 of the Irish Constitution were updated when power was devolved to the Northern Ireland Assembly). Power was devolved (December

1999) to a locally elected (June 1998) Northern Ireland Assembly with a wide range of executive and legislative powers. Posts of executive authority are shared on a proportional basis (the d'Hondt system) and safeguards are in place to protect the interests of both main parts of the community (parallel consent). There is a North/South (Northern Ireland and the Irish Republic) Ministerial Council bringing together those with executive authority to work together by agreement on matters of mutual interest. This is paralleled by a British-Irish Council bringing together devolved administrations in Northern Ireland, Scotland and Wales. The Agreement also includes a range of measures designed to create a 'normal and peaceful society in Northern Ireland'. The most significant of these are:

Prisoners: Under the existing early release scheme, set up in 1995, determinate sentence prisoners were entitled to automatic release at the half way point of sentence. The Agreement allows automatic release at the one-third point[1] and is implemented through a new Sentence Review Body. Those prisoners who belong to organisations which have not declared and are not maintaining unequivocal cease-fires will not be considered for release. Prisoners who qualify will be released on licence and returned to prison if they engage in any further terrorist activity. As a political counterbalance a Victims' Commission has reported on ways to 'recognise the pain and suffering felt by victims of violence arising from the troubles of the last 30 years, including those who have died or been injured in the service of the community' (Bloomfield Report, April 1998: 6).

Decommissioning: Both the British and Irish Governments have taken steps to facilitate the decommissioning process through a Decommissioning Scheme in Northern Ireland and Regulations in the Republic. Participants in the Agreement committed themselves to a total disarmament of all paramilitary organisations by working with the independent International Body on Decommissioning. The objective is to achieve either the provision of information to the Commission leading to the collection and destruction of arms and/or the destruction of arms by persons in possession of them by May 2000.

Policing and criminal justice: Parallel reviews of the policing service and criminal justice systems have been established. The former is an Independent Commission (chaired by Chris Patten, ex-Governor of Hong Kong and minister in Northern Ireland) set up to consider what kind of policing service would be appropriate in Northern Ireland devoid of violence. The latter is a government-led review, with external assessors, which will address the structure, management and resourcing of the criminal justice system to include appointments to the judiciary, the prosecution service and the possibility of a separate Department of Justice. Patten reported in September 1999 to widespread opposition from the Unionists but has been broadly accepted by the Government.

Human rights and equality: A new independent Human Rights Commission has been established to consult and advise on the scope for defining rights supplementary to those in the European Convention on Human Rights which the British Government is in the process of incorporating into United Kingdom law. There will also be a statutory requirement on the public sector to promote equality of opportunity and the creation of a unified Equality Commission embracing existing statutory bodies (Fair Employment Commission; the Equal Opportunities Commission; the Commission for Racial Equality; the Disability Council).

Progress and problems

Significant progress has been made since the signing of the Agreement. The Assembly has been set up with every political party sitting in the same chamber for the first time in Ulster's history, policing has been reviewed, troop levels are being reduced, permanent vehicle check points and army sangars are being closed and paramilitary prisoners have been released. The implementation of some aspects of the Agreement has, however, been fraught with problems. The intention at the outset was that all parts of the Agreement, including those described above, would move forward *in parallel* – this has not happened. A target date for establishing the 'shadow' executive (31 October 1998) as the first stage in the process of devolving power back to locally elected representatives could not be met. Unionists argued that decommissioning of terrorist weapons was a *sine qua non* for progress to be made before the formation of a power-sharing executive and the creation of cross-border bodies. Furthermore, Unionists reminded the Prime Minister (Tony Blair) of his pre-referendum pledges to the people of Northern Ireland, one of which was that those who use or threaten violence would be excluded from the Government of Northern Ireland.[2] For the Unionist community the decommissioning issue is a fundamental confidence building measure necessary to create the trust needed to make further political progress. Republicans (Sinn Féin) counter that this argument represents an excuse on the part of Unionists not to share authority with them and that if the decommissioning hurdle was crossed, some fresh precondition would be put in place. The failure to resolve the decommissioning issue led to the re-imposition of direct rule on 11 February 2000 and the assumption by the Secretary of State of his erstwhile responsibilities.

The SDLP hailed the Good Friday Agreement a success for achieving the goal of 'unity'. Party leader John Hume told his party conference in November 1998 that unity was evident in the referenda North and South which endorsed the Good Friday Agreement and was also central to the operation of the Assembly, its Executive and the North–South Ministerial Council. That is, under the 'sufficient consensus' voting rules[3] of the new Northern Ireland Assembly key decisions cannot be taken unless the Ulster Unionists and the SDLP co-operate.

The Deputy First Minister Seamus Mallon, argues that the principle by which all key decisions will be taken on a cross-community basis is at the core of the Agreement. 'Without cross-community agreement, there can be no significant action. The principle is of course diametri-cally opposed to the old politics which saw each and every decision as a victory for one side or the other' (Mallon, 1998).

Aside from decommissioning which led to the collapse of the Assembly and Executive another controversial issue has been the release of paramilitary prisoners under the terms of the Agreement and the concomitant treatment of victims of violence. When IRA and Loyalist prisoners (the Balcombe Street gang and Michael Stone respectively) appeared at public rallies prior to the referenda, it was seized upon by the 'No' campaigners as triumphalist, proof of what the Agreement meant in practice and evidence of how the victims of violence had been forgotten. The Prime Minister intervened to assuage doubters that sub-sequent legislation would establish 'objective and verifiable tests' as to whether those involved had given up violence before they could take advantage of the accelerated prisoner release scheme. Both govern-ments (British and Irish) acknowledge that the prisoners' issue is highly emotive but point out that it is an indispensable part of the Agreement.

There is, however, a clear acceptance of the need to address the suf-fering of victims of violence as a necessary element of reconciliation. The Agreement itself makes the point: 'it is recognised that victims have the right to remember as well as to contribute to a changed society. The achievement of a peaceful and just society would be the true memorial to the victims of violence' (The Belfast Agreement, 1998: 18 section 12). The mechanism for providing greater recognition for those who have become the victims of 30 years of violence was a report commissioned by the Secretary of State entitled 'We Will Remember Them' (launched 13 May 1998). The appointed Northern Ireland Victims Commissioner consulted with victims and their families, welfare groups of the bereaved and disabled, community groups, churches and political parties. The Government responded to the recommendations of the report with a range of practical measures (amounting to some £2 million) dealing with the economic welfare of victims, accessibility to counselling support and medical services, and funding for groups and organisations which seek to help victims (these measures included the establishment of a new Trauma Unit for young people and families affected by the troubles, and a Victims Liaison Unit to drive the whole process forward). Victims and their families, whilst appreciative of the financial support, were somewhat cynical of the government's new-found concern ('too little, too late'). Some viewed such moves as no more than a necessary part of the political and public relations management of the prisoner release process within which victims were mere pawns in a wider unstoppable agenda for a peace deal.

Israel: the Wye Agreement

In Israel and the Palestinian administered territories there appears to be less optimism for the Wye (Maryland) Agreement (October 1998) brokered by the Americans and hailed as unparalleled since Carter's mediation at the Camp David summit 20 years ago. The Wye Agreement aimed to breathe life into the 1993 Oslo peace plan which, six years on, had not delivered the promise of historic reconciliation to end the Middle East's 100 years of war. As an *interim* measure the Declaration of Principles (September 1993), based on the Oslo Accord, provided for immediate Palestinian self rule in the Gaza Strip and the West Bank town of Jericho, an agreement on self-government and the election of a Palestinian Council, with Israeli sovereignty over Jewish settlements in the Occupied Territories. Talks on the *permanent* status of the West Bank and Gaza were to begin by December 1995. The Declaration of Principles established a five-year transition period within which a final settlement would be negotiated. Under Oslo the Palestinians ceded more than three-quarters of the territory in which they had lived as a majority earlier in the century in return for peace with Israel and, at some future point, the promise of a sovereign state.

The phased implementation of the Declaration of Principles experienced long delays however because of disagreements between Israel and the Palestinians. The Gaza–Jericho Agreement was signed in May 1994 on four main issues – security arrangements, civil affairs, legal matters and economic relations. It included agreement on the withdrawal of Israeli forces from Gaza and Jericho, a transfer from the Israeli Civil Administration to a Palestinian Authority, the structure and composition of the Palestinian Authority (a 24 member appointed body with legislative and executive powers), a Palestinian police force, and relations between Israel and the Palestinian Authority. The Palestinians, according to Peretz (1996), insisted on the Declaration of Principles as the *first step* towards an independent state, whereas Israel treated the agreement as a guarantee of autonomy, *not* of independence.

In September 1995 a further agreement was signed in Washington (the Israeli–Palestinian Interim Agreement on the West Bank and the Gaza Strip, also known as 'Oslo II') to expand Palestinian self-rule in three regions of the West Bank[4] and provide for elections to a Palestinian Council (which would take over from the Palestinian National Authority). The signing of the agreement generated a new wave of optimism. Despite a set-back caused by the assassination of Yitzhak Rabin in November 1995, his replacement, Shimon Peres, redeployed troops from most West Bank towns enabling the first Palestinian elections to take place. In January 1996 elections were held for the Palestinian Council (88 members) and its President. Yasser Arafat was elected Ra'ees (President) of the Palestinian National Authority and the Palestinian Council with more than 90 per cent of the votes. The elections were hailed by the Palestinians as the first important step toward recognised statehood, although what was on offer was little more than a form of home rule.[5]

The dynamic of the peace process, however, came to an abrupt halt. A series of suicide bombings by Hamas to avenge the killing of their master-bomber Yahya Ayyash by Israeli agents in January 1996 left 61 Israelis dead. Peres responded by suspending peace talks. The Labour Government also imposed a five-month closure of the West Bank and Gaza borders depriving an estimated 40,000 Palestinians of work in Israel and barring imports and exports from the self-rule areas. Israeli public confidence in the peace process had collapsed leaving the way open for a new government.

Binyamin Netanyahu denounced the Oslo agreement within days of its signing in 1993 as 'an enormous lie', was against the peace process when he was in opposition, campaigned on a slogan of a 'secure peace', and has reneged on Oslo since reaching office. The election of Likud[6] and Mr Netanyahu's right-wing/religious coalition government in May 1996, the opening of an archaeological tunnel in the heart of occupied east Jerusalem and the expansion of Jewish settlements in the east Jerusalem suburb of Har Homa (Jabal Abu Ghneim) have done little to inspire Palestinian confidence in progress towards final status talks. His coalition government presented policy guidelines to the Knesset after the election which were uncompromising, stating that while:

- the new government is committed to negotiating with the Palestinian National Authority 'with the intent of reaching a permanent arrangement, on the condition that the Palestinians fulfil all their commitments fully';
- 'the government will propose to the Palestinians an arrangement whereby they will be able to conduct their lives freely within the framework of self-government. The government will oppose the establishment of a Palestinian state or any foreign sovereignty west of the Jordan River and will oppose 'the right of return' of Arab populations to any part of the land of Israel west of the Jordan';
- existing settlements in the Gaza Strip and West Bank will be expanded. 'Settlements in the Negev, the Galilee, the Golan Heights, and in Judea and Samaria (the West Bank) and Gaza is of national importance to Israel's defence and an expression of Zionist fulfilment. The government will alter the settlement policy, act to consolidate the settlement enterprises in these areas, and allocate the resources necessary for this';
- the guidelines were uncompromising on Jerusalem, one of the key issues in the final status talks with Palestinians. The new government has declared that 'Jerusalem, the capital of Israel, is one city, whole and undivided, and will remain forever under Israel's sovereignty...the government will thwart any attempt to undermine the unity of Jerusalem, and will prevent any action which is counter to Israel's exclusive sovereignty over the city'. (Ash, 1996)

The message from these policy guidelines was clear. Peace would be pursued but with less urgency, guided by a grudging recognition and the new government's own interpretation of the Oslo agreements. Netanyahu believe that the majority of Israelis remain deeply suspicious about exchanging land-for-peace. Accordingly, he engaged in a delicate political balancing act under pressure from both his right-wing religious allies in the coalition government, particularly settlers' representatives, demanding further expansion, and external pressure from America to inject momentum into the Oslo peace process.

Palestinians insist on a freeze on construction/expansion in return for full negotiations on a Palestinian state. They are convinced Israel is racing to create 'facts on the ground' (a tactic aimed at buying Israelis time to build Jewish settlements in Gaza and the West Bank) before final status talks determine the exact borders and limitations of a future Palestine. Har Homa is a classic example of this policy. The new Israeli settlement midway between south-east Jerusalem and Bethlehem would complete the ring of Jewish-only estates that divide Arab east Jerusalem from its West Bank hinterland. This would make it extremely difficult for east Jerusalem ever to be the capital of a Palestinian state. The status of Jerusalem is one of the most difficult decisions awaiting the final-status negotiators and hence Israeli tactics are seen as deliberately pre-emptive and provocative.

While Netanyahu cited an agreement in January 1997 on Hebron and accompanying pledge by Israel to withdraw in stages from other unspecified parts of the West Bank as evidence of his commitment to Oslo, only 2 per cent of the West Bank was handed over in the first of these withdrawals and it was made clear that Netanyahu's vision for the Palestinians' homeland was scattered non-contiguous cantons in less than half the territory with a grid of Israeli-controlled roads and territory. The Oslo agreements prescribed three redeployments during the interim period, cumulatively transferring the bulk of the West Bank to Palestinian control. The Palestinians' interpretation of Oslo envisaged the three redeployments amounting to some 85 per cent of the West Bank. Palestinian frustration has also grown because of disappointment with the Palestinian Authority which is seen as autocratic, conspiratorial and sometimes brutal in its operation. This led the United Nations Development Programme Officer based in Gaza to comment that for most Palestinians the peace process has caused nothing but hardship. 'People honestly would prefer to go back to the situation before the peace process began. Now, there is no peace and no jobs. Then, there was no peace but jobs' (Ash, 1996: 6).

The net result has been that since Mr Netanyahu's election the peace progress is in limbo. The Oslo timetable, under which Israel was to have withdrawn from swathes of the West Bank, with final status negotiations under way, has not happened. Jewish settlements in the territories have increased and Israel has thwarted economic development in those few areas that have been ceded to the Palestinian Authority. As a consequence, an atmosphere of mutual recrimination exists with Israelis blaming Palestinian terrorism, and Palestinians the Israeli Government's refusal to accept the basic conditions for a settlement. One assessment of Mr Netanyahu's record in government is that he wanted to reach the elections not having given up much territory, yet without having caused the violent destruction or total implosion of the peace process. The comparison is made with Northern

Ireland:

> Israeli and Palestinian peaceniks recalled with wistful irony that the initial breakthroughs in these two ancient conflicts came at the same time, in late 1993. Israel recognised the PLO; Britain agreed to a role for Sinn Féin. In both cases, the accords were predicated on an end to terrorism, and in both cases subsequent terror outrages brought peace talks to a halt. But in Israel, after Mr Netanyahu's accession in 1996, the halts were to a process the government did not truly want to proceed with.
>
> (*The Economist*, 25 April 1998: 48)

The Wye Agreement is meant to pave the way for comprehensive negotiations aimed at a final lasting peace settlement. Under the deal, Israel will withdraw its troops from a further 13 per cent of the West Bank, giving Arafat full or partial control of 40 per cent of the territory.[7] The Palestinian areas are, for the most part, non-contiguous and allow no free passage between them. Jerusalem also remains off-limits to residents of Gaza and the West Bank. The Israeli government is committed under the agreement to the phased release of 750 of the 3,000 Palestinians in its prisons. It agreed to negotiate a further troop withdrawal in the months leading up to 'final status' talks. In exchange, the Palestinians agreed to a detailed 'workplan' under which they will co-operate with the CIA in tracking down and arresting extremists in the Hamas and Islamic Jihad groups. Yasser Arafat agreed to summon a broad assembly of Palestinian delegates to review the Palestinian Covenant, expunging paragraphs calling for the destruction of Israel. Wye, in essence, was a return to the basic land-for-peace formula which underpinned the 1993 Oslo Accord.

The prospects for its success were dismissed by some observers:

> The Israeli-Palestinian arrangement the Americans have brokered is a deal designed to fail. The essence of the Israeli position has been to demand security guarantees so tight that they cannot really be fulfilled. However hard he tries, Arafat cannot give Israel total security against every suicide bomber and every extremist group ... As violations almost inevitably occur, they will provide Netanyahu with built-in opportunities to denounce the Palestinians and suspend any territorial transfers or take an even harder line in the negotiations over final status of the Palestinian entity ... A tight

security pact gives him the chance to bed down even more firmly the principle of reciprocity which he has used to erode the Oslo agreement. Reciprocity, in Netanyahu's definition, means that what Oslo says or implies Israel should do can be evaded, watered down or indefinitely postponed if there is a bomb or a shooting.

(Woollacott, 1998)

A further problem is that the most emotive issues remain unresolved under Wye with no framework for negotiation. Both sides still claim Jerusalem as their capital. The right to return of the original (1948 and 1967) Palestinian refugees now living in Jordan, Syria, Lebanon, the West Bank and Gaza Strip remains a basic PLO demand. The old Labour and Likud governments agree on yielding little more than 50 per cent of the West Bank, retaining the rest for settlements, water resources and security – hence Palestine's final borders will be a fundamental issue to resolve. Such were the difficulties surrounding these matters that the architects of Oslo left them in the hope that when talks began there would be a new relationship between the two sides. The deadline for completing permanent status arrangements was May 1999 but no one believed that date could be met. At that stage, when the five year old Oslo accords finally expired, Yasser Arafat threatened to announce his intention to declare a Palestinian state, with Jerusalem as the eternal capital, blaming Netanyahu for stalling the negotiations. The Israeli Prime Minister, in turn, accused Arafat of failing to crack down on Islamist extremists and claimed that an arbitrary, unilateral declaration of Palestinian State would prompt an Israeli reprisal – the likely annexation of most of the West Bank leaving Arafat with Gaza and a scattering of self-rule cantons. This is hardly conducive to creating an environment within which final status can be negotiated. One scathing analysis of the Wye Agreement suggested:

Most of the Wye River Memorandum is taken up with security arrangements which in effect commit the Palestinian Authority to Israel's security, but not the other way round ... Israel, in the meantime can do what it likes, including the building of more settlements, taking more land, adding to Jerusalem's area, and helping itself to all the West Bank water it wants.

(Said, 1998)

Hamas which made no secret of its opposition to the peace deal reacted with a suicide car bomb in a Jerusalem market killing the two bombers and injuring 21 people. An uneasy 'peace' prevailed as the provisions of Wye limped into existence.

All change?

Netanyahu's fragile coalition (of Likud, Sephardim, Russian immigrants and the Orthodox) came to an end in December 1998 after 30 months in government, during which the peace process had stalled and the country's economy was struggling. Unemployment stood at a six year high of 8.5 per cent and economic growth less than 2 per cent in 1998. The scene was set for a five month long election campaign. In the meantime the 4 May 1999 deadline loomed large. This was the expiry date for the Oslo agreement's five-year interim period, and the date, according to the Oslo process, when Israel and the Palestinians should have reached a final agreement. Arafat, given the imminence of the elections and fearful of handing Netanyahu electoral advantage, postponed a unilateral declaration with suitable endorsements from the Americans and the EU who reaffirmed Palestinians' right to self-determination. Palestinians in turn demanded a freeze on all new settlement construction. According to Israel's *Peace Now* movement, Netanyahu's government had established 17 new 'hilltop' settlements since the Wye Agreement was signed, increasing the West Bank's settler population from 160,000 to 200,000. If this continued a future Palestinian state would find it difficult to expand beyond the 29 per cent of the West Bank which the Palestinian Authority currently and partially controlled.

Israelis did not see peace or economic policies as the key electoral issues as voting took place to promote strict ethnic and religious interests. Although Oslo was perceived as moribund, voters assumed that a new Prime Minister would revive the process. Similarly, the sharp rise in Israeli casualties in Syrian-controlled Lebanon made it imperative that attention be paid quickly to this issue post election.

The elections of 17 May 1999 gave Labour's Ehud Barak a 56 per cent to 44 per cent victory over Bibi Netanyahu in the prime ministerial contest. Separately, his own One Israel Party (Labour plus two satellite groups – Gesher and Meimad) fared worse ending up with just 26 seats in a Knesset of 120 members, compared with the 34 seats that Labour won on its own at the last election. The task of building a coalition (with Shas, a revivalist Orthodox party, and Meretz, a secular party) from the 15 parties now represented in the Knesset was to prove difficult. Likud has 19 seats, sharply down from 32 it achieved last time, when it included two other small parties. Shas, the Sephardic-Orthodox party, thought to have benefited from Likud defectors, increased its representation from 10 to 17, close to overtaking Likud as Israel's second largest party.

Barak promised 'a new dawn' of healing and reconciliation to Israel's divided society. He pledged to bring Israel's soldiers home from the Lebanon within a year by making peace with the Syrians and to pick up the pieces of the Wye Agreement left by Netanyahu. This included promises to fulfil Israel's commitment under Wye by withdrawing from another chunk of the West Bank, releasing 750 of the 2,000 political prisoners, and creating a passage between the West Bank and Gaza. His victory speech however heralded a tough stance towards final status talks with the Palestinians:

- Jerusalem, united under Israeli sovereignty for eternity
- No return under any circumstance to the 1967 borders
- No foreign army west of the river Jorden
- The majority of the settlers in Judea and Samaria in settlement blocs under Israeli sovereignty.

Barak promised that any final status agreement would be submitted to a referendum. He and Arafat agreed on a timetable for an Israeli–Palestinian 'framework agreement' by 13 February 2000 and a fully-fledged 'permanent-status' agreement by September 2000. Palestinian mistrust was fuelled however by the Israelis' refusal to freeze settlement building during the talks. In the meantime renewed peace talks between Syria and Israel got off the ground, central to which was the return of the Israeli seized (1967) Golan Heights in exchange for stringent security guarantees and an embassy in Damascus. Palestinians were given full or partial control of an extra 10 per cent of the West Bank in January 2000 but the framework agreement, due to consider issues such as Jerusalem, refugees, settlements, water and borders, was postponed as attacks by Hizbullah guerrillas in the Lebanon increased, causing Israeli casualties and counter-attacks. The negotiations between Israel and the Palestinian Authority appear not to be going well. On offer to the Palestinians are two cantons north and south of Jerusalem with no territorial contiguity between them, none of them near the city and no access to the border with Jordan. Recriminations abound including a Palestinian view that Barak is no better than Netanyahu.

South Africa: the Truth and Reconciliation Commission

In South Africa the most recent political events have been dominated by the final report of the Truth and Reconciliation Commission (TRC) established under the Promotion of National Unity and Reconciliation Act, 1995. The overall aim was to promote national unity in a spirit of understanding based on 'a need for understanding but not vengeance, a need for reparation but not retaliation' (South Africa's Transitional Constitution, 1993). The intention, therefore, was *not* to punish but to understand whilst at the same time acknowledging that the apartheid state was responsible for torture and murder.

The Truth and Reconciliation Commission aimed to achieve this by:

- establishing the causes, nature and extent of gross violations of human rights which were committed between 1 March 1960 and 5 December 1993 (subsequently extended to 10 May 1994);
- granting amnesty to persons who make full disclosure of facts associated with political objectives;
- establishing and making known the fate and whereabouts of victims of gross violations and by restoring their human and civil dignity by letting them relate those violations and by recommending reparation measures;
- compiling a report of activities of the Commission, containing recommendations of measures to prevent future human rights violations. (Truth and Reconciliation: Terms of Reference)

The Truth and Reconciliation Commission, chaired by Archbishop Desmond Tutu, reported in October 1998 amidst a blaze of controversy caused by the African National Congress (ANC) which attempted, at the last moment, to block its publication.[8] The report was a searing indictment of South African Society under apartheid, handing out savage criticism across the political and social spectrum. At the heart of the report is the finding that apartheid was a crime against humanity:

> The state, in the form of the government, the civil service and its security forces, was, in the period 1960–94, the primary perpetrator of gross violations of human rights in South Africa and, from 1974, in southern Africa. In the application of the policy of apartheid, the state in the period 1960–90 sought to protect the power and privilege of a racial minority. Racism therefore constituted the motivating core of the political order, an attitude largely endorsed by the investment and other policies of South Africa's main trading partners. A consequence was that white citizens in general adopted a dehumanising position towards black citizens, to the point where the ruling order and the state ceased to regard them as fellow citizens and labelled them as the enemy. This created a climate

in which gross atrocities committed against them were seen as legitimate.

(TRC Report, 1998)

The commission ruled that former President P.W. Botha (National Party) carried overall responsibility for security force atrocities from 1978 to 1989, as Head of State and Chairman of the State Security Council. In the latter role he had used language which led to murder. Criticism was not limited to the state. The report was scathing of the judiciary, big business, the media, churches and the medical establishment for failing to take a moral stand under apartheid rule. The judiciary was blamed for collaborating with politicians by enforcing flimsy laws granting 'no bail certificates', uncritically handing out police search warrants, and turning a blind eye to the causes of injuries or death in detention. Business was central to the economy that sustained apartheid. The report singled out the mining industry, which benefited from the payment of low wages to migrant workers, for helping to 'design and implement apartheid policies' (TRC Report, 1998). The broadcast media was seen as a tool of the government. The 'staff code' of the South African Broadcasting Corporation (SABC) allowed any white member of staff to sack any black employee, without reason. Between 1975 and 1985, those black employees who were given disciplinary hearing could opt to be sjambokked (whipped) rather than dismissed. The report condemned the repression of religious communities by the apartheid government but stressed that 'some of the major Christian Churches gave their blessing to the system', in particular the Dutch Reform Church which until 1986 presented apartheid as a biblical instruction. Doctors, surgeons and dentists were also accused of regularly misrepresenting forensic evidence.

Most controversially, however, there was condemnation of the ANC for gross human rights violations, including summary executions and the use of torture. Members of the ANC's armed wing, Umkhonto we Sizwe (MK – Spear of the Nation), committed gross human rights violations, even after the liberation movements were legalised in 1990. The report gave examples of torture in ANC camps in Angola and Tanzania, including the use of electric shocks, melted plastic, and blows to the head and spine with metal rods. The commission found that the killing of defectors or informers, considered 'military targets' by MK, was not justified. The ANC's reaction to have the publication blocked distracted attention from the commission's position that its struggle, armed or otherwise, against apartheid was justified. There was no suggestion of equivalence between the evils of a system which was a crime against humanity and the abuses, however serious and including murder, which ANC members committed.

The commission also found that Chief Mangosuthu Buthelezi (Inkatha Freedom party – IFP) colluded with the apartheid regime and bore responsibility for crimes including the setting up of murder squads and the creation of a paramilitary force designed to wreck the 1994 elections. Winnie Mandela was found to be complicit in acts of 'murder, torture, assault and arson' committed by her Mandela United Football Club.

Reactions to the outcome of the findings were mixed. Archbishop Tutu described it as 'a triumph for truth and humanity'. The ANC's president-elect Thabo Mbeki, on the other hand, said of the Commission 'they are wrong, wrong and misguided'. In terms of establishing the 'truth' about crimes in the apartheid-era the commission, despite its attempts to be comprehensive, of necessity was selective. Even with sweeping powers of search and seizure, and of subpoena, incriminating files were shredded or as the commission described it 'mass destruction of records has had a severe impact on South Africa's social memory'. It therefore relied on voluntary co-operation. In terms of 'justice' one editorial suggested:

> In the sense of bringing the guilty to court and punishment, the exercise has been less effective. Indeed, it has often worked in contradiction to it by allowing villains to ask for amnesty. But the very process of rejecting amnesty has allowed the victims of apartheid and the relatives of the murdered to expose guilty men to the glare of publicity. The exposure of truth is also a form of justice in the court of public opinion, even if it does not lead to conviction and sentence.
>
> (*The Guardian*, 31 October 1998)

The report is expected to lead to a flood of civil and criminal claims against perpetuators who either were not granted amnesty by the TRC (although over three thousand who applied are still waiting for a TRC ruling) or who never applied for it. In terms of 'reconciliation' one response has been:

> A victor who ends a war with this enemy's unconditional surrender can choose to punish the vanquished. Black South Africans, however, did not defeat the white regime; they negotiated it out of office. The

price of the peaceful handing over of power by Mr de Klerk's National Party was amnesty. Even then, South Africans could have offered a blanket amnesty to everybody, drawn a line under the past, and left it at that. But they hatched something more ambitious: selective amnesty to those who confessed, accompanied by an effort to write a truer history... As for reconciliation, a verdict must be on hold.

(*The Economist*, 31 October 1998)

The engine for change

South Africa has come a long way since the collapse of apartheid in 1989 and the announcement by the National Party of its willingness to consider the extension of black South Africans' political rights. Their acquiescence had been brought about by militant political resistance, trade union agitation, boycotts and guerrilla struggle in the black community. In other words 'the economy had been brought almost to its knees... and the business class stared disaster in the face. The captains of industry and high finance, so long the main beneficiaries of apartheid, decided the game was up' (Hain, 1996: 31). This pressure from the business community created the circumstances in which the modernisers in the National Party could seize the initiative for change with Frederik Willem de Klerk ousting his predecessor P.W. Botha in 1989 at the height of an era known as the 'total onslaught' because of the hostility between the government and the exiled ANC. The lifting of the 30-year ban on the ANC and release of Nelson Mandela in 1990 created a climate for political negotiation and change, paving the way for an Interim Constitution in December 1993 and the first multiracial democratic elections in April 1994.[9] The Interim Constitution provided for regional government with limited powers (e.g. housing and secondary education but not police or taxation) in nine new provinces and entrenched power-sharing for the lifetime of the interim government (5 years) by guaranteeing cabinet seats to any party winning at least 5 per cent of the national vote – a Government of National Unity. The junior members of the coalition, Inkatha and the National Party, experienced problems in working with the ANC, trying to serve as partners in government and simultaneously act as an opposition.

Nelson Mandela set out his vision for the attainment of a democratic, non-racial, non-sexist, peaceful and prosperous country in which he referred to four founding stones to build a new society. The first founding stone was national reconciliation and national unity – the need for blacks and whites to live together as equals, and as citizens bound together by a common destiny. The second founding stone was the establishment of a democratic system which ensured that all citizens have an equal right and an equal possibility to determine their future. This prohibited the option of tyranny and dictatorship, and guaranteed the fundamental rights of all. The third founding stone was to end the enormous race and gender disparities in wealth, income and opportunity inherited from the past which detracted from the achievement of the goals of national unity and reconciliation. The fourth and final founding stone was rebuilding and modernising the economy and setting it on a high, sustainable growth path to end poverty, unemployment and backwardness. Mandela himself commented:

> None of us can underestimate the complexity of the challenge that faces us with regard to the laying of these latter two founding stones ... In this context, we must refer to the mood of the masses of our people who correctly expect that freedom must be attended by a better life for all. But because they are poor, these millions understand the effort and time it will take to graduate from walking barefoot to the comforts of a truly decent existence.
>
> It may be difficult to understand the enormous creative force released among the people by the fact that, for the first time in centuries, they have a government which they can correctly claim as their own and whose very reason for existence is to serve the interests of these millions; and that they are builders of a society in which the individual is by law protected against any tyranny from the state.
>
> (Mandela, 1996: 22–3)

Unfortunately that 'graduation from walking barefoot' has been dogged by the twin problems of crime and unemployment. The crime is both random and violent in nature – South Africa's murder rate is about six/seven times that of America, it is a trans-shipment point for drugs from Latin America and Asia heading for the European market. Car-hijacking, guns, diamonds and rhino horn smuggling are linked to crime syndicates. In short, robbery, murder and every other kind of crime are rife and the government appears unable to uphold the rule of law. Unemployment is about 30 per cent or more and the labour market is paralysed as a result of racism and an unskilled workforce. This is compounded by strong unions and restrictive labour protection legislation. Industry has long been protected (almost closed) and, as a result, uncompetitive with a host of trade barriers and monopolised by big conglomerates.

The biggest task, however, is how to tackle the huge inequalities. One report noted that if the white 13 per cent of the population were a separate country its standard of living would rank a comfortable 24th in the world (just behind Spain) according to a United Nations' Human Development Index. Black South Africa, by contrast, would rank 123rd (just above Congo). White South Africans are on average nine times richer than blacks with the wealthiest 10 per cent earning half of the country's income. The World Bank calculates that whites are paid twice as much as blacks, even allowing for differences in skills and experience. This unequal income distribution is paralleled by welfare spending – in 1989 per capita spending on education for whites was R3,082 and only R765 for blacks. The average education attainment of the adult African population is only seven years of schooling (Hofmeyr and Buckland, 1992, quoted in Luiz, 1996). Over one quarter of the black community is illiterate, a legacy of 'bantu education' which forced black students to follow an education system designed to teach only the basic skills necessary for menial labour. A large number of schools are in dire circumstances with limited investment in books and buildings and a culture of disruption still exists from the days when this was a legitimate form of political protest. Attainment rates amongst blacks in the basic school-leaving examination are particularly low although the government no longer analyses examination results by race. A large army of jobless people is unlikely to contribute to the vision of a peaceful law-abiding citizenry as the significant wealth-gap encourages many into opportunistic crime. These inequalities persist and are graphically described by one commentator:

> The truth is that, now that apartheid has gone, life for most White South Africans is almost exactly as it was before, but without the guilt. This goes a long way to explaining the whites' apparent magnanimity in political retreat. White South Africa is still capable of keeping poor black Africa at bay, shopping in suburban malls, wearing smart hats to the races and fortifying itself behind high walls in leafy suburbs with scented names like Saxonwold. Black children still die of tuberculosis, and increasingly AIDS; white children are more likely to drown in the swimming pool.
>
> (Pedder, 1995: 3)

There were great expectations from the grassroots of the ANC in government for jobs, schools, hospitals and houses. In 1994 the ANC promised to build 1 million houses over five years. The goal was to turn peace into prosperity, to move from conflict and crisis to construction and reconciliation. The centrepiece of the ANC's policy was the Reconstruction and Development Plan (RDP) outlined by President Mandela in his first speech to parliament in May 1994 and due to run until 1999. Its policy aims were to meet basic needs, develop human resources, build the economy and democratise the state and society. It established the following targets: redistributing 30 per cent of agricultural land; raising the annual number of houses built from 50,000 to 0.3 m; providing safe drinking water for 12 m persons; providing sanitation for 21 m; creating 0.3 m non-agricultural jobs; reversing privatisation 'contrary to the public interest'; introducing anti-trust legislation; 'de-racializing' business ownership; improving industrial relations. This ambitious plan however met with limited early success:

> The initial failure of the RDP to deliver even incremental improvement in the lives of the poor appeared, however, to owe less to financial constraints and more to the culture of protest which had grown up during the apartheid years and which the new government was finding impossible to dispel. Plead as he might, President Mandela failed to persuade tenants and householders in the black townships that they would have to abandon their boycott of mortgage repayments, rents and service levies before banks and building societies could be persuaded to guarantee funds for the house-building programme.
>
> (The International Institute for Strategic Studies, 1995: 221)

ANC politicians either tacitly or openly supported this type of action which had been integral to their struggle. The ANC experienced problems in moving from a protest and liberation movement to a political party carrying functional responsibilities as a government. The provincial governments (which have joint responsibility with central government for managing areas such as education, health, roads and welfare – but limited revenue raising powers) are also becoming obstacles to delivering the central government's promise of basic services. They are seen as profligate and badly managed.

A central tenet of Mandela's commitment to a stable democracy was the new constitution replacing the interim constitution which had established the Government of National Unity for 5 years after the 1994 elections. According to the interim constitution the two houses of parliament (the national assembly and the senate – a joint sitting was called the Constitutional Assembly) were given until 8 May 1996 to finalise the constitution. This had to be adopted by a two-thirds majority, meaning the ANC and National Party had to reach an agreement. This was reached during the night of 7/8 May 1996. The ANC, National Party, Democratic Party and the Pan Africanist Congress voted for the constitution, the Freedom Front abstained and the African Christian Democratic Party voted against it. After the final constitution was accepted by Parliament (the new constitution came into effect February 1997), F.W. de Klerk announced the National Party was pulling out of the Government of National Unity and assuming the role of opposition, making the ANC the governing party. De Klerk's strategy of power-sharing proved flawed as nationalist politicians were systematically sidelined by ANC sympathisers (black and white) who took up influential positions in government, the army and the police. He retired from politics in September 1997 (Marthinus van Schalkwyk was elected party leader) with his party in disarray and no longer a significant force in national politics. A rift was emerging between those who favoured a regional party based largely on its support in the Western Cape and those who saw the need for a new restructured national party which shed its apartheid image and attempted to address the hostility of many blacks.

This somewhat bleak portrayal, particularly of economic and social issues, should not detract from what has been achieved:

> South Africa has an unnerving capacity to surprise. It has already shown that miracles do happen – for the events that held the world so rapt in 1994 qualify, if any do. To follow that political miracle with an economic and social one was bound to be even more difficult, and so it has proved. Achieving everything the new government promised looked impossible back then, and still does. But South Africa's leaders have put in place some of the measures needed to make the country a more prosperous, more stable and less divided place. South Africa's future may well be unspectacular – neither miraculous nor catastrophic, more an ungainly muddling through.
>
> (*The Economist*, 13 December 1997)

There is, however, increasing pressure for 'transformation' or shifting of power from white-dominated business, media, banks and universities to blacks. Whites, on the other hand, feel much has been conceded; blacks believe change has just begun and is much too slow. Their economic destiny, to that extent, is vested in a white élite. This, in turn, has led to frustration with the pace of change under the ANC. Whilst the euphoria of post-apartheid democracy may well be spent the ANC stills enjoys extraordinary loyalty or as one editorial put it 'for all the unbuilt houses, uncreated jobs and uncurbed crime, it carries a weight of history and mythology that will not be quickly wiped out'. (*Economist*, ibid.)

South Africa's second all-race elections in June 1999 gave the ANC an overwhelming mandate to accelerate Mr Mbeki's (Mandela's successor) programme of 'transformation'. The ANC won 266 of the 400 seats in the national assembly, falling short by one seat of the two-thirds majority which it would require if it sought to make constitutional changes. The Democratic Party, the heir to the country's long white liberal tradition, and perceived by most blacks as a party for rich whites, gained 38 seats to establish itself as the new official opposition. Third place went to Mangosuthu Buthelezi's Inkatha Freedom Party, which won 34 seats, most of them in its heartland of the troubled KwaZulu-Natal province. The biggest loser was the New National Party, rump of the monolithic white party which governed under apartheid. Tainted by this legacy they lost much electoral support to the Democratic Party dropping from 82 seats in 1994 to 28 in 1999. Most of the remaining opposition benches are filled by the United Democratic Party/ Movement (14 seats), a new protest movement. The ANC took all but one of the country's nine provinces (KwaZulu-Natal). In the Western Cape a Democratic Party – National Party opposition alliance excluded the ANC from government.

What the election results demonstrated however was evidence of enduring racial polarisation. Few whites voted for the ANC and few blacks, apart from Inkatha-supporting rural Zulus, voted for any party other than the ANC. Ethnic solidarity was reinforced despite calls by Thabo Mbeki to 'build a non-racial and non-sexist society' following the elections. Before his inauguration as the president of South Africa, Mbeki told parliament that South Africa was a country of two nations – one nation was 'white and relatively prosperous, the other black and poor'. The elections showed little sign of racial reconciliation. Thus far affirmative action legislation introduced by the ANC has resulted in the government hiring blacks and giving contracts to black-owned firms wherever possible, with slight regard to competence. Some within the ANC openly argue that merit should be a secondary consideration. Recent attempts to prevent and eliminate discrimination have been described as an illiberal muddle. Mandela's 'rainbow nation' still seems a long way off.

A model of peace building

This brief overview of recent events in Northern Ireland, Israel and South Africa provides an insight into the efforts invested in tackling ethno-national conflict at the macro level in each of the three countries. Understandably the focus of attention in both academic and journalistic accounts has been at this level. Yet this is a restrictive framework for comparative analysis and policy learning across the three countries. The approach ignores the possibility that whilst macro level accommodation is a necessary precondition for political progress it may not, by itself, be sufficient to achieve the goals of building peace and reconciliation. One alternative conceptualisation is suggested by John Paul Lederach (1996) in his peace building model. Lederach makes three broad observations about peace building in deeply divided societies.

First, there is an over-emphasis on short-term tasks which are often separated from the longer ranging goals of social change necessary to sustain any macro political achievements made. Each political crisis or incident becomes the focus of attention rather than a strategic vision of where the divided society is going. Examples here could be immediate problems over decommissioning in the Northern Ireland context, the political and legal ramifications of the TRC findings in South Africa or the phased withdrawals from the West Bank and prisoner releases in Israel.

Second, Lederach argues there is a hierarchical approach to peace building instead of an organic approach. He presents this as a three level pyramid (see Figure 1.1). At the top level, politicians, the military/police and appointed officials/advisors engage in high-level negotiations with the aim of reaching some kind of political 'solution' or compromise. At the middle level there is input from sectoral leaders e.g. the business community, trade unions, religious leaders, academics and think-tanks. At the grassroots level, NGOs, the voluntary and community sectors and local activists are involved. Lederach makes two observations about the pyramid population. First, the grassroots level is the tier at which many of the symptoms of conflict are manifest – social and economic insecurity, political and cultural discrimination and human rights violation – but the lines of ethno-national conflict are drawn vertically rather than horizontally through the pyramid. In other words, the three levels in the model are not pitted against one another, conflict is cross-cutting. Second, there are two inverse relationships in the conflict setting. Those at the top of the pyramid have the greatest capacity to influence the wider peace building process but are least likely to be affected by its consequences on a day-to-day basis. Those located at the bottom of the pyramid, on the other hand, will be very directly influenced by the outcomes of macro developments but will have limited access to the decision-making process and a narrower view of the wider agenda which may demand bargaining and compromise (Lederach, 1997: 43). Lederach argues: 'my basic thesis would be that that no one level is capable of delivering and sustaining peace on its own. We need to recognise the interdependence of people and activities across all levels of this pyramid' (Lederach, 1996: 45). In short, much of the activity is focused on top level leaders and the macro level political activities in which they are engaged.

This has significant consequences in terms of the pace of change experienced across the three levels. The peace process can be seen as moving, simultaneously, too slowly or rapidly. It will be too slow for

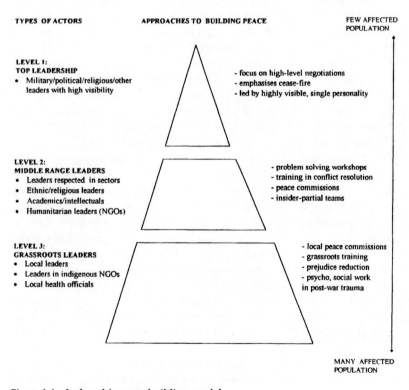

Figure 1.1   Lederach's peace building model
Source: Lederach, 1997: 39.

those whose expectations have been raised by the possibility of peace, according to Lederach, and too rapid for those who feel they have conceded too much and received too little. This has current resonance within the Unionist community in Northern Ireland who complain that the British Government has conceded numerous Republican demands without reciprocal gestures (e.g. handing over terrorist explosives and weaponry). Similarly in South Africa there is frustration with the pace of economic and social reform amongst the black community. The most impoverished would ask what has really changed post-apartheid; and in Israel there is a reluctance to make further 'land-for-peace' concessions on the part of some Jews. A further consequence is what Lederach refers to as 'the identity dilemma' in which people moving from violent conflict to reconciliation must reshape their identity away from one which is defined exclusively in relation to their enemy, but retains the core purpose of 'who they are' and 'what they are about'. In this context their personal and group identities are part of the macro negotiated settlements which are validated or invalidated by what happens at the top level of the pyramid, and over which they have little/no control. This can lead to feelings of marginalisation, insecurity and disillusionment. In this case-study, therefore, some in the Unionist, Afrikaner and Palestinian communities will ask, did Trimble, de Klerk and Arafat respectively 'sell-out' in negotiating agreements with the 'other side' and, if so, how should/will their ethnic identity change (or have to change) as a result? Lederach concludes that the top level official process is incapable of delivering on its own and there is a need for an organic approach which treats peace building as a web of interdependent activities and people across all three levels, rather than hierarchical model. 'The single most important aspect of encouraging an organic perspective is in creating a genuine sense of participation, responsibility and ownership in the process across a broad spectrum of the population' (Lederach, 1996: 48–9).

The *third* component of the model poses the question 'how do divided societies move from transition to transformation?' and ultimately reconciliation (see Figure 1.2). Here Lederach argues that there are important political changes which are integral to the process of transition in divided societies, referred to as the 'technical or task oriented' components of any negotiated settlement. While these political changes are necessary if reconciliation is to be achieved, moving beyond transition to transformation requires a more comprehensive approach involving social, economic, socio-psychological and spiritual changes. Only then can new relationships be built based upon a willingness to

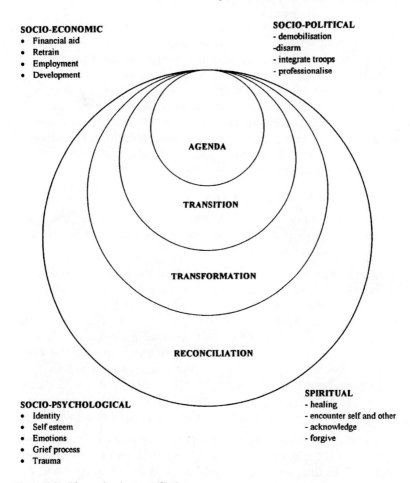

SOCIO-ECONOMIC
- Financial aid
- Retrain
- Employment
- Development

SOCIO-POLITICAL
- demobilisation
-disarm
- integrate troops
- professionalise

AGENDA

TRANSITION

TRANSFORMATION

RECONCILIATION

SOCIO-PSYCHOLOGICAL
- Identity
- Self esteem
- Emotions
- Grief process
- Trauma

SPIRITUAL
- healing
- encounter self and other
- acknowledge
- forgive

Figure 1.2 The web of reconciliation
Source: Lederach, 1996: 50.

acknowledge truth and the past injustices and an openness to offer and accept forgiveness. He summarises his model thus:

> We must move beyond a short-term crisis orientation and toward the development of a capacity to think about social change in terms of decades and generations. We must move beyond a hierarchical focus on politics and toward the construction of a more organic, broad-based approach that creates the space for genuine responsibility, ownership and participation in peace building. We must move

beyond a narrow view of peace building and toward the formation of a web of activities that envision a whole body politic, whole persons seeking change in radically changing environments...The challenge posed by reconciliation is to open up the social space that permits and encourages individuals and societies as collective, to acknowledge the past, mourn the losses, validate the pain experiences, confess the wrongs and reach toward the next step of rebuilding the relationship that has been broken. This is not to forgive and forget. This is not remember and justify. True reconciliation is to remember and change.

(Lederach, 1996: 53–4)

This book adopts the Lederach three-part framework for peace building in its analysis of Northern Ireland, Israel and South Africa. In so doing it will consider:

- macro political developments in each of the three countries, or an overview involving the key stages of moving towards a political resolution of the conflict (the top tier in Lederach's hierarchical model);
- parallel micro developments, through an examination of the better known grassroots activities which are taking place and an evaluation of their contribution to sustaining the wider political process;
- the extent to which each of the three countries have moved (or are moving) beyond the focus on the technical tasks of political 'transition' to social, economic, psychological and spiritual processes of 'transformation' and, ultimately, towards the goal of reconciliation.

The book is therefore structured to reflect this framework. Each country is analysed at the macro and micro levels (Northern Ireland: Chapters 2 and 3; Israel: Chapters 4 and 5; and South Africa: Chapters 6 and 7) in order to explore issues which may provide a basis for transformation and thus *sustain a lasting peace*. We return in Chapter 8 to the Lederach model as a means of drawing out some comparative themes which could promote policy learning within and between Northern Ireland, Israel and South Africa and we reflect on the value of the model as a useful theoretical framework for peace building in deeply divided societies.

2
Northern Ireland: Macro Political Developments

Introduction: the Stormont era

Northern Ireland is part of the United Kingdom of Great Britain and Northern Ireland, has an area of 13,483 square kilometres (5,269 square miles), covering six of the nine counties which make up the Province of Ulster,[10] and a population of 1,648,960 at June 1995 (Department of Finance & Personnel & H. M. Treasury, 1997). This compares with 3,503,000 living in the Republic of Ireland. Based on census data collated in 1991, 42.1per cent of the population is Catholic and 57.9per cent non-Catholic (Jardine, 1994). Most of the population live in the east of the Province, including about 490,000 in the urban area around the capital city Belfast.

The 1920 Government of Ireland Act provided for the creation of two separate 'Home Rule' parliaments in Dublin (for the 26 Catholic counties) and Belfast (for the 6 largely Protestant counties of the north-east) following a prolonged period of pressure in the nineteenth century for limited self government from British sovereignty. The twentieth century saw a continuation of parliamentary and extra parliamentary expression of this pressure and armed opposition to it in the north-east from Unionists. The Act was implemented in Northern Ireland but the Republicans, in the form of the Irish Republican Army, refused to accept it and continued to fight for complete independence. After a truce was signed in June 1921, negotiations with the Southern Irish led to the Anglo-Irish Treaty of December 1921. This resulted in the establishment in 1922 of the Irish Free State with dominion status. The boundary with Northern Ireland was confirmed in 1925.

From 1921 to 1972 Northern Ireland had its own regional government based at Stormont outside Belfast. The constitutional position of

Northern Ireland was unique in that it sent representatives to the United Kingdom Parliament but was subject, in most internal matters, to the jurisdiction of Stormont. The Northern Ireland Parliament, modelled on Westminster, had legislative and spending powers except for those explicitly reserved – war and peace, foreign trade and treaties, many taxes and other matters not exclusively related to Northern Ireland. During 1921–72, the Ulster Unionists held a majority in Stormont and formed the government of Northern Ireland. To maintain the Union constant vigilance was required. Darby describes this process as follows:

> Emergency legislation was introduced on a permanent basis; a police force and police reserve was established which was almost exclusively Protestant; local government electoral boundaries were openly gerrymandered... and a system of economic discrimination was introduced against the Catholic minority in Northern Ireland.
>
> (Darby, 1995: 17)

In reviewing the period 1921–68 John Whyte supports Darby's thesis of a 'consistent and irrefutable pattern of deliberate discrimination against Catholics' in the following areas (rank-ordered): electoral practices, public employment, policing, private employment, public housing and regional policy (Whyte, 1983: 30).

These grievances led to the emergence of the Civil Rights Movement which sought to redress discrimination through public protest in the form of demonstrations and marches. In 1968 one such march in Londonderry protested that the majority Catholic city was gerrymandered in such a way as to be run by Protestants. The march met with a violent reaction from the police and Protestant mobs. In response the Unionist Prime Minister, Terence O'Neill, announced a programme of reform – a points system for housing allocations, an Ombudsman, the repeal of the Special Powers Act (legislation passed in 1922 to deal with illegal political activities), 'one man, one vote' (*sic*) for local elections, and the setting up of an independent housing executive.

The reforms enraged Protestants without appeasing Catholics and although inter-communal violence was quelled in the short-term, disunity amongst the Unionists began to emerge. Prime Minister O'Neill resigned in 1969 suffering a loss in support from the Unionist rank-and-file and his parliamentary party for conciliatory overtones to Nationalists. Militant nationalists/republicans and loyalist terror groups then engaged in campaigns of violence. This led to the British

Government authorising the deployment of units of the armed forces in support of the civil power. As Buckland noted:

> The events of August 1969 marked the beginning of the end for Stormont. Northern Ireland's affairs ceased to be the sole concern of Northern Ireland, as the British Government became increasingly involved ... Traditional animosities were reinforced by the revival of the IRA and a renewed determination on the part of many unionists to uphold their accustomed ascendancy by any and every means. In the end, violence grew at the expense of constitutionalism, as politicians and advocates of compromise lost control to men with guns or industrial might.
>
> (Buckland, 1981: 132)

Several political and military blunders followed, from internment without trial through 'political status' for IRA prisoners, to the shooting of 13 unarmed demonstrators at an anti-internment march in Derry (Bloody Sunday – 30 January 1972).[11] In March 1972, with the inter-communal violence and terrorist actions continuing, the British Government first suspended and then, in 1973, abolished the regional parliament at Stormont and introduced Direct Rule from Westminster (Bew, Gibbon and Patterson, 1979; Arthur, 1987). A new British Cabinet Minister, the Secretary of State for Northern Ireland, assisted by two Ministers of State and two Parliamentary Under Secretaries assumed overall responsibility for the government of Northern Ireland. He/she is directly involved with the political and constitutional matters, security policy and broad economic questions. The major functional areas of government, law and order, economic development, education, health and social services and the environment are shared amongst the other ministers. Buckland further noted:

> The suspension of Stormont and the imposition of Direct Rule took power away from the unionists but did little to restore order and failed to achieve widespread agreement upon the way Northern Ireland should be governed ... Direct Rule became the form of government that divided Northern Irishmen least, but which could not command complete acceptance.
>
> (Buckland, 1981: 159)

Direct Rule arrangements were never intended to be permanent, and successive efforts have been made to restore a measure of devolved government which are only now (in 1999) being realised. The Protestant community acquiesced in the system of Direct Rule when the alternative to power sharing with Catholics seemed unacceptable. Similarly, the Catholic community preferred Direct Rule to the return of Protestant ascendancy. The consequences, however, were a complete absence of local accountability and a very powerful executive (senior civil servants) which controlled Northern Ireland's £8.4 bn public purse.

Direct rule: attempts to reform

Since the inception of Direct Rule in 1972, the stated aim of successive UK administrations was to seek peace, stability and prosperity for the people of Northern Ireland within a framework of harmonious relations with the rest of the United Kingdom, the Republic of Ireland and within the context of the European Union. This approach is described by a senior Northern Ireland Office official as follows:

- promoting agreement among all people who live in the island of Ireland and working with the Irish Government to that end;
- a co-ordinated and coherent approach to all aspects of government policy in Northern Ireland which recognises that the fundamental political, security and economic and social problems are closely interrelated; and,
- policies informed by the principles of equality of opportunity, equity of treatment and parity of esteem, irrespective of political, cultural or religious affiliation or gender. (Bell, 1995: 2)

Underpinning this approach is the principle of consent. Northern Ireland will not cease to be a part of the United Kingdom without the consent of a majority of the people therein. The first attempt to secure constitutional reform, following the introduction of Direct Rule, came in 1973 when a Northern Ireland Assembly was elected by proportional representation and a Power Sharing Executive formed from its members. Negotiations between representatives of the British Government, the Taoiseach of the Republic of Ireland and members of the new Executive secured the Sunningdale Agreement, which protected the rights of the Catholic minority by endorsing Catholics' desire to share power, and created a Council of Ireland, with members drawn from the North and South, to deal with matters of common concern. The Unionist Party leader Brian Faulkner, however, could not secure majority support of his party or Unionist voters for the agreement. This opposition crystallised in the form of a general strike by Protestant Ulster Workers' Council that crippled the Province through widespread intimidation including the control of food and electricity supplies. Grassroots Protestants made it clear through their actions that they would accept no dealings with the Republic in a Council of Ireland, nor would they share power with Catholic politicians. The Power Sharing Executive collapsed in 1974 (Bew and Patterson, 1985).

It was not until 1982 that the Northern Ireland Secretary of State proposed 'rolling devolution' under which an elected Northern Ireland Assembly would gradually assume executive powers in proportion to politicians' willingness to share responsibility (O'Leary, Elliott and Wilford, 1988). Both sides had to agree on how such powers should be discharged, with the endorsement of not less than 70 per cent of the Assembly members. Although all parties fought the elections to the Assembly, the Nationalists (SDLP and Sinn Féin) boycotted it in protest against any initiative that sought only internal solutions (excluding Dublin) to Northern Ireland's problems and Unionists' willingness to work exclusively on quasi-majoritarian terms. With no acceptable proposals for devolved structures emerging from the Assembly and electoral support for Sinn Féin increasing at the expense of the SDLP, the British and Irish Government signed the Anglo-Irish Agreement in 1985 (Aughey, 1989; Connolly and Loughlin, 1986).

Reflecting on the period preceding the Anglo-Irish Agreement O'Day writes:

Violence was endemic but had receded from the levels of the mid-70s; the government of the Irish Republic was less insistent upon its traditional objective of unification, though it did not abandon irredentist aspirations; and accommodation on the ground between peoples in Northern Ireland had not produced the desired results. From the late 1970s British governments increasingly sought to manage the crisis through bi-lateral diplomacy with the Dublin regime ... Britain no longer sought to treat Northern Ireland solely as an 'internal' matter, and London-Dublin negotiations soon assumed a primacy over attempts to secure agreements directly between peoples within Northern Ireland. While the strategy paid dividends in terms of Anglo-Irish relations, it did not end terrorism and it exacerbated concerns within the unionist community. The Anglo-Irish Agreement was a turning point. British refusal to pay serious attention to unionist objections, and the acknowledgement of a role for

the Republic in affairs of Northern Ireland, undermined confidence
in it for many Ulster Protestants.

(O'Day, 1997: 10)

The Agreement asserted that the constitutional status of Northern
Ireland would not change without the consent of a majority of its
inhabitants and established an Intergovernmental Conference between
Britain and the Republic of Ireland as a forum within which the Irish
Republic could forward views on a range of political, security and legal
matters, reflective of the Nationalist perspective in the North. Unionists
were incensed that the Agreement had been negotiated without con-
sulting the Unionist majority, incorporated an Irish dimension and had
the status of international law. The two main Unionist parties, the UUP
and DUP, engaged in a campaign of political disruption and demonstrations that failed to rescind the Agreement, and their relationship
with government ministers plummeted to an all-time low until inter-
party discussions resumed in 1991 (Knox and Connolly, 1988). These
were aimed at securing a consensus on a power sharing local assembly
with new North–South and Anglo-Irish intergovernmental institutions.
The talks got bogged down over procedural and substantive wrangling
and eventually foundered.

With the breakdown in the inter-party talks, both the British and
Irish Governments seized the initiative and issued the Anglo-Irish Joint
(Downing Street) Declaration in December 1993. The Joint Declaration
was agreed between the then Republic of Ireland Taoiseach, Albert
Reynolds and the British Prime Minister, John Major. It set out an agreed
framework devised by both governments and committed them to promote co-operation at all levels on the basis of fundamental principles,
undertakings, obligations under international agreements and guarantees that each government had given and reaffirmed, including
Northern Ireland's statutory constitutional guarantee. It was described
as the starting point of a peace process designed to culminate in a
political settlement. The Joint Declaration stated that ultimate decisions on governing Northern Ireland would be made by a majority of
the citizens therein. The Republic of Ireland would, as part of an overall settlement, seek to revise its constitutional claim to sovereignty over
the six counties of Northern Ireland, and Britain would not block the
possible reunification of Ireland, if it were backed by a majority in the
North. The Joint Declaration, set alongside a flurry of secret discussions
that included an unpublished peace plan devised by the SDLP and Sinn
Féin, acted as a catalyst for the IRA cease-fire.

After 3,168 deaths and 25 years of violence, the Irish Republican Army (IRA) announced a cease-fire on 31 August 1994. This was subsequently followed (14 October 1994) by a reciprocal cessation of violence from the combined Loyalist Military Command, an umbrella group comprising the Ulster Volunteer Force, The Ulster Defence Association and the Red Hand Commando. The IRA announcement claimed its cessation was in recognition of the 'potential of the current situation and in order to enhance the democratic peace process'. The Loyalists, in turn, stated that their cease-fire was 'completely dependent upon the continued IRA cessation, since the Republican cease-fire has yet to be declared permanent'. Britain maintained that it would not enter into formal talks with Sinn Féin until it unequivocally renounced violence and for 3 months after the start of a permanent cease-fire by the IRA.

The two governments responded to the cease-fires with different degrees of magnanimity in an effort to encourage the peace process, on the one hand, but detract from critics, on the other, that such gestures were a 'reward' for terrorism. For example, the ban on broadcasting imposed on Sinn Féin was lifted and the people of Northern Ireland promised a referendum on future proposals for its governance emerging from a framework document drawn up by the British and Irish Governments. Border crossings were opened, financial and economic aid promised from British, European and American sources and an unofficial scaling down of military presence in volatile areas got under way. The Republic of Ireland began a programme of releasing IRA prisoners (with less than 3 years to serve), somewhat misguidedly in the British view, which was seriously set back when a postal worker was shot (November 1994) in an IRA fund-raising robbery. This served only to remind both governments (if indeed they needed such a reminder) that the men of violence were waiting in the wings whilst politicians were given an opportunity to reach an acceptable constitutional agreement. One relic of past failures to reach a compromise was the 1974 Power Sharing Executive. A loyalist backlash against power sharing and the Irish framework (Council of Ireland) had led to the collapse of the administration and the re-imposition of Direct Rule. The preferences of the British and Irish Governments for a future settlement and proposals for all-party talks were subsequently outlined in the Frameworks Document, published in February 1995, which adopted a three strand approach – agreement between parties within Northern Ireland (strand 1), a North–South relationship (strand 2), and an Anglo-Irish (Britain and the Republic of Ireland) agreement (strand 3).

The peace process

The publication of the Frameworks Document represented a promising attempt to bring stability to Northern Ireland though nascent consociational arrangements. The document proposed a number of initiatives including provisions for: a 90 member Assembly for Northern Ireland elected by proportional representation, with substantial legislative and administrative powers; a North/South body comprising elected representatives of the Northern Ireland Assembly and the Irish Parliament; an end to the Republic's constitutional claim over Northern Ireland; increased London and Dublin co-operation through a standing intergovernmental conference, but with no right to interfere with the Northern Ireland Assembly; separate referenda in the North and South with a majority needed in each case for proposals to proceed.

The document was presented not as an immutable blueprint, but as a contribution to the talks process, through either bilaterals or round-table negotiations involving all political parties. While O'Leary described the two framework documents as 'the most far-reaching and intelligent tests yet produced by the two governments, and one must be hopeful that they will lead to fruitful negotiations', he highlighted three problems. The documents were: vague/inconsistent in their commitment on rights, law and the judiciary; devoid of methods for reaching the proposed agreement, apart from the ultimate prospect of referenda and constitutional legislation in the two sovereign parliaments; short on suggestions about what happens if there were no negotiations, or no negotiations which produced an agreement which could be sold in two referenda (O'Leary, 1995).

The Irish Government committed itself to introducing and supporting proposals to amend articles 2 and 3 of the Irish Constitution through the assurance that 'no territorial claim of right to jurisdiction over Northern Ireland, contrary to the will of a majority of its people is asserted' (Hansard, 1995). By the same token the British Government reaffirmed that it would uphold the democratic wish of a greater number of people of Northern Ireland on the issue of whether they prefer to support the Union, or a sovereign United Ireland. The British Government was equally cognisant of either option and open to its democratic realisation. In particular, it pledged not to impede movement towards a United Ireland. Compromise and bargaining between the two governments was obvious. The revision of the Republic's constitutional claim over Northern Ireland, as a placatory measure for

Unionists, was reciprocated with the British position that reunification would not be blocked, a measure designed to appease Nationalists.

The bargain was endorsed by proposals for a new North–South body charged with a range of consultative, harmonising and executive functions. Membership of the new body would be drawn from, and accountable to, the proposed Northern Ireland Assembly and the Irish Parliament. Decisions in the body could only be taken where there was agreement North and South. The Northern Ireland Assembly and the Irish Parliament would therefore have an absolute safeguard against proposals they did not approve.

The Frameworks Document was widely perceived as a contribution by the two governments to the subsequent multi-party talks process. These are described in the Frameworks Document as 'the most comprehensive attainable negotiations with democratically mandated political parties in Northern Ireland which abide exclusively by peaceful means and wish to join in dialogue on the way ahead' (*The Times*, 1 March 1995). Political parties could table alternative proposals to those contained within the Frameworks. Thereafter, a 'triple lock safeguard' against any proposals being imposed on Northern Ireland would operate. First, any proposals must command the support of the political parties in Northern Ireland; second, any proposals must then be approved by the people of Northern Ireland (and the Republic) in referenda; and third, any necessary legislation must be passed by the United Kingdom Parliament.

The view from the Northern Ireland Office was optimistic on the prospects for political progress:

> More now than 20 years of commitment by successive UK adminis-
> trations to the peace, stability and prosperity of Northern Ireland,
> efforts are beginning to pay immense dividends – with the help above
> all of our friends in the Republic of Ireland, the USA and, it must be
> said, the vision of those within republican and loyalist communities
> who could persuade their colleagues to lay down their weapons. In
> parallel, the economy – and all that means – for the life chances of
> everyone in Northern Ireland is prospering as perhaps never before.
> There is, if the paramilitaries on both sides can take the necessary
> confidence building measures, a real prospect of constructive, inclu-
> sive political talks involving all shades of political opinion leading
> eventually to that just and lasting settlement the United Kingdom
> government has consistently pursued.
>
> (Bell, 1995: 20)

The pace of political developments, however, remained decidedly slow. Although bilateral meetings took place between government ministers and all the political parties, an impasse developed with no immediate prospect of round table talks. Despite concessions in August 1995 by the British Government to increase remission for terrorist prisoners to 50 per cent, a commitment to reform policing structures, and a promise to review the need for emergency legislation, little progress was made. Unionists would not enter into political negotiations until weapons were decommissioned. Sinn Féin, on the other hand, insisted on all-party talks and no decommissioning until a settlement was reached. In an attempt to break the log-jam the British and Irish Governments set up an international advisory body (the Mitchell Commission) to identify and advise on a suitable and acceptable method for full and verifiable decommissioning and to report whether or not those holding illegal arms were prepared to work constructively towards achieving this objective.

Competing views were advanced on decommissioning prior to all-party negotiations. One was that this *must* occur as a clear demonstration of adherence to democratic principles and of a permanent end to the use of violence. In this way, it was argued, a start to decommissioning would provide the confidence necessary for all-party negotiations to commence. The alternative view was that decommissioning of arms prior to all-party negotiations was not required before the announcement of the cease-fires, and had it been, there would have been no cease-fires. Those who entered into cease-fires did so in the belief they would lead immediately to all-party negotiations. Prior decommissioning was therefore perceived as merely a tactic to delay or deny such negotiations.

The SDLP leader John Hume, reflecting on decommissioning, stated:

> The whole decommissioning issue has been a very serious and silly distraction. Virtually every political party in Ireland, except my own, was founded by the gun. Where are the guns now ? They didn't decommission to anyone, but they got rid of them. Doing otherwise is to give the appearance of surrendering. I was astonished when this issue was first raised by the Major government.
>
> (Hume, 1997: 20)

The Commission reaffirmed that the paramilitaries would not disarm and, as an alternative, recommended allowing arms decommissioning *during* all-party talks, so long as all participants first signed up to six principles before being admitted to talks.

The six principles (the 'Mitchell principles') were that parties to negotiations affirm their total and absolute commitment to:

- democratic and exclusively peaceful means of resolving political issues;
- the total disarmament of all paramilitary organisations;
- agree that such disarmament must be verifiable to the satisfaction of an independent commission;
- renounce for themselves, and to oppose by others, the use of force, or threat to use force, to influence the course or the outcome of all-party negotiations;
- agree to abide by the terms of any agreement reached in all-party negotiations, and to resort to democratic and exclusively peaceful methods in trying to alter any aspect of that outcome with which they may disagree; and,
- urge that 'punishment' killings and beatings stop and to take effective steps to prevent such actions.

The British Government reacted by side-stepping the major thrust of the Commission's findings published in January 1996, seizing instead upon a relatively minor confidence-building measure in the report – an elected assembly to provide a mandate for talks without prior decommissioning. Nationalists (SDLP & Sinn Féin) and the Republic of Ireland Government accused the British of 'political mugging' and pandering to Unionists in an effort to prop-up their dwindling Conservative majority in the House of Commons. A suggestion by the Irish Government that Dayton-style talks, akin to those in the former Yugoslavia, take place met with Unionist derision. Without notice the IRA called off the cease-fire (9 February 1996) and bombed London's docklands killing 2 people and injuring many others. This was followed soon afterwards by a bomb which exploded prematurely killing its IRA handler.

Predictable recriminations followed in the wake of the cease-fire breakdown. Nationalists accused the British Government of squandering the respite in violence and dragging its heels on political progress. Unionists, on the other hand, felt vindicated in refusing to join round-table talks in advance of decommissioning terrorist weapons. The London bombings were, in their view, good examples of the terrorists' response to not achieving their political objectives and demonstrated the futility of engaging in political dialogue with Sinn Féin. The Government of the Irish Republic felt slighted in the wake of the findings of Mitchell because of the British Government's insistence on elections as a means of achieving multi-party talks. This surprising turn of events had resulted, according to the IRA, from the British Government's failure during the 17 months of the cease-fire to move towards 'an inclusive negotiated settlement'.

Within days of the London bombing, a flurry of activity by the British and Irish Governments produced a consensus on future progress in contrast to previous disagreements on the way forward. Hitherto, the Nationalists and the Irish Government were committed to the *idea* of 'proximity talks' as a precursor to all-party negotiations. Unionists and the British Government preferred elections to a Northern Ireland Convention or Forum leading to negotiations with both governments. By 4 March 1996, two weeks of proximity talks were underway, province-wide elections were announced (for 30 May 1996) to a new 110-strong elected forum without executive powers whose brief was 'to promote dialogue and mutual understanding within Northern Ireland' leading 'directly and without preconditions' to all-party negotiations (Northern Ireland Office, 21 March 1996). The successful parties were invited by the Secretary of State to select, from among their representatives, negotiating teams for talks to begin on 10 June 1996. The elected Forum could not engage in the negotiations, which were free-standing, but could interact with and inform the process at the request of the participants in negotiations. The Forum's life was time-limited to 12 months, renewable for up to a maximum of a further 12 months.

The purpose of the negotiations was to 'achieve a new beginning for relationships within Northern Ireland, within the island of Ireland and between the peoples of these islands, and to agree new institutions and structures to take account of the totality of relationships' (Northern Ireland Office, 1996, Cm 3232). Both governments reaffirmed their intention that the outcome of negotiations would be submitted for public approval by referendums in Ireland – North and South – before being submitted to their respective parliaments for ratification and implementation. Three independent chairmen were appointed: Senator George Mitchell, the former majority leader of the United States Senate, General John de Chastelain, former Chief of Staff of the Canadian Armed Forces, and Mr Harri Holkeri, the former Prime Minister of Finland. In the absence of a new IRA cease-fire, however, Sinn Féin were excluded from taking their place at the negotiating table. This, in turn, was seen by the IRA as a precondition and elections to a 110 member 'peace' forum took place on 30 May 1996 with no cease-fire in place.

In the event, Sinn Féin returned its best electoral result[12] (15.5 per cent) and the Ulster Unionists a relatively weak performance (24.2 per cent). Worst of all, following months of political wrangling and the breakdown in the IRA cease-fire, the British Government was left with a strategy – disarmament talks and political negotiations running in parallel – the same outcome suggested by the Mitchell Commission in January 1996.

The multi-party talks

The Forum first met on 10 June 1996 (without Sinn Féin) and all the delegates committed themselves to the Mitchell principles of democracy and non-violence, including the fringe Loyalist parties (UDP and PUP). It made faltering progress, however, as a result of procedural rows, largely relating to the chairmanship and the role of the Irish Government in the multi-party talks. Attempts to move towards political negotiations were overshadowed by widespread civil disorder over a disputed Orange Order march in Drumcree, Portadown (July 1996) which saw the return of riots, shooting, petrol bombs and barricades to the streets of Northern Ireland. Eventually (29 July 1996) rules of procedures were agreed but delegates were unable to advance into issues of substance because they failed to reach sufficient agreement on the issue of decommissioning of weapons by paramilitaries. The Forum and the talks were formally suspended pending the general elections throughout the United Kingdom in May 1997, having made little progress to date.

In May 1997 a new Labour Government was elected to Westminster with a landslide victory ending 18 years of Conservative rule. The size of the Labour mandate (44 per cent vote and 419 seats) nullified the political influence exerted by the Ulster Unionists over the previous administration. In the same elections two prominent Sinn Féin leaders (Gerry Adams and Martin McGuinness) were elected to Parliament. Both subsequently refused to swear an oath of allegiance to the Queen and could not therefore take their seats in the Commons. At the same time Fianna Fail, a party seen to be more sympathetic to nationalists, was elected in the Republic of Ireland. The size of the Sinn Féin vote (16.1 per cent) and its new position as the third largest political party in Northern Ireland (behind the Ulster Unionists and the SDLP) demanded a new response from the Labour Government.

The Government's position was outlined by Prime Minister Blair on his first official visit to Belfast following his election. Northern Ireland was to be one of the new government's highest priorities. It would remain part of the United Kingdom for as long as that was the wish of a majority with the principle of consent accepted by all constitutional parties in Ireland, North and South. In this way, if a majority decided in favour of a United Ireland, the Government would respect that, but it recognised this was unlikely for the foreseeable future. The immediate challenge was to arrive at a settlement that commanded agreement on both sides of the communities with the vehicle for so doing, the talks process. The Prime Minister stressed the need to reach agreement on the decommissioning issue and move into discussions on the substance of a settlement. The talks resumed in June 1997 with a clear directive to resolve the issue of decommissioning, endorse proposals for an agenda and launch the 'Three Strands'. The new Labour Secretary of State (Mo Mowlam) immediately authorised contacts between civil servants and Sinn Féin, ostensibly to clarify the new government's position, but in fact to negotiate with the party.

The British and Irish Governments put forward their proposals for decommissioning in which they undertook to bring about 'due progress' on decommissioning *alongside* progress in the substantive political negotiations. Mechanisms for achieving further progress on decommissioning would be established in the form of an Independent Commission: to consult on schemes for decommissioning and present proposals to the government; to undertake tasks that may be required to facilitate, observe, monitor and verify decommissioning and to receive and audit arms, and make reports; and the setting up of two liaison sub-committees of the talks plenary, one on decommissioning and another on confidence-building measures. These proposals failed to achieve 'sufficient consensus' (the support of representatives of a majority of each community which is necessary for approval under the talks rules – in short, that parties representing a majority of each community, unionist and nationalist should concur) when put before the talks. The two governments made clear their determination to press on with the talks process and an Independent Commission was set up with a view to commencing work alongside substantive negotiations.

The negotiations between the government and Sinn Féin resulted, according to the latter, in their demands being met over four crucial issues. Sinn Féin would be admitted to all-party talks on the same basis as other parties; those talks would be completed within a fixed time frame; the government would not require decommissioning of weapons before or during negotiations; and confidence-building measures would be introduced such as a relaxation in security and concessions for 'political prisoners'. The result was the IRA cease-fire effective from 20 July 1997 – 'an unequivocal restoration of the cease-fire of August 1994'. Its renewal was met with the same degree of surprise as its collapse in February 1996. It was greeted however with considerable scepticism and hostility by the UUP and DUP respectively. The former described it as a tactical ploy aimed at getting Sinn Féin into talks but reserving the right, should negotiations not go their way, to re-engage in violence. As the DUP deputy leader (Peter Robinson) commented, 'all we have is a restoration of a phoney cease-fire'.

On 29 August 1997 the Secretary of State announced that Sinn Féin would be invited into the talks process, since in the light of the IRA's resumption of its cease-fire they now, in her view, met the requirements of entry. The Ulster Unionist Party first threatened to boycott the talks then rejoined them saying it wanted to confront Sinn Féin to expose 'their fascist character'. At the same the DUP and the UK Unionist Party withdrew. Sinn Féin attended the talks for the first time in September and subscribed to the Mitchell principles of democracy and non-violence. There was clearly disapproval within the Republican ranks. An Phoblacht, the republican newspaper, published an interview with an IRA spokesman in which he reiterated that there would be no decommissioning ahead of a political settlement. He also claimed that the IRA 'had problems' with the Mitchell principles of non-violence which had been endorsed by the Sinn Féin leaders. This provoked a Unionist backlash and accusations that Sinn Féin were duplicitous in a bid to secure entry to the talks.

Both the British and Irish Governments set out their thinking on two key issues in the talks process. On the question of *consent*, they emphasised that it would be a guiding principle for them in negotiations out of which no outcome was excluded or predetermined. They reaffirmed that the aim of the negotiations was to achieve a new and lasting agreement, addressing the totality of relationships, commanding the consent of unionists and nationalists. They emphasised that the talks rules, binding on all participants, required that any agreement must command sufficient consensus among participants. On the question of *decommissioning*, they remained totally committed to the implementation of the Mitchell Report in all aspects and indicated that both Governments would like to see decommissioning of some paramilitary arms during negotiations, as progress was made in the political talks. This would be seen as a major contribution to confidence building and a momentum towards agreement (Northern Ireland Office, 1997a). In September 1997 the talks agreed a procedural motion by which

discussion moved on from decommissioning, an agenda for negotiations was agreed and the three strands of substantive negotiations were
launched. At the same time an Independent International Commission
on decommissioning was set up by the two governments.

The objective of the Commission is to facilitate the decommissioning of firearms, ammunition, explosives and explosive substances in
accordance with the Report of the International Body (Mitchell) and
the legislation already enacted in each jurisdiction (UK and Republic
of Ireland) – the Northern Ireland Decommissioning Act 1997 and the
Decommissioning Act 1997. Among the privileges and immunities
granted to the Commission, its members and staff, are immunity from
suit and legal process and immunity for its premises in Belfast and
Dublin and for its documents.

The Secretary of State was upbeat about the move to substantive
negotiations:

> Today we have turned an important page in the history of Northern
> Ireland. The new chapter we shall be writing will involve inclusive
> and substantive negotiations, taking place in a peaceful atmosphere.
> Such talks have the potential to bring huge benefits to all the people
> of these islands and especially the people of Northern Ireland... The
> machinery is now in place for fair and effective negotiations, capa-
> ble of addressing all the issues of concern to all participants and
> leading to a political settlement which will be widely acceptable. No
> one has anything to fear from seeking such a settlement. Everyone
> has much to gain.
>
> (Northern Ireland Office, 1997a)

The talks were hailed as different to any others which had been
attempted since 1970. For the first time they were taking place with IRA
and Loyalist cease-fires in place. They embraced the broadest spectrum of
political opinion, a reference to the involvement of Sinn Féin, fringe
Loyalists and other smaller parties (Women's Coalition and Labour). The
government also promised to give 'due weight' to the views of the DUP
and the UK Unionist Party despite their withdrawal from the process.
Moreover, in considering new arrangements for Northern Ireland, there
was an opportunity to learn from plans for devolution in Scotland and
Wales.

Strand 1 of the talks was expected to address and seek to reach
agreement on relationships and arrangements within Northern Ireland.
This included the constitution of any elected institutions, the method

of election, their role and responsibilities, their relationship with the executive, accountability, checks and balances against abuse, finance, and the relationship with the Westminster Parliament, The European Union, political institutions in the Republic of Ireland and the proposed Scottish Parliament and Welsh Assembly.

The pace of the talks, however, remained decidedly slow despite the direct involvement of the Prime Minister in supporting the efforts of participants. Inviting Gerry Adams, Sinn Féin's President, to Downing Street in December 1997 was part of that process in 'taking risks for peace'. The Prime Minister suggested that unless Sinn Féin returned to violence he intended to treat them exactly like all other participants in the talks process. The UDP & PUP, front parties for loyalist paramilitary groups, had also met Mr. Blair. Some comfort was taken from the fact that the UUP remained within the process having accepted the talks format, and George Mitchell as Chair, when they had once opposed both. The Ulster Unionists also said that they would never enter substantive negotiations with Sinn Féin, while the IRA retained its weapons (*Economist*, 1997). But no decommissioning by the IRA or loyalist paramilitaries had taken place, yet the UUP entered into substantive negotiations. The Prime Minister insisted, however, if no agreement was reached by May 1998 he intended to put a proposed settlement to the province's voters in a referendum.

What we are aiming for is a settlement which commands the consent of both communities. Any settlement must be negotiated. Let me recall that the negotiations are governed by the principle of sufficient consensus under which all conclusions must have the support of parties representing a majority of unionists and a majority of nationalists. Finally, any settlement must be endorsed by the people of Northern Ireland in a referendum and by the British Parliament. So the 'triple lock' is in place, as strong as ever. Fears about an imposed settlement are entirely misplaced. And the basic elements of a settlement are reasonably clear – a devolved Assembly and mutually beneficial North–South arrangements in the context of a broader-based agreement addressing the totality of relationships within these islands – although there will of course be fierce argument about the details and some will be arguing for a united Ireland as they are perfectly entitled to do. There is nothing for any democrat to fear from these negotiations.

(Tony Blair, *Belfast Newsletter*, 13 September 1997)

The British Government stressed its role as a facilitator for agreement in the talks and guarantors that, for as long as Northern Ireland remains part of the United Kingdom, they will work with parties to make it a fair and just place to live. They pointed to a comprehensive programme for change to operationalise these principles – a series of confidence building measures:

- legislation will be in place before the next marching season (summer 1998) to secure local accommodation, including powers to re-route, through an Independent Parades Commission in a bid to avoid the disturbances surrounding Drumcree and other contentious marches;
- the European Convention on Human Rights will be incorporated into UK law and Northern Ireland parties encouraged to develop a Bill of Rights;
- changes in policing structures will take place to increase confidence across the whole community and make them more accountable alongside the creation of an independent complaints system – a police ombudsman;
- a fairer prisons systems will be established (transfer of prisoners to be near their families; shorter time between life sentence reviews);
- significant military de-escalation throughout Northern Ireland will continue to take place at a pace in keeping with the level of violence (no military patrols in Belfast, Londonderry and Newry town centres – RUC foot patrols unaccompanied in West Belfast);
- a review of emergency legislation has already made changes – the removal of the internment provisions, the provision for police interviews with terrorists suspects to be audio recorded, reduction in the number of cases heard by Diplock non-jury courts;
- government will respond to the Standing Advisory Commission on Human Rights report on employment equality issues to shape future policy on fair employment and provision for the unemployed and socially disadvantaged.

This programme of changes was therefore an attempt by the British Government to support the best efforts of politicians in negotiations and build confidence in the community. In essence, for Unionists, negotiations would centre on changes to the Irish constitution and a replacement for the Anglo-Irish Agreement. Nationalists wanted a new relationship between unionism and nationalism within the island of Ireland and North–South arrangements which would help to accommodate the Irish nationalist identity of the minority community in Northern Ireland.

In the absence of progress within the talks, the British and Irish Governments tabled, in January 1998, a paper entitled *Propositions on Heads of Agreement* for debate and discussion in an effort to promote substantive political progress. Both governments suggested that although the paper emerged from them, it was based upon views expressed in bilateral meetings and round table discussions which had taken place with all parties. The propositions paper was therefore their 'best guess at what could be a generally acceptable outcome' (Northern Ireland Office, 1998). It contained suggestions for the key elements of a settlement and was intended to make it easier for parties to engage in the detailed negotiation on specific aspects of its content.

In brief, the propositions were:

- balanced constitutional change to the Irish Constitution and British constitutional legislation;
- a Northern Ireland Assembly elected by proportional representation exercising devolved and executive responsibility over at least the six Northern Ireland departments;
- a new British–Irish Agreement to replace the existing Anglo-Irish Agreement;
- an Intergovernmental Council to deal with the totality of relationships, including representatives of the British and Irish Governments, the Northern Ireland administration and the devolved institutions in Scotland and Wales;
- A North/South Ministerial Council to bring together those with executive responsibilities in matters of mutual interest in Northern Ireland and the Irish Government;
- suitable implementation bodies and mechanisms for policies agreed by the North/South Council;
- standing intergovernmental machinery between the Irish and British Governments, covering issues of mutual interest, including non-devolved issues for Northern Ireland;
- provision to safeguard the rights of both communities in Northern Ireland, including a Bill of Rights for Northern Ireland to achieve full respect for the principles of equity of treatment and freedom from discrimination, and the cultural identity and ethos of both communities;
- effective and practical measures to establish and consolidate an acceptable peaceful society, dealing with issues such as prisoners, security in all its aspects, policing and decommissioning of weapons.

The propositions secured support from the SDLP and Alliance parties but caused problems for the Ulster Unionists and Sinn Féin. For the

Ulster Unionists the nature and extent of executive powers for any cross-border institutions created anxieties of a key role for the Republic of Ireland government and the spectre, ultimately, of moves towards an United Ireland. For Sinn Féin a Northern Ireland Assembly smacked of an internal settlement, totally unacceptable to republicans. As political dissension broke out the Province experienced a vicious and random campaign of murders by Protestant paramilitaries against innocent Catholics with no republican connections. The violence had spiralled following the assassination of LVF leader, Billy Wright, inside the Maze prison on 27 December 1997. The Ulster Democratic Party, political representatives for the UFF (Ulster Freedom Fighters) which was directly linked to the nationalist killings, was expelled from the talks for breaching the Mitchell principles.

There were, however, signs of optimism particularly in the strength of the Anglo-Irish relationship and signals that Sinn Féin might be prepared to compromise. The British and Irish governments had built a solid relationship with unity of purpose on the Northern Ireland issue. Blair delivered politically for Ahern on prison transfers and the new Bloody Sunday enquiry. Ahern was also able to deliver to Blair on a range of issues including an agreement that articles 2 and 3 of the Irish constitution *will* (not simply *could*) be changed as part of an overall settlement and general acceptance on the details of the Heads of Agreement.

Comments (February 1998) by Sinn Féin leaders displayed a new sense of realism. Martin McGuinness looking ahead to the end of the talks said:

> In May (1998), when the settlement will be signed up to, it clearly will not be the case that we will have a united Ireland. But that settlement will be part of an irreversible process towards a united Ireland.
>
> (McGuinness, quoted in L. Clarke, 1998: 15)

Other Sinn Féin leaders (Mitchel McLaughlin) endorse this view and highlight electoral and demographic trends leading inexorably to a united Ireland.

Ruane and Todd (1996) have argued that the actions and policies of the two governments will be a critical factor in confirming or disconfirming that there is now a real potential for resolving the conflict. In assessing the peace process they describe the different approaches involved:

> For some it is simply a practical accommodation to the current balance of power. The past twenty-five years of political and military

struggle have revealed to the different protagonists the extent and limits of their power and the relative stability of the current balance of power. On both sides there has been a change in strategy – a pursuit of traditional goals by other means, at least in the short term ...

Others – in both communities and in all parties – view the peace process quite differently. They see a real potential to bring the long destructive conflict finally to an end and are genuine in their expressions of moderation and generosity, their desire for reconciliation. For them the peace process is a first step to a permanent resolution of the conflict and an agreed settlement would represent major progress in that direction. There are many in both communities who fluctuate between these two poles in response to events and to their reading of others' attitudes.

(Ruane and Todd, 1996: 295)

The unpredictable nature of events on the ground could always precipitate an environment which was less than conducive to constructive negotiations and compromise. This made it difficult for politicians to deliver the outcomes of the multi-party talks to their constituents who, living in an atmosphere of fear, oppression and alienation, construe 'solutions' as 'sell-outs'. There is, none the less, a 'war-weariness' amongst the people of Northern Ireland and a realisation that the multi-party talks represented the best chance for peace. The performance of the fringe Loyalist parties (UDP and PUP) at the talks did much to assuage Nationalist fears by their attempts to persuade the men of violence to lay down their arms and call a halt to the brutal and random sectarian killings of Catholics. Although Sinn Féin indulges in the rhetoric of a united Ireland, there is a tacit acceptance that this is not achievable, at least in the short-term. But hard-liners still exist on both sides. Their actions, despite their limited numerical strength, has in the past and will in the future influence the political agenda despite the best intentions of key political actors not to be distracted from their goal of a settlement to the conflict.

3
Northern Ireland: Micro Grassroots Activity

Introduction

The formal position of the United Kingdom Government is that it seeks to secure peace, stability, reconciliation and prosperity for the people of Northern Ireland. It endeavours to achieve this through:

- promoting agreement among all people who inhabit the island of Ireland and working together with the Irish Government to that end;
- a co-ordinated and coherent approach to all aspects of government policy which recognises that the fundamental political, security, and economic and social problems of Northern Ireland are closely inter-related; and
- policies informed by the principles of equality of opportunity, equity of treatment and parity of esteem, irrespective of political, cultural or religious affiliation or gender. (Department of Finance & Personnel & H. M. Treasury, 1995)

What is important from this official statement of the government's position is a recognition that addressing political problems at the macro level is, in itself, insufficient. In other words, even if progress can be made on political, constitutional and security issues, the underlying community divisions will still exist and need to be addressed. If this does not happen they will threaten and eventually undermine achievements secured at the macro level. Any progress at the political level therefore needs to be consolidated by government initiatives to bring about equality, promote reconciliation and mutual respect for the separate traditions and cultures which exist within Northern Ireland; in short, to create a community which accommodates peoples' differing beliefs, aspirations and traditions. This has been referred to as the 'hearts and minds' strategy. Central to this strategy is a policy of improving community relations between Catholics and Protestants. This twin-track macro/micro approach is operationalised through the Central Secretariat which is located in the Department of Finance and Personnel (pre-devolved government under Belfast Agreement) as a discrete command within the Northern Ireland Civil Service. It provides support to the head of the civil service and central advice and guidance to the Secretary of State and Ministers on major policy issues affecting the Northern Ireland Departments.

The main objectives of the Central Secretariat are:

- to contribute to the achievement of a workable and effective political accommodation in Northern Ireland, acceptable to all the parties involved in its discussion and negotiation;
- to ensure that all sections of the community enjoy equality of opportunity and equity of treatment, to develop cross-community contact and co-operation, and to encourage the development of mutual respect, understanding and appreciation of cultural diversity.

The Central Community Relations Unit (CCRU), set up in September 1987, is in turn located within the Central Secretariat and provides policy advice to the Secretary of State on all community relations issues. It is charged with formulating, reviewing and challenging policy throughout the government system with the aim of improving community relations and has direct responsibility for primary community relations policies and programmes. The Department of Education for Northern Ireland (DENI) also has an important role in developing and implementing community relations policies and programmes in the education sector and through the arts, museums, sport and recreation. Overall the government has sought to implement a three-part approach to micro developments – measures to ensure equality and equity, education initiatives and those aimed at improving community relations. We consider each in turn.

(i) Equality and equity

Equality of opportunity and equity of treatment has now become a major concern for the government in Northern Ireland. On all major social and economic indicators – employment, unemployment, education, skills – Catholics experience much greater levels of disadvantage.

An analysis of the 1991 census data confirmed the level of inequality:

(a) The Catholic rate of unemployment remained higher than that of Protestants. Among men, Catholics were 2.2 times as likely to be unemployed in comparison with Protestants. Catholic women were 1.8 times as likely to be unemployed as Protestants. At the level of electoral ward analysis, 75 per cent of wards have Protestant male unemployment rates at or below 20 per cent whereas only 44 per cent of wards have Catholic rates at or below 20 per cent. Almost a third of wards have Catholic male unemployment rates above 30 per cent, whereas only 8 per cent of wards have Protestant male rates at these levels;

(b) There was Catholic under-representation in administrative and management occupations. Protestant men were more likely to be found in non-manual categories in comparison with Catholic men. Protestant men were over-represented in security and protective service occupations, managerial and administrative occupations, and skilled engineering occupations. Catholic men were over-represented in skilled construction trades, labouring occupations, and on government employment and training schemes;

(c) Protestant men were more likely to have vocational qualifications than Catholic men, and were slightly more likely to have graduate level qualifications. Catholic men were also over-represented among those with no qualifications;

(d) Catholic unemployment rates, for men and women, were higher than those of Protestants for each level of qualification.

The analysis concluded that:

(e) There have been substantial increases in Catholic representation in the areas of white collar, professional, managerial and administrative occupations. As yet, however, very few of these increases have taken Catholics up to, or beyond, their representation in the economically active population. There is, therefore, evidence of an expansion in the Catholic middle class. However, Catholics have yet to get a similar advance in senior decision-making positions in public services as a whole or as senior managers in larger private sector concerns. There is no evidence, as far as Catholics are concerned, that 'fair participation' has been achieved;

(f) The two most striking differentials between Protestant and Catholic profiles are the substantially higher experience of Catholic unemployment and the domination of Protestants in security occupations. (Cormack, Gallagher and Osborne, 1993; Gallagher, Osborne and Cormack, 1995)

These differential experiences sustain feelings of disadvantage, discrimination and alienation among Catholics, which in turn influence attitudes to political and security issues. Political 'solutions' must therefore include policies and programmes aimed at tackling and removing differentials and, as importantly, ensuring that current government programmes do not have a differential impact on one community at the expense of the other. What follows is a description of policies devised by government to tackle issues of equality and equity.

Targeting social need

A major government initiative, Targeting Social Need (TSN), was launched in February 1991 by the Secretary of State, who said:

> If we genuinely wish to address the issues of social need...and achieve a reduction in community differentials, we must target our resources. The objective of the TSN initiative is to tackle areas of social and economic differences by targeting government policies and programmes more sharply in those areas or sections of the community suffering the highest levels of disadvantage and deprivation. Since the Catholic section of the community suffers higher levels of social and economic disadvantage, the targeting of need should have the effect of reducing existing differentials.
>
> (Peter Brooke, Secretary of State: quoted in CCRU Paper 'Community Relations In Northern Ireland', 1996)

The objective of TSN is, therefore, to direct resources more precisely on Northern Ireland's most disadvantaged areas and people. In successive public expenditure surveys, TSN has been confirmed as a continuing priority of promoting self-sustaining economic growth. An important effect of this should be to reduce social and economic differentials between the two major blocs within the community. TSN is not, however, a programme or set of programmes itself, but an underlying principle which guides allocations across many programmes. The Secretary of State was, however, at pains to point out:

> I must stress that the programme is about targeting resources and policies to address disadvantage and is *not* about positive discrimination which would be unlawful under existing law. However, since

the Catholic section of the community generally suffers more extensively from the effects of social and economic disadvantage, the targeting of need will have the effect of reducing existing differentials.

(Peter Brooke, Secretary of State: quoted in McGill, 1996)

Therein lies a confusion about the precise purpose of TSN. Osborne
(1998) points out that an opposing view exists within the higher levels
of the civil service that socio-economic need and, increasingly, alienation is to be found in the Protestant community. As a result, it would
be wrong for TSN to be so explicitly aimed at one community. The
problem, however, given the high levels of segregation in Northern
Ireland is that when composite rankings of social disadvantage are
devised at the electoral ward level most Catholic areas emerge at the
top (Robson, Bradford and Deas, 1994). This geographical approach to
disadvantage side-steps the charge of a religion-specific policy of targeting social need.

The commitment of government departments to the principles of
TSN has, however, been controversial. McGill (1996: 5) examined the
implementation of TSN in three of the six Northern Ireland departments – agriculture, economic development and education, to assess
the extent to which 'public expenditure is skewed towards disadvantaged areas and people'. His conclusions were highly critical of TSN as
practised by central government departments. Specifically he found that:

- the Department of Agriculture had no data on the poorest family
  farms, no idea of where social need existed and no plans to use
  deprivation indices (Robson, 1994) to influence the allocation of
  resources;
- the Department of Economic Development had a target of locating
  75 per cent of inward investment projects (not jobs) 'in or adjacent
  to' disadvantaged areas. Not only was this found to be 'absurdly
  vague' but as these TSN areas have 82 per cent of the registered
  unemployed, even meeting their own target would further widen
  the gap between these and other areas;
- spending by the Department of Education is skewed towards
  middle-class children, exacerbated by the selection of children for
  secondary and grammar schools. Voluntary grammar schools receive
  social deprivation funding, even though they are among the most
  privileged schools in the United Kingdom.

McGill concluded that 'the policy has failed to make much impact on
many areas of government' (1996: 57) and noted that some departments

had taken the view that they were not concerned with the religious affiliation of their clients. Without monitoring differentials between Catholics and Protestants, it was, he suggested, clearly impossible to remedy them.

In a more comprehensive review of the implementation of TSN by government departments between 1991 and 1995, Quirk and McLaughlin (1996) outlined the Secretary of State's position that TSN had to be seen as a long-term commitment which would not be 'quick and easy'. They referred to a previous study by the Northern Ireland Council for Voluntary Action (NICVA, 1994) which found little evidence of monitoring systems capable of establishing the differential impacts of government programmes and concurred with its conclusions:

> The TSN policy is potentially the most significant policy initiative in the area of social need, deprivation and disadvantage ever taken by Government ... However, it has yet to take root in all departments or to make real impact where it is most needed ... Unless Government establishes new ways of progressing the policy and of challenging departments to implement it with vigour and enthusiasm, it may unfortunately remain a nice idea existing in the margins of Government and the minds of a few committed individuals.
>
> (Northern Ireland Council for Voluntary Action, 1994: 6,
> quoted in Quirk and McLaughlin, 1996: 158–9)

The evaluation of TSN by Quirk and McLaughlin was part of a broader employment equality review undertaken by the Standing Advisory Commission on Human Rights on behalf of the Secretary of State. The researchers were scathing in their condemnation of civil servants whose role included the implementation of TSN in the main departments of government. They attacked officials for assuming an ambivalent approach to the way the initiative was operationalised – on the one hand targeting, community differentials and, on the other, targeting all need, regardless of community, despite knowing that a 'religion-blind' approach was ineffective in reducing community differentials.

Their research concluded:

> there was little evidence that TSN, as it was initially framed politically, has had a substantial influence on spending and decision-making of departments. This is not surprising, given the reluctance of most departments to monitor or research expenditure, programmes

and policies in terms of their impacts on the Catholic and Protestant communities in Northern Ireland. TSN has not been, in our view, a public expenditure priority – rather it is a principle awaiting definition, operationalisation and implementation.

(Quirk and McLaughlin, 1996: 183)

Two special initiatives, 'Making Belfast Work' and the 'Londonderry Initiative', have been highlighted as examples 'at the forefront of the government's Targeting Social Need strategy' (Making Belfast Work, 1995). The Making Belfast Work (MBW) initiative was launched in July 1988 in response to severe multiple deprivation (endemic problems of unemployment, low skills levels, poor educational achievement, poor health and a depressing physical environment) deep-rooted in a number of areas of Belfast. MBW has two primary aims: to increase opportunities for residents of MBW areas to secure employment; and to improve the quality of life for these residents. By March 1997 a total of £200 m had been allocated to the initiative, resources over and above those already deployed within departmental budgets on TSN. Examples of projects supported under MBW included financial aid to establish community businesses in East Belfast, building a training centre (Springvale) for young people and adults to acquire IT skills, financing nursery unit accommodation, and providing advance factory accommodation in West Belfast suitable for a variety of manufacturing activities.

The Londonderry Initiative is a similar scheme in an area of high unemployment which seeks to tackle various aspects of urban decline, including physical dereliction, social deprivation and economic difficulties. By March 1997 a total of £23 m had been allocated to the initiative, over and above mainstream departmental expenditure. The main aims of the initiative are to attract private sector investment to the city, help people to secure jobs, improve their employability, refurbish the physical environment, and promote the image of the city at local, national and international levels. Examples of projects supported under the initiative included: the provision of a new primary school and nursery unit in the heart of the City (the Fountain Estate); a secondary schools programme in two schools (one on the East Bank of the Foyle and the other on the West Bank) with the aim of improving the employability of their pupils; a youth programme targeted at those aged 10–17 years who were involved in deviant behaviour.

Here again the government's approach to equality and equity came in for criticism. An evaluation of MBW described the strategy as comprising three basic ideas: the need for job creation, local community involvement and central government control. It concluded:

> In terms of the key objectives MBW has not been very successful. The initiative has not made significant in-roads into the lack of jobs and long-term unemployment in the disadvantaged areas. The majority of the jobs created by the initiative to date have been in the social and community services rather than in commercial or business enterprises and consequently are often low paid or part time.
>
> (Birrell and Wilson, 1993: 51)

The evaluation also highlighted 'some degree of success' and made suggestions for consolidating achievements (Birrell and Wilson, 1993: 54). It acknowledged the benefit of targeting deprived areas but wanted more internal differentiation at the level of neighbourhoods. There had been a welcome emphasis on social deprivation as a multi-disciplinary problem which required a combined approach from the relevant government agencies, and there was some success with community involvement, despite the difficult conditions in West Belfast.

Quirk and McLaughlin (1996) reached similar conclusions on the lack of success of TSN:

> Making Belfast Work, the Londonderry Initiative and the Rural Development Programme have to be regarded as the principal face of TSN. Significantly, both MBW and the Londonderry Initiative predate TSN and while all three initiatives are clearly targeted on areas of multiple deprivation, in practice, the TSN impact of these programmes has been minimal both in terms of outputs and their effectiveness in changing the spending priorities of departments and agencies.
>
> (Quirk and McLaughlin, 1996: 178)

Attempts by government at improving equality of opportunity and equity of treatment have not therefore been well regarded. We now turn to another central plank in the government's approach to these issues – fair employment.

Fair employment legislation

Concerns over fair employment in Northern Ireland were part of a series of grievances highlighted by the civil rights movement of the late 1960s. The Cameron Commission (1969), an enquiry set up to investigate the causes of the disturbances surrounding the civil rights marches, listed 'well founded grievances' as their source, of which job discrimination was one (Buckland, 1981: 135). An important element of the Unionist Government's ongoing reform package at the time was to establish a Parliamentary Commissioner for Administration and a Commissioner for Complaints. Their briefs included investigating allegation of religious discrimination in employment. Following the imposition of Direct Rule in 1972, British Government concerns over fair employment led to the creation of the Fair Employment Agency under the Fair Employment Act 1976. Its role was the elimination of discrimination on the grounds of religious belief or political opinion and the promotion of equality of opportunity. The Agency met with a hostile reaction from the Unionist community and seemed less than effective to Nationalists because of the heavy demands placed upon it by investigations carried out within a fairly modest budget. Moreover, there was a perception that it was relatively ineffective as the legislation was based on voluntary compliance with fair employment guidelines. Other pressures conspired to push the pace of fair employment reform. The Northern Ireland Civil Service embraced a comprehensive system of monitoring employees and an equal opportunities policy. There was an acknowledgement on the part of Government that Catholic disadvantage was significant in both employment and more specifically unemployment. Irish-American pressure groups, through American companies doing business in Northern Ireland, exerted commercial leverage on the British Government to adhere to the MacBride principles of employment (Cormack and Osborne, 1991).

The cumulative effect of these pressures led to the Fair Employment (Northern Ireland) Act 1989 which strengthened the previous legislation by establishing two new enforcement bodies, the Fair Employment Commission (replacing the Agency) and the Fair Employment Tribunal. In addition to the aims of the 1976 Act the legislation had four new objectives:

- the active practice of fair employment by employers;
- the close and continuous audit of that practice by new and stronger enforcement agencies (in this regard employers with more than 10 employees must register with the Commission and submit annual returns on the religious composition of their workforce);
- the use of affirmative action, and goals and timetables, to remedy under-representation;
- the use of criminal penalties and economic sanctions, to ensure good fair employment practice (in this regard the tribunal can compensate

individual victims of discrimination up to £30,000 – this limit was subsequently increased to £35,000 and by 1995 removed). (Department of Economic Development, 1989: 5)

The revised Fair Employment Act of 1989 has established 'arguably what can be seen as not only the most stringent anti-discrimination legislation in the UK but also in Europe' (Osborne, 1998: 185). Initial evidence on the effectiveness of the new legislation based on monitoring returns showed that between 1990 and 1993, the proportion of Roman Catholics in monitored employment rose from 34.9 to 36.6 per cent. The Roman Catholic element of the economically active population was estimated to be 39 per cent. Almost 4,000 public and private sector concerns were registered with the Commission for monitoring purposes. This represented all public authorities and private sector firms with over 10 employees. Although employers were not required to submit the results of their three year reviews of their employment practices to the Commission, some 700 did so. Of these, 38 per cent had affirmative action programmes in place (Department of Finance & Personnel & H. M. Treasury, 1995: 69).

More recently at a reception to mark the twenty-first anniversary of the fair employment legislation, the Secretary of State remarked:

Discrimination can be a destructive force both economically and politically and it is only by eliminating such distrust that we will be able to build a lasting peace and secure future for everyone in Northern Ireland.

Northern Ireland's anti-discrimination legislation, which is there to protect all communities, is recognised as being amongst the strongest in the world and has played an important part in improving equality in employment over the last 21 years.

Dr Mowlam explained that between 1990 and 1996 the numbers of Catholics in monitored employment had risen from 34.9 to 38 per cent and added:

Set against an improving economic background, these figures tell an encouraging story. The employment imbalance is narrowing. However, the government knows there is still more that has to be done. Unemployment is still a blight on the lives of too many, particularly amongst the Roman Catholic community, but we have started to do something about it through the New Deal[13] which is

designed to bring hope and a better future to people right across
the country.

(Northern Ireland Office, 1997b)

During the passage of the Fair Employment (NI) Act 1989, Government gave a commitment to undertake a comprehensive review of
employment equality after 5 years' experience of the operation of the
Act. An Employment Equality Review was undertaken by the Standing
Advisory Commission on Human Rights in 1995/6. This considered the
effectiveness of the fair employment legislation and the institutions
and procedures which it established in promoting equality of opportunity and fair participation in employment between the Protestant and
Catholic communities in Northern Ireland.

A number of technical considerations arose in the review centred
around issues such as fair participation and the merit principle (Cassidy,
1996; McCrudden, 1996, respectively). Fair participation is not defined
in the legislation and its determination depends on the circumstances
of each particular case. The term means that employers should be
working to ensure that equality of opportunity in their employment is
offered to both communities and, where it is not, sustained efforts
should be made to promote it through affirmative action measures and,
if appropriate, setting goals and timetables. Employers are required to
have a written policy on equality of opportunity in employment which
is based on the principle of selection according to merit (Department
of Economic Development, 1989).

The review of the legislation found different conceptions of merit
and differing views as to what their status was (McCrudden, 1996: 43).
Similarly, there was a call for clarification as to how fair participation
and associated concepts were operationalised (Cassidy, 1996: 60). In a
summary review of the role of the Fair Employment Commission,
Metcalf concluded:

> The FEC was faced with a substantial programme of work when it
> was established in 1990. With an approach influenced by its aim of
> securing fair participation at all levels of employment and an
> emphasis on voluntary compliance, it has substantially fulfilled the
> specific task within the Act.

(Metcalf, 1996: 165)

Metcalf went on to recommend important changes in light of the review
such as the expansion of the remit and powers of the FEC so that it
could act more directly on unemployment and economic development;

the need for employers to have to consider and propose affirmative action measures irrespective of their determination of fair participation; and an extension of the Commission's powers to enable enforcement of affirmative action, irrespective of the determination of fair participation.

Policy appraisal and fair treatment

A recent addition to this concerted approach on equality and equity issues is Policy Appraisal and Fair Treatment (PAFT). PAFT is concerned with securing equality of opportunity and equity of treatment regardless of religious belief, political opinion, gender, marital status, having or not having a dependant, ethnicity, disability, age or sexual orientation. Some of these groups are afforded protection in law against discrimination but PAFT is not confined to questions of legality and encompasses wider issues of fairness. Under the PAFT initiative, guidelines came into effect for all Northern Ireland government departments, the Northern Ireland Office and their agencies in January 1994. The guidelines aim to ensure that those responsible for the development of policy and the delivery of services do not unfairly or unnecessarily discriminate against those specified sections of the community. This approach replaced an equal opportunity proofing process which had been introduced in 1990 and criticised for focusing too narrowly on personnel issues, principally gender and religion, with particular reference to the government as an employer. That is, proofing implied a check-list approach at the end of the process whereas PAFT aimed to ensure fair treatment pervaded decision-making and implementation of policies. The new guidelines indicate that discriminatory action is that which results in different treatment of one group as opposed to another, either to its advantage or to its detriment, for example between people of different gender or religion. The *prevention* of direct discrimination alone is not enough to promote equality of opportunity and fair treatment.

Within the overall aim of securing equality and equity the Government set itself the following objectives:

- to promote a positive and proactive approach to providing equality of opportunity and equity of treatment;
- to ensure that there is no unlawful discrimination or unjustifiable inequality in any aspect of public administration;
- to incorporate a fair treatment dimension into all policy-making and consideration of new provision for services;

- to take account of fair treatment aspects when reviewing existing policies and delivery of services;
- to monitor, as appropriate, the impact of government policies. (Central Secretariat, 1993)

The PAFT initiative was seen by government as complementary to Targeting Social Need whose principal aim, as mentioned, is to reduce unfair social and economic differentials by targeting resources more effectively at those in greatest need. PAFT is wider than TSN in that it is not confined to socio-economic issues and takes account of the impact of government's actions on a broader range of social groups. In implementing PAFT, government departments and agencies were asked to take into account any aspect of policy or service delivery which could in practice affect some people less favourably than others, so that consideration could be given as to whether such treatment would be unlawful, unjustifiable or undesirable and, where appropriate, the viability of alternative approaches assessed. The guidelines point out that there may be instances when a policy proposal or course of action which has discriminatory effects may be justified, e.g. unequal treatment may be justified where it constitutes lawful affirmative action to remedy the adverse effects of past discrimination. Departments and agencies were asked to regularly monitor and report on a yearly basis their actions in implementing PAFT.

The Employment Equality Review's research found a mixed picture of commitment to PAFT within government departments/agencies and concluded:

A PAFT initiative which is only partly adopted is likely to be particularly damaging politically. The message sent out by the guidelines – a commitment to equity in policy making – will be perceived as more of a gesture than a fully incorporated dimension to policy.
(Osborne, Gallagher, Cormack and Shortall, 1996: 150)

In particular the researchers drew attention to confusion over the status of the guidelines and their implementation. Departments carried out PAFT appraisals in different ways, there was poor central co-ordination of the initiative and little political priority was attached to it.

Other proposals have subsequently emerged to put PAFT on a statutory basis and suggestions that a duty be imposed on government to reduce material inequality between relevant groups (McCrudden, 1996). This has been operationalised by the statutory equality obligation now contained in section 75 of the Northern Ireland Act 1998. Further proposals have argued that government policies in Northern Ireland should be subject to a new set of policy appraisal guidelines in respect of communal separation and sharing, referred to as PASS (Policy Appraisal for Separation and Sharing), in addition to the PAFT guidelines. The thinking behind proposals for PASS is that equal priority should be given in government policy-making to fostering better community relations and reducing, or at least not increasing, the degree of separation between members of the two communities (Hadden, 1997). The second part of the government's approach to micro peace building has concentrated on education as a means of tackling community division.

(ii) Education initiatives

Integrated education

There exists in Northern Ireland two religiously homogeneous systems of education, Catholic and Protestant (Gallagher, 1989). Controlled or state schools are predominantly Protestant and maintained schools Catholic. A third category, which includes most Protestant and all Catholic grammar schools has voluntary status. The categories have implications for public funding levels of both recurrent and capital expenditure in the schools. At the onset of the current conflict such rigid religious divisions in schooling prompted questions about whether the education structure was intrinsically divisive (Morgan et al., 1992: 10) and about the possibility of setting up a school system which could accommodate both Protestants and Catholics (Akenson, 1970: 40). Mainline Protestant churches initially contributed to the mood for change by publishing statements of support for the ideals of integrated education, though when it came to matching rhetoric with action they were less than enthusiastic. The Catholic church remained fiercely defensive of their own denominational schools (Dunn, 1990: 84).

In 1974 the first pressure group for integrated education was founded. The All Children Together (ACT) movement comprised parents of school age children (many of them educationalists) who were committed to an education structure which could cater for their own specific interests. The group had little success from the outset in persuading both Protestant and Catholic churches of the merits of integrated education. They did manage, however, through one of their members (Lord Dunleath) to secure a legislative amendment to the Education and Library Board's Northern Ireland Order (1972) leading to a new category of school termed 'controlled integrated' (Dunn, 1990: 85). Despite initial optimism arising from this, Protestant church opposition meant that nothing resulted and, out of frustration, ACT established their own integrated school in Belfast in 1981 (Lagan College). A charter set up at the school's inception prohibits Catholic/Protestant enrolment drifting beyond 40:60/60:40 ratios.

From modest beginnings the integrated school movement quickly gathered momentum. In an *ad hoc* fashion, pressure groups sprung up within communities and by 1992 there were 4 integrated secondary schools and 14 integrated primary schools, accounting for 3,600 pupils (out of a school population of 336,000). Integrated status is definable in these schools through a unique enrolment pattern, management structure and integrated ethos. On their formation all of the integrated schools had private or independent status. The Department of Education for Northern Ireland only considered allowing them into the state system when they had proven their viability through acceptable enrolment figures and evidence of pre-school children on a waiting list (Morgan et al., 1992: 14). The Education Reform (Northern Ireland) Order 1989 now provides 100 per cent funding for two types of integrated schools, grant-maintained integrated schools and controlled-integrated schools.

Since provision was made for the establishment of integrated schools in the Education Reform (NI) Order 1989, 14 existing schools and 19 new schools have been granted integrated status. Six controlled schools have been given conditional approval to integrated status. The total enrolment currently stands at over 7,000, (from a school population of 350,000) with the number expected to increase to over 8,000 by 1999 (Department of Finance & Personnel & H. M. Treasury, 1998: 174). Development to date has taken place largely through the establishment of new grant maintained integrated schools. A review, undertaken by the Department of Education in 1996, of the arrangement for the support and development of integrated education, led to:

- revisions of the viability criteria for new integrated schools, increasing the intake and long-term enrolment requirements for primary and secondary schools; and
- the introduction of new provisions to facilitate the transformation of existing schools to integrated status, subject to fulfilling certain conditions relating to parental consent, viability and commitment to, and awareness of, the process of integration. Transforming schools will also be expected to achieve an appropriate religious balance, over time, in both pupil intakes and overall enrolment and in staffing and representation on the governing body.

Meeting the future demand for integrated education will therefore be through the transformation of existing schools as opposed to new capital build projects as tended to be the case hitherto. Alongside the integrated education movement, changes in the curriculum have sought to establish the theme education for mutual understanding.

Education for mutual understanding (EMU)

During the period of 'educational enlightenment' in the early 1970s, not all educationalists agreed that the formation of new integrated schools was the only way of tackling community relations in education. Some believed (Dunn, 1990; Malone, 1973; Skilbeck, 1973) that given the inextricable link between religion and politics, segregated schools would continue to predominate in Northern Ireland. On this basis, they argued that community relations should be addressed *within* the state and maintained schools (Dunn, 1990: 87).

This analysis led to a number of school-based projects, during the 1970s, which attempted to gauge improvement in negative social attitudes through the teaching of a more objective curriculum (Greer, 1976). Research concluded that, whilst most schools in Northern Ireland were clearly segregated along religious lines, and that while contact was minimal, the similarities between the two systems were more easily detectable than the differences (Darby et al., 1977; Dunn et al., 1984). These findings suggested that improving community relations within segregated schools would be best achieved through both the curriculum and the development of inter-school contact. As Dunn argued: 'it committed the system for the first time, to a public policy of using education for community relations' (Dunn, 1990: 87).

Curriculum reforms followed in the 1989 Education Reform (Northern Ireland) Order. In line with education reforms in Great Britain, the Order specified a new common curriculum. Included within this curriculum were six education themes. Two of these themes, 'education for mutual understanding' and 'cultural heritage', were unique to the Northern Ireland programme. Guidance for EMU work proposed that, through the development of study programmes within subject areas of the curriculum and through the values which inform the school ethos and relationships within the school, pupils should:

- learn to respect themselves and others;
- appreciate the interdependence of people within society;
- know about and understand what is shared as well as what is different about their cultural traditions;

- appreciate how conflict might be handled in a non-violent way. (Northern Ireland Curriculum Council, 1989)

A further feature of the reform programme was to broaden parental choice to opt for integrated education for their children.

An evaluation of EMU (Smith and Robinson, 1996) found that schools, by and large, adopted a minimalist approach to its implementation, sufficient to meet their statutory requirements but little more. The evaluators concluded:

> There are overriding concerns about the extent to which the themes are evident at classroom level and the effectiveness of a cross curricular strategy for the implementation of EMU...The impact of EMU continues to be limited by the fact that teachers find it elusive. No clear agenda has emerged...Two important areas for educational development are noticeably absent from most current activities undertaken as part of EMU. One is a focus on civil and human rights and the other is a concern to encourage young people's understanding and participation in political processes. Civics, human rights and education for political participation are particularly relevant strands of EMU at a time when the broader society supports a commitment to political dialogue rather than political violence. During the initial statutory years of EMU within the curriculum there is little evidence that teachers have been able to develop progression towards approaches to address the more controversial aspects of EMU.
>
> (Smith and Robinson, 1996: 82–3)

The researchers refer to the challenge that now exists for EMU to move beyond the 'polite exchanges' which take place into areas of meaningful discussion on controversial social, cultural, religious and political issues. The second strand of the schools based approach was to encourage inter-school contact, which we now examine.

Cross-community contact scheme (CCCS)

The cross-community contact scheme, introduced in 1987 and funded by the Department of Education for Northern Ireland promotes ongoing contact (rather than one-off type ventures) between schools, youth, community and sports groups. The emphasis is on continuing systematic programmes of work and activities which help to break down the traditional barriers, to dissolve the myths of history and culture, and to encourage children and young people from different backgrounds to work together for a common purpose (Central Community Relations Unit, 1991: 4). It affords young people the opportunity to meet and mix with peer groups from different religious backgrounds in a non-threatening way. Criteria for inclusion in the scheme include the following:

- the programme must be coherent, ongoing and systematic;
- the programme must result in cross-community contact which is purposeful and requires a genuinely collaborative effort to achieve its aims;
- activities should involve new contacts or be a development of an existing contact programme;
- the participants must, as far as possible, be mixed on a religious basis within the ratio 60:40/40:60;
- those participating must be under 25 and engaged in full-time or part-time education;
- the programme must include the same group of participants throughout. (Department of Education, Community Relations Branch, 1992)

The scheme has achieved high take-up rates from a modest base in 1987. There are now some 700 schools (from an initial 170 schools) involved in the cross-community contact scheme. This represents approximately 54 per cent of all schools in Northern Ireland. The administration of the scheme was transferred to the Education and Library Boards from September 1996 and is now an integral part of the Boards' Curriculum Advisory and Support Service. Expenditure on CCCS in 1997–8 was £1.8 m (Department of Finance & Personnel & H. M. Treasury, 1997: 186).

The cross-community contact scheme is closely related to the delivery of the cross-curriculum themes of education for mutual understanding and cultural heritage. Although EMU can operate at the intra-school level, many schools have taken the opportunity of developing and extending EMU programmes by establishing inter-school links through the cross-community contact scheme. Such links, while not mandatory, have been encouraged by the Department of Education:

EMU can involve work within a single school, and this is important in establishing attitudes and in encouraging curricular initiatives with an EMU dimension. But its importance also derives from its role as a preliminary to projects between institutions, involving pupils and teachers from two or more schools and from both communities, meeting together for a common purpose.

(Department of Education for Northern Ireland, Circular 1987/47)

The cross-community contact scheme was evaluated as part of the research which assessed the impact of EMU. The researchers highlighted an important distinction between the number of *schools* from government records which were involved in the scheme and the number of *pupils* who had participated in the cross-community contact programmes. They estimated that in 1994–95 less than 20 per cent of primary and 10 per cent of secondary pupils participated. Whilst acknowledging that it might be unrealistic to expect every pupil to participate in a programme every year, they suggested schools be encouraged to concentrate on a small number of annual programmes which offered progression and quality of experience. They concluded:

> Department of Education records of the scheme suggest that many schools have evolved inter-school programmes with particular age groups, or in particular subject areas, which work well and are repeated year after year. Some schools have operated such programmes since the scheme was established in 1987. However, the records provide limited evidence about the educational benefits and quality of programmes.
>
> (Smith and Robinson, 1996: 44–5)

The Department of Education also provide financial support towards core funding for around 20 voluntary bodies or non-governmental organisations operating reconciliation programmes for young people. The recipients of the larger awards included Harmony Community Trust, Churches Peace Education Project, Community Relations in Schools, Positive Ethos Trust – EMU Promoting School Project and the Northern Ireland Children's Holiday Scheme. The third part of the government's approach to micro peace building deals with attempts at improving community relations.

(iii) Community relations

The community relations approach grew out of a failed attempt by the Stormont Government to win over Catholics to the reform programme of the moribund Unionist regime in the late 1960s and early 1970s through the establishment of the Community Relations Commission. With the collapse of Stormont, the introduction of Direct Rule and subsequently a power sharing executive, the role for the Commission changed, support for it declined and its staff became disillusioned when the real commitment to tackling divisions within the community appeared lacking. The Commission was finally dissolved in 1975 and no formal expression of government support for community relations existed until the emergence of the Central Community Relations Unit.

The Central Community Relations Unit was established in 1987 by the then Secretary of State to report directly on all aspects of relations between the two main traditions in Northern Ireland. The intention was to ensure that, at the centre of the decision–making process in Northern Ireland, crucial community relations issues, in their very widest sense, were given the fullest possible consideration.

The Unit has three broad roles:

- challenge – to ensure that major policy decisions are taken only after careful evaluations of their possible effects on community relations;
- review – to carry out periodic reviews of the most important policies and programmes to assess their impact on community relations; and
- innovation – to develop new ideas about improving community relations and about how best to support those on the ground who are working to improve relations and reduce prejudice.

Definitions of community relations and the approach taken to it within Northern Ireland are best summarised by the first Chair of the Community Relations Council in Northern Ireland:

> Community relations, simply defined, endeavours to bring the two sides of our community towards greater understanding. It is concerned with the building of trust and the reduction of prejudice. Though it cannot be superimposed on bigotry, the movement nevertheless thrives by harnessing the accumulated common sense, resolve and energy of individuals. In exploring cultural traditions we address the specific problems – and the rich opportunities – of our diversity. No case is argued for a common culture but rather that the full spectrum should be explored and celebrated; there are many more colours than orange and green.
>
> (Hawthorne, 1991: 5)

This definition is seen by others as a rather narrow interpretation limited to promoting a harmonious existence between different groups, with the intended goal of integrating minority groups into the wider community. Frazer and Fitzduff (1986) argue that community relations is a much wider concept which concentrates on the idea of equality of basic rights and opportunity for all groups, whilst simultaneously encouraging cultural diversity.

The community relations budget for 1997–8, including EU monies, for specified community relations programmes administered by CCRU, the Department of Education and the Department of Finance and Personnel was £12.7 m (Department of Finance & Personnel & H. M. Treasury, 1997: 251). These resources support a range of initiatives which are designed to improve community relations at province-wide and local level as follows:

(a) a district council community relations programme which grant-aids local programmes designed to encourage cross-community contact, mutual understanding and awareness of cultural diversity;

(b) funding for the Community Relations Council (CRC) set up in 1990 as an independent, voluntary, charitable body to promote better community relations and the recognition of cultural diversity in Northern Ireland. CRC provides support, facilities and recognition for community organisations operating at the local level. The community relations work supported by the Council falls into three categories – cultural traditions, work and community, and reconciliation. The Council seeks to broaden the appreciation of cultural diversity in Northern Ireland as a means of fostering increased tolerance and mutual understanding between the two communities. It takes the view that the rich diversity of cultural traditions such as music, literature, folklore, history, drama, language, visual arts and dance, should not be regarded as a source of division and conflict but rather as a heritage which all can respect, and even share. The Council also seeks to recruit all organisations which are part of the life of the community to help in the work of creating greater tolerance and understanding. This includes community groups, district councils, trade unions, business, sports bodies and tenants associations. Finally, the Council provides funds, training and contact networks for the groups which have been working to achieve peace and reconciliation through organised cross-community contact. CRC's budget for 1997–98 is over £2.5 m;

(c) support to a number of reconciliation bodies which promote cross-community contact;

(d) a cultural traditions programme which explores how the existence of different cultural traditions can be handled in ways which are positive and constructive, rather than threatening or divisive. This includes policy development in relation to the Irish language – to encourage interest in, and appreciation of it, to highlight the contribution which it has made to the cultural heritage of the whole community and to work towards the removal of obstacles to its use by those who wish to do so;

(e) a capital programme which supports and encourages the development of community based facilities, accessible to the main sections of the community.

This whole approach to community relations is underpinned by the contact hypothesis (Allport, 1954). It has been argued that the separate institutional arrangements for services such as housing and education in Northern Ireland are, to some extent, responsible for perpetuation of the conflict. The contact hypothesis argues that segregation of national, ethnic, racial or social groups within a single society fosters hostility or, at least, inhibits interaction by blocking off communication. Without this, it is impossible for individuals to discover that many of their beliefs, concerns and experiences are essentially similar. Poverty and unemployment in Northern Ireland, for example, do not recognise religious boundaries (although the two communities have differential experiences of them). The contact hypothesis asserts that the fundamental problem in inter-group conflict is individual prejudice caused by ignorance of the other community, and since these are educational and psychological problems, they can be remedied through contact. Early attempts at intervention to encourage cross-community contact in Northern Ireland came in the form of children's community holidays where kids, usually from deprived single identity areas, were selected for a funded vacation. Research findings on the value of this approach suggested:

> We have no doubt that many interpersonal friendships are formed which may transcend the religious divide. What is less clear is whether this experience can have any real and lasting impact on subsequent Catholic-Protestant relations. Thus while we do not wish to rule out interpersonal contact programmes altogether...we caution practitioners to be modest in their expectations of such interventions. Thus, in policy terms, we urge the implementation of inter-group contact, but also acknowledge that some positive contact may be better than none at all.
>
> (Hewstone and Brown, 1986: 41)

Such a view finds support from Lockwood (reported by Trew, 1989: 100), who argued that 'the contact thesis offers hope in a no-hope situation'.

We consider two major initiatives here as examples of the grassroots community relations approach to peace building – the district councils' programme and support to a number of reconciliation bodies which promote cross-community contact.

District councils' community relations programme

In 1989 the CCRU invited councils to participate in a community relations programme whose objectives were to develop cross-community contact and co-operation, to promote greater mutual understanding, and to increase respect for different cultural traditions. CCRU offered 75 per cent grant-aid for the employment of community relations staff by councils, provided financial support for appropriate cross-community activities, and assisted with the development of local heritage and cultural activities. A budget of £1.5 m was allocated to the programme in 1990/1 with incremental increases thereafter as more councils joined the initiative (funding for the programme in 1997/8 amounts to almost £2 m per year).

The specific conditions laid down for participation were:

- councils had to agree on a cross-party basis to participation in the scheme;
- councils had to draw up a community relations policy statement;
- the policy statement and individual projects undertaken had to be agreed to on a cross-party basis;
- community relations officers had to be appointed to administer the scheme and their posts advertised under this title;
- projects had to include cross-community contact, mutual understanding, or cultural diversity.

The first council joined the scheme in February 1990 and within two years all 26 councils in Northern Ireland were participating. The nature of projects undertaken by community relations officers was contingent upon the extent of support at local authority level. The potential for the programme to address issues which were at the heart of the divisions in Northern Ireland, and its location within the remit of local government where it assumed a certain political aura, provoked a degree of suspicion among some councillors. Working within such an environment, community relations officers were often directed into 'soft' community relations work such as organising community arts festivals, summer activity schemes for children or big publicity events usually in the form of concerts, performances or sports programmes. These events, whilst bringing Protestants and Catholics into contact did little to explicitly address core community relations issues – often there was little or no meaningful interaction.

In councils where good relations between politicians from opposing parties were evident, through for example 'responsibility sharing', the environment was often more conducive to focused community relations projects, including small group workshops, residentials and inter-group activities which attempted to confront negative social attitudes and stereotypes. Community relations officers within these authorities were usually given a relatively free hand to direct the programme and supported through the establishment of community relations sub-committees and broader council policies which encouraged officers to tackle divisive issues. Generally though, community relations officers claimed that successful implementation of projects at district council level demanded a delicate balance between the promotion and development of community relations and accommodation of political sensitivities within councils. As one officer put it 'You swim with the tide and when no one's looking you jump out and do something and then jump back in again quickly' (Knox and Hughes, 1994).

Any attempt at classifying the diverse range of projects undertaken by community relations officers in councils is fraught with difficulties. In general, however, four broad types of projects were evident:

1. High profile community relations. Projects under this category are generally one-off events aimed at promoting the community relations function through public relations. They tend to attract large numbers but are not part of a long-term developmental strategy. Examples include: concerts, sports events and plays.

2. Inter/intra community development. Projects here include both single identity (Catholic or Protestant, but not both) and cross-community work. Single identity or intra-community projects recognise that polarised communities first need to address their own prejudices and misunderstandings prior to engaging in cross-community work. Inter-community development on the other hand builds upon a network of established groups interested in pursuing common goals that straddle the sectarian divide (e.g. health, housing, roads, or economic development issues). Good community relations is seen as an important by-product of this process. An example is cross-community economic development groups established to tackle issues which affect the economy of both their communities.

3. Cultural traditions. Projects under this heading attempt to capitalise on the cross-community benefits that accrue to groups with a shared cultural interest in sport, music, dancing, drama, and so on. The approach focuses on what binds communities rather than what

separates them. Examples of this type of project are cross-community drama groups, inter-district music twinning and heritage trails.
4. Focused community relations. By definition, projects under this heading are much more directive and aim to tackle, head-on, controversial community relations issues. The approach is premised on the idea that people adopt an avoidance strategy and steer clear of politics and religion, particularly in mixed (Protestant/Catholic) company. This approach suggests that such issues, if left unresolved, compound insidious sectarianism and bigotry. Examples of projects in this category include anti-sectarianism and prejudice-reduction workshops in which the most divisive issues are confronted and discussed in an atmosphere of trust and respect for opposing views.

An evaluation of the district council programme was able to exploit the staggered involvement of councils in the initiative by comparing, quantitatively, attitudes to community relations within authorities which were involved in the programme and those which hadn't at that point joined the scheme. The research concluded:

> Evidence from the surveys suggest an improvement in attitudes toward Catholics and a greater tolerance of the other tradition both over time and between councils participating and not participating in the programme. The significant difference between the two types of councils (participants and non-participants) highlights the impact of the programme. Given the objectives of the initiative 'to promote greater mutual understanding and respect for different cultural traditions' such evidence is encouraging support for those charged with implementing the programme.
>
> (Knox, 1994: 614)

Over and above the intrinsic merits of the individual projects, the programme had a significant symbolic value according to the research. First, establishing community relations as part of the remit of Northern Ireland's 26 councils was a major achievement by CCRU and an endorsement of the programme's objectives. Such an achievement was all the more significant when set within the context of the vitriolic political battles that have taken place in some councils over the presence of Sinn Féin councillors. Second, the initiative forced community relations on to the policy agenda of local authorities. As the only remaining democratic institution of government since the demise of the Northern Ireland Assembly, debating community relations matters in councils created a public awareness of the initiative's importance. Doing so in those local authorities, whose track record of discrimination amongst the workforce has been poor, was even more important. Third, a number of councils have now engaged in *de facto* power sharing or 'responsibility sharing'. This involves rotating the post of chair or mayor between political parties, and in some cases proportional representation arrangements on committees. Such a public expression of good cross-community relations between politicians was both an endorsement of the initiative's principles and an open display of 'leading from the front'. The research concluded that the benefits of cross-community example at the political level although difficult to measure, had contributed to a more favourable social climate which was seen as important in reducing prejudice.

Reconciliation bodies

Another major bottom-up initiative is the 'Community Relations Measure' within the Physical and Social Environment Sub-Programme (PSEP), 1994–9, of the European Commission. The PSEP contains a range of measures (community relations, urban regeneration, targeting social need, community infrastructure) assisted by the European Regional Development Fund (ERDF) and the European Social Fund (ESF). The programme aims to tackle a range of internal problems perceived to be hindering economic growth both for Northern Ireland as a whole and for specific communities within the region. In particular, the existence of a deeply divided society and years of inter-community tension and violence were seen as major impediments to economic growth. For this reason, assistance was provided to further the work of improving community relations within the region. The EC allocated 20.43 m ecu (approximately £17 m) to the community relations measure which was administered through CCRU with the primary objective of 'providing opportunities for purposeful and meaningful cross-community contact with a view to reconciliation between the main sections of the Northern Ireland community' (European Structural Funds, 1994: 3).

Under the first phase of PSEP the EC provided over £10 m grant-aid to fund a range of community relations projects located in a number of reconciliation bodies. Some projects/programmes received joint funding from CCRU and PSEP. An evaluation of the initiative generated a taxonomy (see Table 3.1) which usefully describes the various types of community relations work undertaken and their relative merits.

These categories are discussed briefly in *order of importance* derived from the evaluation.

Table 3.1 A taxonomy of community relations programmes

Type of programme	Rationale	Organisations
Key reconciliation bodies	Bodies (public, voluntary, independent) set up with a specific community relations' brief	– Community Relations Council – Corrymeela Community – District Council Community Relations Programme
Community development and community relations	Organisations, agencies and projects established originally with a community development brief, now incorporating a community relations agenda	– Central Churches' Committee for Community Work – Cornerstone Community – Harmony Community Trust – Co-operation North – East Belfast Community Development Centre – City of Belfast YMCA
Cultural traditions	Bodies involved in the support of language, history and race relations as a means of promoting mutual respect and understanding of diverse cultures	– The Ulster Society – The Ultach Trust – Federation for Ulster Local Studies – Race Relations: Chinese Welfare Association
Education, training and personal development	Projects, programmes or bodies with an education, training, personal development remit, some of which have a community relations component	– Women's Education Project – Community relations training programme: NICVA – Columbanus Community of Reconciliation – Irish School of Ecumenics – Forum for Community Work Education
Publicly funded grant schemes	Grant schemes funded by government and/or European money and administered through agencies	– Community Relations Council Inter-Community Grant Scheme – Inter-Community Contact Scheme: NIVT – Physical and Social Environment Programme

Table 3.1 (*Continued*)

Type of programme	Rationale	Organisations
Reactive community relations	Organisations established in response to specific paramilitary atrocities and in support of a public mood towards peace and reconciliation	– Families Against Intimidation and Terror – The Peace and Reconciliation Group (Derry) – Community of the Peace People – The Peace Train Organisation – Women Together for Peace

Source: Knox, 1995.

1. *Key Reconciliation Bodies*: The success of programmes within the key reconciliation bodies is, in part, attributed to their more stable financial circumstances but also to their strategic planning and long-term community relations goals. Lead-in times are long and investment costs high in this policy area, which seeks to alter attitudes and behaviour towards 'the other' community. Moreover, a core of professional staff, trained and experienced in community relations and conflict resolution work, has now emerged in these organisations. This contrasts with the committed workers in voluntary organisations, many of whom have inadequate training and resources to implement projects, but are none the less enthusiastic to 'do something'. The key reconciliation bodies are also more likely to target groups or geographical areas for community relations work. They can more effectively deploy their resources and are better able to assess the impact of programmes. Again, this contrasts with some voluntary organisations who see Northern Ireland in its entirety as their target group and judge their own success by community relations activity levels, regardless of its relative effectiveness.

2. *Publicly funded grant schemes*: The contribution which this funding has made to infrastructural capital projects is important. Although funds have not been so generous as to allow major investment, purpose-built 'neutral venues' or cross-community facilities appear to have made a significant impact on community relations policy and the capacity of officials to operationalise mutual understanding between the two communities. The flexibility, scope and size of grant-aid has

afforded innovation, experimentation and the dissemination of wider good practice than would otherwise be the case. This is seen as important in a policy area where cause-and-effect relationships are not, as yet, well established. Notwithstanding some of the difficulties outlined in relation to voluntary bodies, small-scale, sometimes one-off grants can be made to voluntary groups on a trial-and-error basis. This is based on the principle that a new idea is worth investing some resources in, in order to assess whether it has potential for improving community relations.

3. *Community development–community relations*: The cross-cutting nature of many community development issues created an obvious foundation for both communities to promote greater mutual understanding. Community development work is also seen as a useful, and in some cases necessary, prerequisite for community relations, particularly in single identity communities, so common given the sectarian geography of Northern Ireland. It is important that single identity groups feel comfortable working together on community issues before embracing more difficult cross-community problems. It isn't always clear, however, where community development ends and community relations begins. Some organisations have behaved opportunistically when funds for community relations were available and tried to incorporate a cross-community agenda. The issue, however, is the extent to which these bodies have been genuine in their efforts to pursue community relations as part of their ongoing role or remain no more than token participants. Policy activists and officials seem to acknowledge that this approach is a useful mechanism for the furtherance of community relations goals but not all programmes under this heading have made the transition from community development to community relations.

4. *Cultural traditions*: These are programmes largely involving the use of language, history, arts, culture, sports and drama as a means of promoting mutual respect and understanding of diverse cultures. As with most things in Northern Ireland, however, these are not innocuous activities. Protestants and Catholics have their own versions of history, play different sports and are even associated with two distinct languages. The validity of promoting both traditions in an effort to demystify, foster and sustain cross-cultural awareness within and across communities is unquestionable. The key issue here, however, is how far and how quickly can the debate shift from an emphasis on a 'within' community focus to cross-community activities. Crudely described, it is easy to get single identity support for an Irish language group;

extending that support to the Protestant community is problematic. One criticism commonly levelled at this type of approach is that rather than promoting both cultures, single identity communities simply access funding and produce 'better educated bigots' with an even narrower and exclusive grasp of their own identity.

5. *Education, training and personal development*: Some community relations education and training schemes under this category have been seen as too narrowly focused or élitist in their mode of delivery. Such a model of education promotes greater understanding of issues germane to the conflict, taught to postgraduate students, or those interested in the intellectual underpinnings of cross-community issues. Whilst laudable in their objectives, both can be criticised as having a rather small and select target market. The rationale for this approach is that programmes are aimed at leaders and community activists who are likely to be influential and whose newly acquired knowledge will permeate their work and 'trickle down' to community level. It isn't clear that such a link has, as yet, been well established.

Training on offer appears to range from programmes which see the practitioner in need of personal development, those which attempt to teach activists reconciliation and conflict-resolution skills, through to programmes which aim to improve facilitation and enabling skills of community relations workers at the level of group activity. Because the role of practitioner is an evolving, eclectic and unstandardised one, trainers have felt overwhelmed by the variety of needs, diversity in backgrounds of those now involved in community relations work and the very different organisational contexts within which they work and practise.

6. *Reactive community relations*: Whilst it is accepted that much good public-spirited work has been and is taking place in these bodies, some of which is dangerous (dealing with paramilitaries), voluntary and unacknowledged, their reactive role, by definition has contributed little to long-term community relations goals. They may well be symbolically important, having captured the imagination and support of the public (who in Northern Ireland and beyond has not heard of the Peace People?), but their capacity to make a sustained and focused contribution is questionable. Many of these organisations have acted as a conduit for the expressed revulsion of the public to anti-social or heinous activities of terrorists. Their contribution has been immediate and effective but, at the same time, transient and ephemeral.

Whilst the taxonomy cannot claim to be exhaustive, it does however provide a summary framework of the various types of community relations and peace building activity going on at grassroots level. A more recent addition to this type of work is the European Union Special Support Programme for Peace and Reconciliation.

The European Union Special Support Programme for Peace and Reconciliation

In autumn 1994, following the cease-fires, a special European Commission task force was set up to find ways to assist Northern Ireland and the border counties towards maintaining the momentum for peace and reconciliation. The task force concluded that the European Union had a clear interest in supporting the peace process, not simply for the benefit of Northern Ireland as a region, but for the European Union as a whole. As a result, the Commission adopted a 5-year (1995–9) proposal, the Special Programme for Peace and Reconciliation in Northern Ireland and the Border Counties, to be implemented in the form of a community initiative.

The overall aim of the programme is 'to reinforce progress towards a peaceful and stable society and to promote reconciliation by increasing economic development and employment, promoting urban and rural regeneration, developing cross-border co-operation and extending social inclusion' (Eurolink, 1995). Total expenditure for the first 3 years (1995–7) amounted to 416m ecu (£350m). with the programme containing a number of innovative features. In addition to government departments there is a range of delivery mechanisms. Of particular note is the Northern Ireland partnerships sub-programme under which 26 district partnerships (coterminous with local authority boundaries) have been formed for the purpose of preparing and managing action plans best calculated to advance the aims of the initiative in their local areas. These partnerships comprise one third each, local councillors; community/voluntary representatives; business and trade union interests, as well as statutory organisations. A report by Northern Ireland's three MEPs (Paisley, Hume and Nicholson) gave an early assessment of the programme:

> There can be no doubt that the partnership element of the Special Peace and Reconciliation Programme has been a major success. The concept had been conceived of as an experiment, initially in the economic development context, later extended to other social spheres, with the objective of stimulating co-operation between

communities and different interest groups, including district councils at local level ... Partnerships have made the most obvious contribution to the programme's basic objectives of peace and reconciliation.
(Report to Jacques Santer, President of the European Commission, 1997: 14–15; I. Paisley, J. Hume and J. Nicholson)

There are several reasons for the success of this partnership model in tackling peace and reconciliation issues. A vast amount of goodwill and energy has been invested by district partnership members in pursuit of a common vision of a more stable and equitable society at the *local* level. This, in part, has emerged through frustration at the lack of progress by elected politicians (MPs) to move the administrative, political and security agenda forward. The voluntary/community sector, in particular, has demonstrated a major commitment to making partnerships work. Although at times their grassroots knowledge and ongoing community development work antagonised local councillors who occasionally felt usurped, each sector quickly accepted the complementary skills they brought to the process. The partnerships have successfully challenged the traditional cross-cutting cleavages in Northern Ireland society – Unionist/Nationalist; business/trade unions; voluntary/public/private; male/female; urban/rural. As one independent evaluator noted:

The district partnerships have managed, in adverse political circumstances, to bring together a wide variety of actors (politicians, social partners, administrators, voluntary organisations) to plan local social and economic development plans in a socially inclusive way.
(Harvey, 1997: 65)

The social inclusion component of the partnership programme has been singled out as making a particular contribution to the goals of peace and reconciliation (Hughes, Knox and Murray, 1998). Specifically this involves targeting all marginalised and vulnerable groups (women, young unemployed people, ex-prisoners etc.) with the aim of bringing them back into society and the economy, thereby promoting reconciliation.

Pycroft (1996) provides an interesting example of the use of local partnerships in post-apartheid South Africa where alliances are being formed between the public and private sectors, civic associations, trade unions, international donor agencies and NGOs to assist in institutional

capacity building and local community empowerment. Similarly partnerships in Northern Ireland have tapped the latent energy within the
public, private and voluntary sectors stifled by years of impotence in
the face of sectarian violence.

Micro approaches to peace building

Several points emerge from the discussion of the various approaches
described within this chapter.

(a) The major orientation to micro peace building in Northern
Ireland has been heavily dominated by the involvement of the United
Kingdom government and latterly European funded initiatives. Since
the government is perceived by one section of the community to be
a key protagonist in the conflict, their motivation is regarded with a
degree of suspicion. Even amongst Unionists, the community relations
approach has been criticised as a strategy aimed at diluting their culture – the creation of 'Prod-olics', a new hybrid species which com-
bines Protestants and Catholics.

(b) The availability of government funding and support for reconciliation initiatives has not led to the emergence of non-governmental
organisations much in evidence in both Israel and South Africa. Their
existence depends on attracting outside finance which affords them a
considerable degree of independence in their aims. This is not to suggest the absence of an NGO sector in Northern Ireland. On the contrary, Northern Ireland has a thriving 'industry' in quasi-autonomous
non-governmental organisations (quangos) whose role and number
have increased dramatically under Direct Rule. Yet there are significant
differences. Quangos in Northern Ireland still receive most of their
funding from government sources – the Community Relations Council
is a good example. Even though it is set up as an independent, voluntary, charitable body, more than 75 per cent of its income is derived
from the Central Community Relations Unit, a central government
source. This suggests that quangos function at arms-length from government as opposed to independent operators.

(c) Whether the government's approach to micro peace building has
been a reaction to a failed street-level movement or has at least, in part,
contributed to its lack of development (through generous funding) is
difficult to assess. The three elements of bottom-up activity which
occur to a greater or lesser extent in Israel and South Africa, *peace movements*, *women's groups* and *church activity*, have achieved very limited
sustained success in building peace in Northern Ireland.

Bloomfield (1997), for example, in describing the Peace People, a mass protest movement set up in 1976 after the death of three children by a car involved in a shooting incident, argued that 'within a few years, what had been by far the highest-profile peace group to emerge from the conflict settled into the role of a small, low-profile group' (Bloomfield, 1997: 62). He draws on contemporary evidence which substantiates this view:

> The overall effect of peace groups has been peripheral ... a group like the Peace People has made some difference but has in no way substantially altered the overall situation. Other groups too may have affected hundreds or even thousands of individuals, but they have not altered the overall situation in society either.
>
> (Dawn, 1978: 24, quoted in Bloomfield, 1997: 62)

A similar story is true when assessing the role of women's groups in peace building. Morgan and Fraser (1995), for example, point out that groups which evolved around a commitment to peace have not been exclusively female but had women in their majority. They argued:

> Such groups have been able to mobilise mass action and demonstrations for the cessation of violence over a brief period, but they have found it difficult to translate this into sustained political action. It appears to be possible to arouse intense public emotion in opposition to violence but much more difficult to focus the rather amorphous response which is generated in such contexts into a programme with political and social power.
>
> (Morgan and Fraser, 1995: 89)

The ambivalence of churches to cross-community activity is also striking in the Northern Ireland context. There is little ecclesiastical encouragement for inter-congregational activity and, in some cases, active hostility to the idea, most clearly manifest in the reaction of the Catholic church to integrated schooling. Where cross-community work does take place it has been initiated by individual clerics. Researchers describe the involvement of churches as follows:

> Discussions on the task of the churches in a divided society have seldom taken place except between clergy. There is very little evidence that parishes and congregations provide places for serious debate on the function of churches in inter-community relationships.

In a society in which community divisions mirror denominational divisions this is a notable omission. It may be that the churches fear serious institutional division in the event of discussions on this subject becoming widespread. It is clear that neither clergy nor laity have sought to open up such discussions.

(Morrow, Birrell, Greer and O'Keeffe, 1994: 260–1)

A similar view is expressed by Fitzduff when she points out that 'for much of the conflict, with a few honourable exceptions, churches have either denied that addressing the conflict was their business' or have given a religious endorsement to political and cultural allegiances (Fitzduff, 1996: 31). It has therefore been very difficult for them to put much emphasis on cross-community and reconciliation work.

Had government intervention through direct (CCRU) or indirect means (CRC and various funding schemes) not occurred, then a more vibrant NGO sector may have emerged. Whether this would have been more successful in tackling sectarian differences is impossible to say.

(d) What we can say, however, is that government intervention measures aimed at peace building through equality and equity, education and community relations have met with mixed success. Those initiatives located directly in government departments with responsibility for their implementation vested in the hands of civil servants have been most heavily criticised as paying lip service to peace building, broadly defined. Targeting Social Need, Making Belfast Work, Policy Appraisal and Fair Treatment do not appear to have met their equality and equity objectives. Fair employment, the responsibility of a quango (FEC), has been more successful but faced systemic problems in the Northern Ireland labour market through its attempts to redress employment imbalances. Despite claims of success with education initiatives, the figure of less than 2 per cent of children attending integrated schools must be seen as disappointing by those advocating this approach. Similarly EMU and cross-community contact schemes have to address major questions about the quality and type of experience resulting from these initiatives. The community relations approach, whether through the district council programme, the Community Relations Council, the various reconciliation bodies or the European Special Support Programme, has been more successful. Rooted in schemes which operate at the level of individual communities and administered at the local government level, through quangos or in the voluntary sector, evidence suggests they have, in general, contributed to an improvement in peace building relations. This conclusion would not, however, be widely accepted. Critics argue that the events of Drumcree, Harryville, Bellaghy and Dunloy (all flash-points during the traditional marching season) demonstrate a policy failure to promote respect for different cultural traditions, a core objective of the community relations approach. Community relations practitioners, in response, claim that this merely validates the importance of their continuing work and the long-term nature of building and sustaining peace.

4
Israel/Palestine: Macro Political Developments

Background to the conflict

The area of Israel, including the Golan Heights and East Jerusalem, is 21,946 square kilometres (8,473 square miles) with a population estimated in 1997 of 5.53 m. On 14 May 1948 the British Government terminated its mandate, and the Jewish leaders proclaimed the State of Israel. The West Bank has an area of 5,879 square kilometres (2,270 square miles) and a population of about 1.12 m. The Gaza Strip has an area of 363 square kilometres (140 square miles) and a population of around 748,400. The precarious state of the ongoing peace process needs to be viewed in the historical context of relations and attitudes between Israelis and Palestinians. This chapter will attempt to unravel the dynamics and origins of this 'prime and tragic example of the way two nations, competing over the same territory, approach a political conflict not only with conflicting interests but with conflicting mythologies, cultures and histories' (Rothman, 1992: 10).

The events leading to the creation of the state of Israel in 1948 provide an important insight into the shaping of political perspectives amongst Jews and Arabs. During the early period of the British Mandate (1920–48), tensions were running high between the indigenous Palestinian Arab population and the Zionist Jewish settlers. During the Great War, both sides vied for political favours from the British in an attempt to protect their different world views (Smith, 1996). The Balfour Declaration of November 1917 which promised to grant a national home for the Jews in Palestine signified the direction favoured by the British and it indicated the strength of the International Zionist lobby. The inter-war years witnessed the strengthening of Muslim-Christian groups against Zionist plans and while the British encouraged such activity locally, the view in London was firmly fixed on creating a Jewish state in Palestine.

Political tension heightened towards the end of the 1930s when the British declared its intention to divide Palestine between Arabs and Jews. Reaction amongst the Palestinian Arabs led to an armed uprising (1937–9) against British forces which was subsequently quashed. Arab fears that they would be over-run by Jewish settlers were eased following the publication of a White Paper in 1939 which proposed to limit Jewish immigration in Palestine to 75,000 over a five year period. This decision, however, outraged Jews and a campaign of violence was waged against the British and the Arabs in Palestine only to be halted by the outbreak of World War II in September 1939. During the intervening years, substantial numbers of Jews were smuggled into Palestine and when the war ended and the scale of the Holocaust against Jews became known, the United States began to demand that the British government relax its immigration policy in Palestine, requesting that 100,000 Jews be admitted at once. In 1947, the British position in Palestine was unacceptable to all shades of Zionist opinion and they requested that the United Nations take back the mandate and decide the future of the country.

By November of 1947, the United Nations ruled that Palestine be divided into Arab and Jewish states. The partition plan was opposed by Palestinians not only on the grounds that the proposed Jewish state was larger than the Arab state but because Palestinians were acutely aware of the ideological consensus amongst Zionism, that Palestine should one day contain a Jewish majority and that they, in effect, 'could hope to figure, at best, as an excrescence on the body politic' (Finkelstein, 1995: 12). The impact of the war on Zionism, and in particular, the Holocaust redoubled its desire for a Jewish homeland: 'The Zionists believed more firmly than ever that a state in Palestine was their due, not only on the basis of past heritage, but even more so in the light of the Holocaust' (Smith, 1996: 136). The UN decreed that the plan would come into effect in May 1948 and during those months Arabs and Jews prepared for war. Consequently, neighbouring Arab nations invaded the new state and a war with Israeli forces ensued until the Armistice agreement of 1949. The war, in effect, created an area of two distinct halves, one for Jews and one for Arabs, but not in accordance with the UN resolution. During the war, Israeli forces captured sections of land previously allocated by the United Nations to the Palestinians. Most Palestinian Arabs remained on land subsequently annexed to Jordan (the West Bank) or ruled by Egypt (the Gaza Strip) while some left for various Arab states or for other countries (Landau, 1993). Within the newly declared State of Israel, however, there remained a small Arab population made up largely of peasants and agricultural workers and this population, while being granted Israeli citizenship, was placed under military rule.

Thus the formation of the state of Israel created a disparate Palestinian population which has, in one way or another, been engaged in a conflict with the new state at a number of different levels. Between 1948 and 1967, the conflict chiefly manifested itself in terms of a battle between the Arab world and Israel which was largely supported by Western forces. The Six Day War of 1967 marked a watershed in the redefinition of the Arab-Israeli conflict amongst all sides. Palestinians in the West Bank, Gaza and East Jerusalem found themselves under Israeli occupation and they realised that their struggle would not be won by relying on Arab nations. The Israeli administration believed that the land gains made, further secured its borders and that it now had the ultimate bargaining chip which would end the Arab-Israeli conflict – 'land for peace'. At the same time, the war resulted in the beginnings of the 'Palestinisation' of the 'acquiescent' Arab population which found itself under Israeli rule some twenty years previous.

The following section gives a flavour of the historical basis upon which the conflict is understood by each side and will provide an insight into the dynamics of the conflict today.

The Israeli position

The Israeli psyche stems from the peculiarities and strengths of Zionism, a distinctive form of nationalist ideology developed in the late nineteenth century (Kellas, 1991: 129), which is 'rooted in the Jewish experience of exile and opposition, isolation and rejection, the Holocaust and the recurring war with Arabs' (Smith, 1996: 157). The institutionalisation of Zionism in the shape of the new state and the character of Israel's first Prime Minister, David Ben Gurion, are useful starting points which help explain the way in which Israel defines and perceives its conflict with the Arab world. Ben Gurion set about creating a state that would end any notion that the Jews were a weak race or that they would ever be compelled to submit to constraints placed upon them by others. The hostile environment within which the new state found itself and the failure of the Arab nations to recognise Israel's 'divine right' to exist provided Ben Gurion with justification for refusing to allow the 1948 Palestinian war refugees to return to their homes and it enabled the state to place Arab inhabitants of Israel under military control. Two key objectives dominated the politics of the new state: securing the borders and the in-gathering of exiles. The notion of 'exiles' denotes the Zionist belief that Jews were now coming home.

At the practical level of governance, a 'state in waiting' or what was described by Lustick (1980) as a 'proto-type state' had already been created, and institutions which had helped secure the Jewish 'homeland' were given semi-governmental status. New political institutions of government were speedily put in place. The development of the party political process within Israel needs to be understood in relation to the operation of the stable, one party government which existed between 1949 and 1977. As Kaminer (1996) notes, political party support operated at a level well beyond that of voting. Political parties, for example, provided essential services such as housing, employment and health through their close links with trade unions. Thus the unity of Zionism, while scrambling to achieve a state in terms of the linkages between civil society institutions, and elements of government, has sustained because 'what unifies Israeli Jews is stronger and more important than what divides them' (Krauz quoted in Ben Rapfael and Sharot, 1991: 187). The development of democratic norms such as free and fair elections resulted in what Flamhaft (1996: 115) describes as 'the most stable country in the Middle East...with effective political institutions, high level of popular participation in politics...and a political system that is widely accepted by its citizens'. The essential ingredients of the Israeli state were therefore democracy and a home for all Jews but these ingredients were not taken for granted: 'Not only were they hard to obtain but many Israelis believe that Israel's enemies – some of whom have never accepted Israel's boundaries – are relentlessly trying to destroy the Jewish state' (Flamhaft, 1996: 115). This deep sense of 'siege mentality' permeated Israel's newly emerging political culture and it continues to shape the landscape in which security and military might are paramount to domestic politics. Smith (1996) notes the development of Ben Gurionism which, he argues, was evident following Britain's refusal to allow greater number of Jews into Palestine in 1939 and which is based on 'a distinction between Israel and world Jewry on the one hand; and the *goyim* or non-Jews on the other. If the latter did not fulfil their perceived obligations to Israel, they would at best be ignored, at worst fought' (Smith, 1996: 157). In the case of the Arab world, Ben Gurion and the Israeli administration believed that 'they had to show the power of Israel time and again until they were compelled to concede its military superiority and sue for peace' (Smith, 1996: 157).

The Palestinian position

Palestinian nationalism, like Zionism, can be traced back to the turn of the century and the Palestinian question 'can be related to Western cultural penetration in the form of nationalism and political penetration in the form of colonial rule' (Hassassian, 1996: 262). The Zionist project was a catalyst for Palestinian nationalism but it never contributed to its creation (Hassassian, 1996: 263). The success of Zionism over Palestinian nationalism is attributed not only to the powerful world interests supportive of Zionism but to Arab disunity: 'At times, Arabs fought against Arabs, while their Zionist enemy confronted them with unusual stubbornness and determination to reach the ultimate goal – creating a Jewish state in Palestine' (Hassassian, 1996: 262). The 'Catastrophe' of 1948 resulted in the hibernation of Palestinian nationalism as it sought refuge in neighbouring Arab states, who were themselves fearful that the Palestinian refugees would undermine political stability within their societies. However, the creation of the Palestinian Liberation Organisation (PLO) in 1964, and more particularly, the Israeli occupation of the West Bank, Gaza and East Jerusalem in 1967, witnessed the rebirth of Palestinian nationalism as distinct from Pan-Arabism. As Friedland notes:

> even where there is no sense of nationhood before the establishment of the colony, colonialism creates it. It accomplishes it by treating all indigenous residents with equal contempt ... In Palestinian society, nationalism grew out of the systematic repression exercised by the Israeli military occupation.
>
> (Friedland quoted in Hiltermann, 1991: 11)

The PLO became 'the institutional expression of Palestinian nationalism' and through its history has created an organisational framework 'within which all Palestinian cultural, social, educational, political and military activities are integrated' (Hassassian, 1996: 258). Since the early 1970s, the PLO has pursued a dual strategy of armed struggle and diplomacy as a means of solving the Israeli-Palestine conflict. In terms of solutions however, it has moved from a position of liberating the lands taken by Israel in 1948 (total liberation strategy) to the acceptance of a two state solution and the rejection of terrorism (Mohammad, 1997). Inside the territories the political strategy of the PLO was based on the mass mobilisation of Palestinians against the occupation through the creation of 'parallel institutions' (Ahmad quoted in Hiltermann, 1991: 13) which provided essential services for Palestinians in defiance of the Israeli civil and military administration while, at the same time, diplomatic efforts were being pursued at the highest level towards a resolution. The fear of 'normalising' relations with Israel has always featured in Palestinian grassroots thinking and such activity has never been fully supported by the PLO, although the intifada did result in increased contact with Israeli organisations. At a much wider political level, Palestinian society, as represented by the PLO, has always viewed itself as more secular, less autocratic and subsequently more democratic than other Arab states. Palestinian academics (Hassassian, 1996; Said, 1990), while stressing that Palestinian democracy cannot be compared with the Western style of democracy, have attempted to expand the international debate on the PLO which generally portrays the organisation as exclusively terrorist in nature.

The Palestinian Israeli position

The Arab-Israeli dynamic of 1948–67 ignored the plight of the Palestinian Arabs left inside Israel, a population that was 'emotionally wounded, socially hurt, politically lost, economically poverty stricken and nationally hurt' (Mar'i quoted in Darweish and Rigby, 1995: 2). Moreover, Palestinian Israelis[14] found themselves being ruled 'by a powerful, sophisticated majority against whom they fought to retain their country and land' (Mar'i quoted in Darweish and Rigby, 1995: 2). Throughout their history, the Palestinian Israelis have been subject to the inevitable contradictions of a state which attempts to balance democratic practices with Zionist beliefs. Between 1948 and 1966 the Israeli government imposed military rule on the Arab population and the government set about claiming the land of those Arabs who had fled and confiscating land from the resident population on the grounds of national security. The justification for such measures stemmed from a belief within Israeli government circles that the Arabs represented a 'fifth column' which could only be controlled by tight security measures. Having secured such a mechanism, Israel began the dual task of creating an appropriate system of government and, more importantly, of initiating *aliya* (the in-gathering of exiles).

The Israeli Arab community, which represents 18 per cent of the population in Israel, was described by Lustick (1980) as an acquiescent minority between 1948 and 1967. However, the 1967 war re-established links with Palestinians on the West Bank and Gaza and this, in turn with the emergence of the PLO, led to an increasing sense of

Palestinian identity. The interaction of Palestinian national identity and Israeli citizenship has led many to argue that Israel Arabs are in a perpetual state of identity crises (Darweish and Rigby, 1995; Ghanem and Ozacky-Lazar, 1990). Israeli academics (Smooha, 1992, 1994) report an increase in the 'Israelisation' of this community following the intifada in 1987 which has intensified as a result of the Oslo peace process. Palestinian academics (Rouhana, 1990; Mar'i, 1990) distinguish between 'Israeli-ness' which relates to citizenship, and the Palestinian component which is rooted in a deep sentimental attachment to Palestinian nationalism. They argue that both can exist in tandem – a view not shared by Israeli Jews who believe that citizenship and national identity are inseparable.

In terms of political issues, Palestinian Israelis demand full equality within the state, they seek recognition as a national minority and they support the establishment of a Palestinian state alongside Israel. The creation of the state of Israel and the contradictory nature of it being both Jewish and democratic represents the most fundamental source of disagreement and discrimination between Arabs and Jews in Israel. Historically, Arab political parties in Israel have sought to garner the support of the PLO. Within the current peace process, however, the future position of the Israeli Palestinian issue was not on the agenda of either the Government of Israel or the PLO. Indeed, the PLO's recognition of a two state solution legitimised the Israeli sub-identity of Palestinians in Israel: 'This was viewed as a clear indication that the PLO had accepted the status of Palestinians in Israel as Israeli citizens and would help them to become reconciled to a permanent status as a national minority' (Darweish and Rigby, 1995: 16). Hermann, an Israeli academic writing in 1996, stated 'the feeling in the Jewish public is that if we are making territorial concessions, we don't want to compromise over the Jewish identity of the state. This means that whoever expects the peace process to bring about total equality in the relations between Jewish and Arab population within the state, is making a terrible error' (Hermann, 1996: 102).

Peace efforts

The creation of the state of Israel has had a profound influence on the interaction between Israeli Jews, Palestinian Israelis and the Palestinians of the West Bank and Gaza. Indeed their different interpretations of the nature of the state continue to dominate relations and understandings of the conflict today. For many, the Oslo Agreement represented an historic opportunity at resolving each conflict. Although Oslo was negotiated between the PLO and the Government of Israel in respect of the Occupied Territories, it created an expectation amongst the Israeli Arab community that decisions would be taken by the Israeli government on issues relevant to their demands within the state. (The issue of the Israeli Arab position will be specifically dealt with in Chapter 5.) The following section examines efforts made to advance peace between the government of Israel and the Palestinian people of the Occupied Territories.

Since 1967, various proposals have been made in an attempt to resolve the Palestinian-Israeli conflict, each reflecting the differing interpretations of the nature of the conflict itself.[15] The main impetus for resolving the conflict has been largely determined by outside actors, particularly the United States which favoured a Jewish state in the region, and the underlying assumption has been that for peace to be achieved, the PLO would have to renounce violence and accept the legitimacy of Israel's right to exist. Arab and Palestinian academics (Hassassian, 1994; Mohammad, 1997) have consistently pointed to trends within the PLO, from as far back as 1973, which indicate a movement within that organisation towards diplomacy over violence. It should also be borne in mind that the Arab world fully endorsed the legitimacy of the PLO as the sole legitimate representatives of the Palestinian people (1974) and as Kelman pointed out, the PLO's function was 'no different from the function of any legitimate government of a sovereign state' (Kelman quoted in Flamhaft, 1996: 36).

> For the Palestinians in the territories as well as those in the Diaspora, the PLO was certainly not just an organisation but the symbol and embodiment of Palestinian nationhood. This was true even for those Palestinians who were less enthusiastic than others about the PLO leadership.
>
> (Flamhaft, 1996: 36)

The refusal of the international players to accept the validity of Palestinian national rights and negotiate with the PLO was reflected in the Camp David Agreements of 1979. It indicated the asymmetry of powerful world opinion against the Palestinian position. The Palestinian intifada[16] (uprising) of 1987 provided a rude awakening to forces maintaining that the Israeli/Palestinian conflict could be solved without negotiating with the PLO. The two key dynamics which underpinned the intifada, the internal pressures of Palestinian life under Israeli domination and the 'Palestinian exile presence' which 'interacted dialectically with regional and international powers' had finally merged. 'From now on there was to be no turning back, as the Palestinian sense of irreversibility took hold: the occupation had to end, political independence had to be declared, the sacrifice had to be made' (Said, 1990: 14).

The Israeli response to the popular uprising was one of brutality and military oppression. Defence Minister Rabin believed that the Israeli Defence Force (IDF) could contain the problem and that the Palestinians would ultimately 'come to their senses'. Rabin and the Israeli authorities failed to understand that the intifada was not an aberration which would pass but that it had become a very definite 'way of life'. A 'way of life' which was to last, in one form or another, until the beginning of the Madrid Peace Process of 1991. Certain elements of the Israeli mainstream, including members of Rabin's Labour Party, realised that the intifada required a political response, military might was not going to suffice, and that, more than ever before, a 'land for peace' compromise was required. Subsequently, the Israeli peace movement which had become dormant following protest activity during the war in the Lebanon was reactivated. As Cygielman remarked:

> While terrorism had only increased Israel's resolve to fight, and hardened its opposition to all Palestinian demands, the stubborn 'war of stones' started to change the Israeli state of mind.
>
> (Cygielman, 1994: 13)

The Israeli Government of National Unity was rigidly holding the line of not negotiating with 'terrorists'. However, 'the die was cast' (Said, 1990) and external PLO forces seized the moment and convened a Palestinian National Convention (PNC) which marked out the PLO's peace strategy – a strategy which found favour with the international community, particularly the USA. The decision by King Hussein of Jordan to relinquish all claims to the West Bank in July 1988 paved the way for the PLO to declare the establishment of the Palestinian state, alongside Israel, on the basis of UN Resolutions 242 and 338.[17] In so doing, the PLO was accepting the right of Israel to exist and committing itself to the pursuit of finding a settlement based on peaceful means. Arafat was also to make it clear that the PLO had rejected the use of terrorism.

> The State of Palestine, declaring itself a peace-loving state committed to the principles of peaceful coexistence, shall strive with all

states and peoples to attain a permanent peace built on justice and respect of rights.

(Extract from Declaration of Palestinian Independence, November 1988)

By the end of 1988, the United States, on the basis of the decisions taken by the PNC, engaged in direct discussions with the PLO. A new peace dynamic was emerging in the region and international efforts were directed towards convening an International Conference, under the auspices of the United Nations, bringing together the key players in the Middle East for peace talks. Israel maintained its stance of refusing to engage with the PLO despite growing internal pressures from mainstream Israeli peace forces and America's engagement.

Towards the end of the 1980s, internal divisions began to emerge within the PLO and in the territories over the future direction and purpose of the intifada. One school of thought argued that the intifada could be used as a bargaining chip for peace and that this could be advanced through contacts with the Americans. Conversely some Palestinians felt that engaging in a US inspired peace deal was 'crossing the red line' and argued that the intifada could be used as the fuel to ignite Arab revolution. In any event, the PLO's decision to support Iraq during the Gulf War against the combined forces of the United States and prominent Arab states left the PLO in utter financial turmoil at the end of 1990. It is estimated that this decision cost the PLO $120 million in annual donations, leaving it financially crippled and politically weak (Usher, 1995). The only thing that could salvage the desperate situation inside the PLO was the 'peace process' that followed from the Madrid Conference of 1991 (Usher, 1995: 2). The Madrid Conference (October 1991–Summer 1993) consisted of nine rounds of bi-lateral and multi-lateral talks between Israel, Syria, the Lebanon and a joint Jordanian-Palestinian delegation. The then Israeli Prime Minister Shamir had insisted, prior to taking part in the conference, that he would not negotiate with the PLO and that the Palestinian delegation would have to come from the territories and be approved by Israel. The PLO's acceptance of such conditions reflected the weakness of its position (Usher, 1995). The discussions 'produced little discernible progress' but created, according to Milton-Edwards (1996), an 'environment for peace' which was to have an imprint on Oslo. Somewhat paradoxically she remarked:

> The Palestinian and Israeli negotiators at the Madrid process came to the process with a semblance of a popular mandate and throughout

the two year period that the talks carried on, this mandate from the
Palestinian and Israeli people was constantly tested, measured and
debated. This baggage of public debate, no matter how difficult and
tortuous, endowed the process with a greater measure of representation than had ever been achieved in past attempts to mediate and
resolve the Palestinian-Israeli conflict.

(Milton-Edwards, 1996: 200)

The testing of this mandate for Israel occurred mid-way through the
process when the Labour Party won the June 1992 election on a platform of 'peace within nine months'. The defeat of the Likud Party under
Shamir paved the way for a much more pragmatic response to solving
the conflict facilitated by the new coalition partner, the left wing and
pro-peace Meretz Party. In December of 1992, Rabin passed a bill permit-
ting official contact with the PLO and almost nine months later Israel
had agreed and signed up to the Oslo Accords.

Implementing the Oslo Agreement

The Oslo Agreement provides for a two phase solution to the
Palestinian-Israeli conflict and the Accord itself comprises two docu-
ments: the Declaration of Principles (DOP) and the letters of Mutual
Recognition. The letters of mutual recognition formally endorse the
legitimate political rights of (i) the Government of Israel and (ii) the
PLO 'as the representatives of the Palestinian people'. Arafat's letter to
Rabin is a re-statement of his previous position, accepting UN
Resolutions 242 and 338, rejecting terrorism and affirming 'that those
articles of the Palestinian Covenant which deny Israel's right to exist ...
are no longer valid'.

The first phase of the DOP relates to the establishment of self governing arrangements in the West Bank and Gaza for an initial period of
five years during which time permanent status (phase two) negotiations would be completed on outstanding issues: 'Jerusalem, refugees
settlements, security arrangements, borders, relations and co-operation
with other neighbours, and other issues of common interest' (Article V:
Paragraph 3). Both sides agreed to the Gaza/Jericho First Plan and some
seven months after the signing (4 May 1994), Israeli troop deployment
began. Six days later, the first ever Palestinian police force entered Gaza
and on 13 May, military and civilian powers were handed over from
Israel to the new Palestinian Authority (PA). The transfer of authority

was not confined to Gaza and Jericho. 'With a view to promoting economic development in the West Bank and Gaza Strip, authority will be transferred to Palestinians on the following spheres: education and culture, health, social welfare, direct taxation, and tourism' (Article VI: Paragraph 2). For the PLO, statehood was according to Arafat 'within their grasp' (quoted in Usher, 1995: 5) and the new Authority began the state building process of establishing ministries and assessing the damage of the occupation.

Following the implementation of the Gaza/Jericho plan, Israeli and Palestinian negotiators set about discussing the 'Interim Agreement' which dealt with, *inter alia*, the election of the new Palestinian Council and the transfer of powers and responsibilities from the Israelis to the Council. Difficulties began to emerge between the two sides regarding which areas would be transferred to Palestinian control. In order to protect Israeli settlements and Israel's security, the Interim Agreement (Oslo II – 8 Sept. 1995) expanded self-rule to six West Bank towns (Jenin, Tulkarem, Qalqiliiya, Nablus, Ramallah and Bethlehem). Troop re-deployment was completed by December 1995 but as PASSIA noted: 'In fact, however, the PA gained effective control of only 4% of West Bank land ($200\,km^2$) and limited administrative responsibility for some 98% of the West Bank population' (PASSIA, 1997: 213).[18]

The Interim Agreement also provided for elections to the new Palestinian Council which took place in January 1996. With a turnout of 80 per cent, the results were a major victory for both Arafat (88 per cent) and his Fatah party (60 per cent). The instalment of the Palestinian Council triggered the second phase of the process, the initiation of 'permanent status' negotiations which commenced in May. However, the *process* was already under severe strain with the Palestinians accusing the Israelis of violating key elements of the Interim Agreement on civilian and security matters – the deployment of troops from Hebron, the continued use of closures, the restriction of access between Gaza and the West Bank and continued land expropriation, representing the key stumbling blocks. Israel complained about anti-Israeli incitement, activities of the Palestinian security forces and non-payment of debts by Palestinians to Israel.

The admission by Arafat that the Oslo accord represented the best deal possible for the Palestinians contrasts sharply with the initial optimism and euphoria that swept through the West Bank and Gaza following the historic signing ceremony on the White House Lawn.

Peace will have an immediate effect on Israel's ability to reach its
most important current goal, the focus of the aspirations of the
Zionist movement, the in-gathering of exiles.

(Yitzhak Rabin, August 1993, quoted
in Twite and Hermann, 1993)

I know many of you here think Oslo is a bad agreement. But it is the
best we can get in the worst situation.

(Yasser Arafat, July 1994,
quoted in Usher, 1995)

Whilst internal Palestinian forces criticised the deal brokered through
the secret Oslo channel, the political events inside Israel which resulted
in the election of a Likud government in May 1995, compounded the
belief amongst Palestinians that Israel was not ready for peace. The failure of Palestinian and international pressure to prevent Israel from
'establishing facts on the ground' with respect to settlement activity in
Arab East Jerusalem confirmed that not only was the issue of Jerusalem
lost but that the Oslo process could not deliver the ultimate prize – a
Palestinian state. At the opposite end of the spectrum, peace brought
increased levels of violence and suicide bombings against Israel mock-
ing a process which promised 'peace and security'.

Oslo and the Palestinians

Arafat's peace strategy had always been one of high risk given the situation that he and the PLO found themselves in at the beginning of the
1990s. Accordingly, the PLO opted for the DOP that would enable them
to establish 'statehood facts on the ground' – setting up a Palestinian
parliament and taking control of internal security through a Palestinian
police force. Arafat's contention prior to signing the DOP, that a
Palestinian state was 'within our grasps', was received with cautious optimism by the grassroots. However, from the very outset, critics argued
that the ambiguities and open-endedness of the agreement would
enable Israel to consolidate their fundamental objectives of maintaining
vast tracks of Palestinian land. Key amongst the critics was Dr Haidar
Abd al-Shafi who headed the Palestinian delegation during the Madrid
process. Dr al-Shafi argued that the first pitfall of the Oslo Agreement
was the secret manner in which it was negotiated: 'secrecy has widened
the rift among the Palestinian people'. Although recognising the
importance of the preamble of the DOP which mentions the legitimate

and political rights of the Palestinian and Israeli people, he contends that the DOP failed to challenge or address Israel's illegal claim to the territories. This allowed 'for implicit or perhaps explicit recognition of a separate entity for settlements' (al-Shafi, 1994: 17) which would result in the 'batunisation'[19] of the West Bank and Gaza, curtailing the possibility of a Palestinian state free from Israeli control. Palestinian delegates to the Madrid conference, for example, insisted that the transitional government should have jurisdiction over the entire Occupied Territories 'because we refused to allow settlements to be an independent entity or to be under the authority of any other party during the transitional stage since this would influence the final outcome of the peace process' (al-Shafi, 1994: 15). The Centre for Palestinian Research and Studies (CPRS) argued that the most damaging aspect of the Accord was the postponement of fundamental issues on Jerusalem, settlements and refugees, for reasons similar to those expressed above. Israel's ability to 'create facts on the ground' and its expansionist agenda. The failure of the agreement to explicitly state that there should be no additional settlement activity made it very difficult for Palestinians to believe that a state was 'within their grasp' (CPRS, 1994).

The signing of the Oslo II agreement provided evidence that the Israelis would not be dismantling settlements and that it would use security arguments to justify holding territory. For example, Netanyahu, once again, stated that there would not be a Palestinian state, rather as his advisor, David Bar Ilan, explained 'he (Netanyahu) wants the Palestinians to have as much self rule as possible, as long as it does not endanger the security of Israel' (Bar Ilan, 1996: 10). On the question of settlements, Bar Ilan claimed, 'do not forget, the very open and all-encompassing limitation which says that Israel can keep all the areas of the settlements, which is very small, and everything that it may consider essential for its security – and that can encompass a large area' (Bar Ilan, 1996: 16).

Oslo and the Israelis

Rabin and the Israeli government were acutely aware of the difficult position faced by Arafat and grasped his 'weakened condition to achieve concessions (even if unwritten) that he might not have offered otherwise. Whereas a weakened PLO in the 1980s justified to Americans and Israelis its continued isolation, a wounded Arafat now encouraged recognition when the alternatives were considered' (Smith, 1996: 318). With regard to the modalities of the agreement, since the intifada

Israel wanted to 'get Gaza out of Tel Aviv' because it was strategically unimportant and seen as a 'hotbed' for Islamic fundamentalism. The decision to include the West Bank town of Jericho was, from an Israeli viewpoint, much more significant as it represented the implementation of 'land for peace' which had currency amongst members of the Labour party, especially Yossi Beilin and Shimon Peres. As General Gazit remarked, 'if you Palestinians have been worried that all Israel wants is to get rid of the Gaza Strip while maintaining, keeping, holding and annexing the West Bank, the introduction of Jericho says: don't be worried' (Gazit, 1994: 37). Smith (1996) provides an insight into the reasoning behind staggering the negotiations – an issue discussed by the Rabin Cabinet in July 1993. The decision to opt for interim arrangements was taken on the grounds that (1) it would provide a test of the Palestinians' ability to rule and (2) 'afforded Israel an opportunity to consolidate control of territory considered essential, namely Greater Jerusalem, because Arafat had left Jerusalem under Israeli auspices until final talks began' (Smith, 1996: 324).

With respect to the creation of a Palestinian state, Gazit believed that Oslo offered the potential that 'theoretically, there is nothing in DOP that forbids Israel to demand that the next phase, after the interim 5 years, should be the complete annexation to Israel of all the territories, that it should be, if you want, the Greater Israel position' (Gazit, 1994: 37). Interviews undertaken with Rabin (October 1993) suggest that both he and Peres favoured some form of confederation with Jordan:

> There is nothing (in the Accord) about a Palestinian state or a capital in part of Jerusalem. I stick to my position: no Palestinian state, Jerusalem must remain united under Israeli sovereignty and be our capital forever … I don't believe there is room for an additional state between Israel and Jordan.
>
> (quoted in Smith, 1996: 324)

The dangers of an open-ended agreement became problematic with the election of the Likud Party which always espoused the Greater Israel position. However, Bar Ilan argued that with regard to final status issues there was very little difference between the Labour and Likud positions, 'in the interim agreement we object to many points that Labour accepts, but on the final status we seem to agree on many things. Labour says we are willing to call it a state as long as there are limitations. The point is not whether you call it a state but what the limitations are going to be' (BarIlan, 1996: 14).

The realities of Oslo

The introductory section of this chapter dealt very briefly with the historical background to the conflict leading up to Oslo. The impact or the 'realities of Oslo' are best described by Smith:

> Most Israelis and Palestinians want peace but many differ in their conceptions of what constitutes peace, coexistence, or achievements of maximalist objectives. Many remain captive to their adherence to aspirations attained or denied in the agreements of World War I and 1948. Current peace efforts are challenged by the existence of settlements...and the emergence of Islam as a force in the forefront of developments...Islamic, as opposed to Arab, approval of peace with Israel is not impossible, but the fact that it requires consideration indicates what has occurred in recent years...True peace, as opposed to the promise to officially sanctioned peace, remains a distant hope with many pitfalls prior to realisation, but the fact that it is being considered at all is a major achievement.
>
> (Smith, 1996: 333)

Despite the fine, if not ambiguous, words of the DOP, the political realities on the ground have not provided much comfort for either the Palestinians or Israelis. The historical factors defining each protagonist's interpretations of the conflict have not been diminished by the actions of 'the other side'. Israelis feel less secure as a result of Hamas attacks and Palestinians continue to live under a new form of occupation. The officially sanctioned peace has not as yet filtered down to the grassroots. Indeed, because the prospect of peace raised expectations, frustration and pessimism prevail. Lucy Nuseibeh, Director of the Palestinian Centre for the Study of Non-Violence, provides the historical context for the downturn in optimism amongst Palestinian society:

> After the first agreement (Oslo I – Sept. 1993) there was euphoria...People thought, 'now at last'...they were out in the streets waving flags and olive branches...But then, when the second agreement (Oslo II – Sept. 1995) was signed, people were absolutely appalled at the sight of that map. They felt everything was sold out...But then, when there was a date for the elections (Jan. 1996), people forgot about the sell out and became very happy and involved and they were able to think that, at last, something positive was

happening ... there was still a lot of hope ... Then when this closure business started and the bombs happened (Feb. 1996), it kicked people down much further than I have ever seen them before ... when people saw how that agreement could be abused and used as a tighter means of control than the Israelis had ever had before and what was worse, there was no way to fight it.

(Interview by authors, November 1996)

The above quotation reflects the ebbs and flows of the peace process with respect to Palestinian society. It also indicates the extent to which daily living is regulated by Israel. The closure of territories which dates back to the period during the Gulf War took on greater significance in April 1993 and it has now become a regular feature of the 'collective punishment' against Palestinians seeking entry to Israel. The use of closures by the Israelis is justified on the grounds of national security and it has tended to be used after violent attacks or when violence is predicted. However, it has had a devastating impact on the economy of the Palestinian Authority – some 60,000 Palestinians are denied access to employment in Israel and the import and export of goods is prohibited. Since the Oslo II agreement, Israel has been imposing 'internal closures' which 'is more severe and crippling ... as it leaves close to two million Palestinians virtual prisoners in their respective towns and villages' (Nakhal, 1996: 119). Not surprisingly, closures and internal closures[20] have had an impact on the ability of Palestinians to engage in peace or coexistence activity (see Chapter 5).

During the intifada, the Israeli authorities were responsible for 1,500 deaths and while the level of violence used by the security forces against Palestinians has fallen significantly, a number of flash point incidents during the peace process have caused deep anger about the role of the IDF and armed settlers. The first major crises after Oslo draws together these two prime concerns. In February 1994, an Israeli settler, Baruch Goldstein, shot dead 29 Palestinians at prayer in a mosque at Hebron; and:

what became evident in Hebron's bloody aftermath, at least to Palestinians, ... was just how little Oslo had changed (and by implication, would change) the modalities of Israel rule ... In the eight days following the massacre, 33 Palestinians were killed by the army (IDF) as protests erupted in Gaza, Jerusalem, Nablus, Ramallah and, of course, Hebron. Over one million Palestinians were confined to the West Bank and Gaza as Rabin sealed off the territories, once more sending their perilous economies into free fall.

(Usher, 1995: 20)

It has been argued that the atrocities at Hebron provided the PLO with a prime opportunity, which was subsequently missed, to initiate discussions on the reformulation of the DOP with respect to settlements. This issue and the status of Jerusalem have dominated the politics of the Palestinian street:

> The end of the peace process to the Palestinian mind is, among other things, the termination of the Israeli occupation of the West Bank, East Jerusalem and the Gaza strip. At the same time, Palestinians consider Jewish settlements in the territories as the essence of occupation. Such a paradox makes it difficult to view peace and settlements as compatible.
>
> (Al-Khatib, 1996: 55)

The Israeli government's attitude to peace has always been conditioned by security concerns. Such a view is entrenched by the continued use of suicide bombings by Hamas and sustained attacks in the run up to the Israeli General Election of May 1996 which left 58 Israelis dead as a result of bus bombings. Furthermore, the hardening of Israeli public opinion, in spite of the assassination of Yitzhak Rabin some six months earlier by a right-wing Jewish extremist, was confirmed with the election of Netanyahu who promised to 'thicken the Jewish settlements in Hebron'. As a result of fear over their security, very few Israelis, including those in the peace camp, would be prepared to criticise or campaign against closures which are at best 'a necessary evil'. The peace process has further deepened divisions within Israel between secular and religious Jews. Naomi Chazan, during a conference presentation in Northern Ireland, remarked that the peace process had shattered the forces which had previously united Israeli Jews – the belligerent Arab world – 'one outcome of the peace process is that Israelis were forced to start defining themselves in terms of themselves rather than the enemy and that has been the greatest difficulty of all'. At this level, fears were expressed amongst Israeli Arabs who argued that their position has become more precarious as a result of a process which amounts to the further Judaisation of Jews. In this context Rabin's comments on the 'in-gathering of exiles' may provide a worrying glimpse of what lies ahead for Israel's Palestinian community as the peace process progresses. The expectation that the Arabs' position inside Israel would be improved in tandem with peace is 'very unrealistic when you look at the attitudes within the Jewish population. As regards winning internal equality here for Arabs, not in terms of budgets but regarding their ability to influence the collective, opinion polls and personal interviews with Jews show that even if the peace process moves forward, the Arabs will face the same barriers, or even bigger ones' (Hermann, 1996: 102). The following chapter examines relationships at the micro level and various efforts by grassroots organisations to contribute to peace building.

5
Israel/Palestine: Micro Grassroots Activity

Introduction

The way in which each protagonist defines the Palestinian/Israeli conflict has created a series of different grassroots responses towards a resolution. That is, the dynamics of occupied and occupier, majority versus minority, powerful and powerless, victim and perpetuator remain central to understanding the reaction of grassroots organisations and their attempts at peace building. Within Israeli society, grassroots efforts operate under the banner of either 'coexistence' or 'peace'. Coexistence work deals with relations between Jewish and Palestinian citizens of Israel, while peace activity is defined in terms of relations between Israelis and Palestinians living in the lands occupied after 1967. Palestinian citizens of Israel were initially partners to coexistence activity but political developments within that community have created new forces acting against the 'Jewish' notion of coexistence. For Palestinians from the territories, peace amounts to ending the occupation, and civil society (the grassroots) has acted as a functionary towards this end through 'out administering' the enemy. This chapter will examine the *dynamics*, the *politics* and the *impact of the peace process* on the Israeli and Palestinian grassroots.

Coexistence in Israel

The key dilemma for state planners and Zionist politicians has always been the extent to which the government can 'accommodate' the Israeli Arab population while at the same time protecting the Jewish Zionist character of the state. The advent of political forces amongst Palestinian Israelis during the late stages of the 1960s, such as re-establishing contact with Palestinians on the West Bank, resulted in a questioning of the true purpose of 'coexistence'. At the same time, the growth of right-wing elements following the Six Day War increased levels of hostility towards the Arabs of Israel whilst strengthening the Jewish character of the state. Understanding the politics of coexistence requires an examination of the interplay between Arabs and Jews at both the macro and micro level.

> How one defines Arab and Jewish coexistence varies in accordance with one's starting point – for Jews coexistence relates to the containment of restive and dissident Arabs, while for Arabs it is how to effect change without being brandied disloyal, and for the system itself, coexistence is determined.
>
> (Smooha, 1990: 112)

Professor Smooha's comments reflect the problems associated with the concept of coexistence in Israel. We provide a background to the 'politics of coexistence' by examining changes in the nature and purpose of micro level activity.

The politics of coexistence

Coexistence can be classified into four historical periods. The first period (1948–66) was driven by government and is understood in terms of the desire of the Jewish authorities to co-opt Arabs into the new state. Activity classified under the heading of coexistence between 1948 and 1966 generally involved contact between establishment forces amongst the Israeli Arab population and mainstream Zionist political forces including the ruling Labour Party, the Histardut and key municipal authorities such as Haifa (Abu-Nimer, 1993: 392). The fragmentation of the Israeli party political system at the beginning of the 1960s resulted in the growth of a number of Jewish organisations which sought to explore new avenues of relations between Arabs and Jews, principally through the use of the educational system (Givat Haviva and the Van Leer Institute). In the second period, between 1966 and the end of the 1970s, coexistence took the form of educational activity outside the brief of the Israeli government but within mainstream Zionist thinking with respect to classification types of the Arab community.

A number of points need to be made in relation to the Israeli domestic scene during the 1970s which profoundly influenced and shaped Jewish public attitudes towards Palestinians and Arabs in general.

The period witnessed a growth in right wing political parties and interest groups, especially those with a messianic mission who argued that the 1967 war was an example of 'God delivering his people the promised land'. There was a subsequent hardening of Jewish attitudes towards Arabs as a result of violent attacks on Israel carried out by the PLO and the devastating impact of the 1973 War which proved that Israel was not militarily infallible (Bar On, 1996: 72). The election of a Likud government (1977) confirmed that Israeli Jews were less inclined towards either relenting on giving up the Occupied Territories or on agreeing to the demands of the Israeli Arab community. During the 1970s, the third period, 'coexistence' and 'peace' activity hibernated as a result of the harsh realities of the macro-political environment.

The final period of the 1980s created new dynamics for 'coexistence' which shape the nature of activities today. Such serious concerns were expressed at the increasing levels of racist, anti-democratic and anti-Arab sentiments being expressed amongst the Jewish youth population, that the Ministry of Education began providing support to projects and programmes which sought to reduce or eliminate these feelings and attitudes (Abu-Nimer, 1993). The educational activities were defined by the Ministry in terms of 'intercultural interaction with respect and equality through knowledge, attitudes and approaches to openness, understanding, tolerance to other cultures, new skills and training' (Ministry of Education Report, 1994 quoted in Abu-Nimer, 1993: 130). In 1985, a Unit for Democracy and Coexistence was established within the Ministry with the task of centralising, approving and co-ordinating coexistence activity throughout the schooling system. Organisations with a track record in delivering such programmes expanded their activities and there was also a blossoming of new organisations in the field to provide for encounters, curriculum development and teacher training. Maoz (1995) estimates that by the end of the 1980s, more than 50 organisations were involved in coexistence projects. The vast majority of these organisations were managed and controlled by Jews and approval was required from the Ministry of Education before programmes could be implemented.

At roughly the same time and in response to a differing and diverging political environment, 'professional organisations sprang up to meet the specific needs of different occupational groups within the Arab population: social workers, medical practitioners, lawyers and educators' (Darweish and Rigby, 1995: 10). Arab political forces were signalling that 'coexistence without equality' was a sham and failed to reflect the political realities and needs of a community growing in political assertiveness (Maoz, 1995). Progressive Jewish organisations also realised that coexistence activity in the educational sphere was not enough. A dual approach developed which sought to enhance inter-personal relations through traditional means, while addressing the needs of the Arab population through promoting equality and reducing socio-economic differentials between the two communities. Activity drawn up without the input of the Arab community was recognised to be, at best, patronising and, at worst, part of a ploy to control the Arab population. Table 5.1 is drawn from the 1996 report of the Abraham Fund, a charitable institution with a coexistence remit, as a guide to the type of

Table 5.1 Coexistence projects (examples) funded by the Abraham Fund

Activity heading	Example of activity
Community Organising	Home advocacy in Beit Saffafa: educates Arab residents about equal access to entitlements and services through public information meetings, community action groups, door to door visits and a drop-in centre
Culture	Theatre Co-operation, joint Arab/Jewish productions, video workshops
Economic Development	Centre for Jewish–Arab Development – business support, investment loans
Education	Curriculum development, early childhood education projects, encounters, teacher training
Encounters	Association for the Aged, youth leadership training, women's training, school and university encounters
Environment	Educating the Galilee: Teaching Environmental Conservation
General Social Services	Haifa Rape Crisis Centre, Institute for the Advancement of Education in Jaffa, Pregnancy Advisory Service
Health	Employment of Arabic Speech Therapist, Galilee Society for Health, Research and Services – Self-Help Groups for Arabs
Public Policy	Sikkuy – Association for the Advancement of Equal Opportunity
Religious Affairs	Interreligious Co-ordinating Council
Women's Issues	Isha l'Isha – Women in a democratic Society – Leadership Training
Youth Social Services	Haifa Children's Rights Information Centre, Ombudsman for Children and Youth in the Arab sector

activity undertaken under the 'coexistence' banner in Israel. We use some of these projects to explain and illustrate the advances made towards re-defining the role of coexistence activity.

The dual process of coexistence

A number of projects under the heading of human relations and semi-structural activity, focus on the dynamic of relations between Arabs and Jews inside Israel. This is due to the fact that:

> the conflict operates at all levels of society and in all fields of life. It's a conflict about resources, about land and about the status of the minority, it is about the very nature of the state...I think that the ethnic character of the state is the main source of the conflict. It is the main source of the discrimination against the Arab minority...It's not just an ideology...its the implementation of the ideology in the state.
>
> (Ghanem, a Palestinian Israeli, interviewed by authors, December 1996)

As a guide to understanding the relationship between Arabs and Jews, Darweish (1996) summarised key areas of dispute between Palestinian citizens of Israel and the Jewish state. Like Ghanem, the key area is the definition of the state as 'a state for the Jews'. The consequences of this definition impacts on all aspects of life for Israeli Arabs. For example, the symbols used representing the state are all Jewish, the national anthem refers to the 'return to Zion' and an electoral law, passed in 1984, prohibits candidates standing for election if they implicitly or explicitly reject the existence of Israel as a state of the Jewish people. Darweish and Rigby (1995) outlined additional areas of discrimination in terms of taxation law, land expropriation, military service, security grounds, education and institutional discrimination. On the issue of education, they write:

> The profoundly discriminatory nature of the education system is evidenced by the State Education Law of 1953 which depicts one of the aims of the elementary education system as being to emphasise 'the value of Jewish culture...loyalty to the state and the Jewish people'. There is also extensive discrimination in the fields of educational facilities, classrooms hours, vocational training and technical education, higher education and appointments to posts within the educational system.
>
> (Darweish and Rigby, 1995: 18)

Israeli Palestinian attitudes towards coexistence within the educational environment have changed in accordance with the wider political environment and new priorities for advancement have emerged such as demands for educational autonomy (Ghanem and Ozacky-Lazar, 1990).

Education and coexistence: a human relations approach

The Israeli education system is divided into three streams – state secular, state religious and religious. The Arab population is educated separately and a Unit for Arab Education exists within the Ministry of Education. Both the state secular and Arab schools are regulated and inspected by the Ministry on curriculum delivery and it is within this area that coexistence/encounter work has operated. The use of educational encounters as a mechanism for improving relationships between Arabs and Jews is based on the contact hypothesis model of human relations. The underlying assumption is that increasing physical inter-group contact results in changes in the mutual attitudes of interacting members and inter-group relations (Knox and Hughes, 1994). Two key questions are relevant: firstly, is this type of activity another, more subtle attempt, by the Jewish authorities at controlling Israeli Arabs and secondly, how effective is this type of activity given the nature and extent of discrimination practised by the state against Arab education?

Palestinian researchers argue that the Israeli educational system represents a central plank in the government's policy of controlling the Arab population and that the system attempts to neutralise Palestinian identity (Abu-Nimer, 1993; Al-Haj, 1990). Evidence used to support this view relates to the absence within the curriculum of Arab or Palestinian identity or culture, the overriding values and ethos of the system which are exclusively Zionist and Jewish, coupled with systematic and institutional discrimination against the Arab education system in general (Al-Haj, 1990). Research undertaken by Al-Haj provides a sense of the paradoxical nature of the Israeli government's position between, on the one hand, promoting coexistence/educational encounters and, on the other, implementing policies which deliberately discriminate against the Arab educational system (interviewed by authors, March 1997). An inherent contradiction also exists between formal curriculum activities and informal curriculum which promote Arab–Jewish relations. Coexistence within this context is interpreted as mere tampering at the edges, as the system continues to be a 'vehicle for nation-building' amongst Jews whilst for Arabs 'it remains an encouragement towards passivity and co-optation' (Al-Haj, 1990). An Israeli education-alist summarised the position thus:

> In Israel, both the curriculum and the textbooks, with their explicit and hidden messages were directed at promoting unity, survival, loyalty, patriotism, etc. In the non-curricular parts of the system ... many new initiatives, programmes and activities have developed which focus on education for democracy, tolerance, coexistence and peace ... Most of these excellent initiatives bear witness to a real process of change. But with all due respect to the fireworks, the essence of education still lies in the grey daily routine of learning and instructing the attitudes and identity building disciplines ... Hence, the principal challenge of education for peace is an examina-tion, and then a sweeping change of the contents of curriculum, of textbooks and teacher training, in other words, the backbone of reg-ular studies. The main challenge is still ahead of us.
>
> (Bitan, 1996: 14)

Criticism has also been levelled at the delivery of coexistence pro-grammes, particularly the way non-governmental organisations (NGOs) have accepted the assumptions of the Ministry of Education which has, for the most part, sought to exclude discussions of key structural and political questions which dominate Arab/Jewish relations at the macro-level (Katz and Khanov, 1990). Maoz (1995) undertook an extensive evaluation of dialogue activity in the Van Leer Institute and two points are worthy of note. Past evaluations of coexistence activity failed to address and challenge the *power relationship* which existed between Arab and Jewish participants. Maoz provides an interesting insight into the dynamics of relations between Jewish directors of educational pro-jects and facilitators. The former group sought to use their influence to eliminate any discussion of 'hot' issues, or those related to the political conflict, arguing that the virtues of the coexistence projects were 'co-operation, good citizenship and loyalty to the state' (quoted in Maoz, 1995: 15). Political encounters were negative because 'they contradict the dominant legitimate (Israeli government) version and bring up sub-versive and threatening versions' of events (quoted in Maoz, 1995: 16). As a result, Jewish Directors virtually excluded discussions on political issues 'in favour of joint activity on neutral educational projects'. The impact of the decision to avoid political issues resulted in harsh criticism from participants and facilitators, with Arab participants arguing that to exclude politics from encounters ignored 'the true reality of Jewish-Arab

relations in Israel'. In a more extensive study of six intervention programmes,[21] Abu-Nimer (1993) found that the majority of Jewish and
Arab *facilitators* defined the conflict in Israel in terms of controversial
political issues – the Jewishness of the state of Israel, the recognition of
the Palestinian Israeli population as a national minority and the pursuit of an equality agenda, the relationship between Palestinians in the
West Bank and Gaza and Palestinians in Israel – but the Jewish *directors*
of the same programmes tended to stress the cultural dynamic as an
important dimension to the conflict. Only two of the six organisations
planned and designed encounter models to include political issues. The
other designs excluded these issues and focused mainly on cultural
components which were viewed by most practitioners as being less
important. The issue of the Jewishness of the state, for example, was
not formally addressed in four out of the six programmes, leading one
Arab facilitator to remark that, 'the workshop is only effective when
Arabs and Jews are engaged in a discussion about the definition of the
state because it is the core issue' or expressed in a different way:

> Those Jewish facilitators who truly understand the conflict and
> observe what is happening between Arabs and Jews not only in the
> encounter context but in general, will reach the conclusion that a
> Jewish state definition is the source of the conflict between Arabs
> and Jews.
>
> (Quoted in Abu-Nimer, 1993: 285)

The argument that educational coexistence activity between Jews and
Arabs is part of the larger system for controlling the Arab population is
persuasive and a commonly held view amongst Israeli Palestinian academics and community activists. It relates directly to macro-political
issues:

> In the economy, in culture, in politics, in every field we can see the
> ethnic character of this state. The Jewish majority is dominating in
> every field of life and also in these (educational coexistence) institu-
> tions. These institutions are mostly owned by Jewish concerns and
> they are part of the domination ... I mean it is hard to think that
> these institutions will succeed in their efforts ... when the entire sys-
> tem is an ethnic one ... So one cannot win against the machine of
> the state.
>
> (As'ad Ghanem, interviewed December 1996)

The failure of the state to address the 'educational gaps' and attempts at undermining Arab and Palestinian identity through the imposition of a curriculum which espouses Jewish values has resulted in demands for complete educational autonomy for the Israeli Palestinian population. The rationale underpinning calls for autonomy, for example, are based on the notion that the integration of Arabs within Israeli society can only be achieved from a position of 'strength, not from a position of weakness' (Al-Haj, interviewed March 1997) and that 'without the feeling of collective identity we would be weak…So in order to succeed, we have to be strong…Only then dialogue makes sense' (interview with Palestinian Israeli community worker, November 1996). This leads us into the second tier of coexistence activity which is best described as semi-structural and which has grown out of the desire on the part of the Israeli Arab population to 'develop our own grassroots, as a community, and around common issues' because 'that is the only way we can change policy, to change Israel and to end discrimination' (interview with Palestinian Israeli community worker, November 1996).

Semi-structural coexistence

Although there has been an increase in the number of organisations involved in educational projects under the coexistence banner during the 1980s, a parallel process was taking place within the Israeli Arab community which clearly suggested that 'dialogue was not enough'. This political position solidified during the intifada of 1987 as Palestinian Israelis increased demands for equality and a recognition of national rights. Institution building was identified 'as a political tool for achieving our goals…the moment we realise there is no longer a need for this tool we will convert it into the open for Jews and Arabs' (Darweish and Rigby, 1995: 23). The drive for equality, however, could only be achieved through attempting to influence government policy and by mobilising Arab forces inside Israel. The Israeli Government's response to calls for separate institutions in education and social services was outright opposition across the political spectrum but certain progressive non-governmental organisations acknowledged and sought to support the need for such a development.

One such body is the New Israel Fund (NIF) which, amongst other things, sees its goal as empowering Israelis to create a 'state based on freedom, justice and peace as envisaged by the founders of Israel'. The underlying assumption of the New Israel Fund is that Israel's very democracy is tarnished by the continuation of discriminatory practices

against the Arab minority. Whilst it could be argued that the organisation operates out of a partial self interest in protecting the fabric of
Israeli democracy, on the other hand, it promotes ideas which are most
unpopular to the majority of the Jewish population. The NIF operates a
dual approach of (i) encouraging dialogue and encounters (human
relations work) while (ii) providing support to Arab organisations on
an equality agenda.[22]

The Equal Access Project is an example of semi-structural coexistence
work because it aims to reduce the socio-economic gaps between Israeli
Arabs and Israeli Jews. The classification 'semi-structural' is derived
from the fact that progress towards full equality could only realistically
be achieved through significant government action on the issue by
way of legislative changes and the transfer of public expenditure to
Arab communities. The Equal Access Project convened the first national
conference on education for Arab parents and educators which led to
the establishment of the Arab Union of Parents' Organisations. The
Union itself is mandated to obtain greater resources for Arab education
and to organise and empower Arab parents at the local level, 'as Jewish
parents' committees have done for decades' (NIF, 1995).

Another example of coexistence work uses economic development
activity as a means of promoting coexistence. The Centre for Jewish
Arab Economic Development (CJAED) was established in 1988 and
operates at three levels. The business unit attempts to promote economic partnerships *between* Arabs and Jews. It also promotes economic
development activity *within* the Arab sector through provision of business loans, business planning advice and assistance in obtaining Israeli
government benefits. The training unit offers a range programmes to the
Arab community on exporting, tourism and women's entrepreneurship.
The most significant aspect of the centre's work is directed towards
increasing private and public sector investment in the Arab sectors
through working with municipal authorities. In 1995, the centre spear-
headed a campaign which resulted in the reduction of 'artificially high
government mandated prices for industrial land in Arab municipalities
to a level comparable to prices in neighbouring Jewish towns' (CJAED,
1995). Coexistence can only operate in an environment of full equality
between all citizens of the state and this belief is reflected in 'a balanced representation of Jews and Arabs, and of men and women, on the
Board of Directors and professional staff' (CJAED, 1995). The centre is
fully aware of the limitations of its work in changing government policy:

> Our long term goal is not to change policy in the government. If it
> happens, well, that's a by-product ... There are other organisations

doing that and frankly, in some ways, they are hitting their heads against a wall...Instead of wasting our time in that direction, we focus our energies on actually changing the direction on the ground and actually working with people directly rather than working on the government.

(Interview with CJAED Director, December 1996)

In spite of the diversification of coexistence activity, decisions related to funding projects which seek to address imbalances have caused concerns amongst some Jewish funders. The first relates to the efficacy of providing funding to projects beyond the limits of the non-governmental sector. Certain funders believed the task of reducing the socio-economic gap could only be achieved through massive state action. Others have suggested that this reasoning is a smoke screen for funders not wanting to be brought into direct conflict with the authorities on issues of policy. The second dilemma relates to a belief that organisations would be encouraging separation rather than coexistence through Arab empowerment and fears were expressed that such positioning might be viewed as threatening to the state. As one evaluator of coexistence work noted:

I think that it is probably true that in any society there is much more work at the superficial levels and less at structural levels. That certainly gets into one of the causes for hesitation by Jewish supporters of coexistence work. How Jews view coexistence raises fears when you talk about empowerment and structural change...there is something threatening when a minority starts talking about structural change vis a vis the majority.

(Interview with Havassey, December 1996)

The view that separation and coexistence are mutually exclusive indicates a belief that coexistence is to be controlled by the Jewish majority. However, the view that semi-structural activity shares the same political rationale as other forms of coexistence work is not persuasive in that it is undertaken outside the control of government regulators and ministries and most significantly, the identification of the need stems from the Israeli Arab community. There are, however, certain 'objective limitations' to semi-structural activity which also apply to educational activity. These are:

- Their development has been hampered by the lack of infrastructure and resources, and hence lack of stability and professionalism in their operation;

- They are extremely limited in reaching only a small part of the population; and
- They lack institutional support and nation-wide legitimation from the authorities and the public. (Hall-Cathalla, 1990: 135)

Coexistence and peace

There has always been a reluctance amongst Israeli peace activists to link the activities of coexistence and peace. The argument being that the conflict inside Israel is one of majority/minority relations, and therefore coexistence is the goal, while the conflict between Israel and the Palestinians in the Occupied Territories relates to a conflict over national identities, and hence peace is the objective.

> Many commentators mistakenly assert that four or five dozen peace organisations were active in Israel during the decade [1980s]. In fact, most of these should properly be described as coexistence groups working to improve relations between Israeli Arabs and Jewish citizens.
>
> (Bar On, 1996: 183)

Peace organisations have tended to ignore the relationship between Palestinians inside Israel and those on the West Bank and Gaza. Israeli coexistence groups, on the other hand, argue that their activity with Palestinians inside Israel places them in a unique position with respect to understanding the Palestinian identity, a position which has not, by and large, been afforded to the majority of peace activists. Jewish coexistence activists point to the lack of understanding displayed by the peace camp during the Gulf War with respect to the Palestinian and Arab position which tended to support Iraq.

The signing of the Oslo Accord was viewed by those involved in coexistence work as a vindication of their efforts and it gave them a renewed sense of legitimacy but political circumstances soon began to dominate their activities:

> A few years ago when I was saying that I was working here [Givat Haviva] and dealing with Jewish/Arab issues I was seen almost like a traitor in the eyes of Jews. After the peace agreement was signed with Arafat, I was viewed almost like a heroine and now [December, 1996] I am neither a traitor but neither am I a hero.
>
> (Interview with Myriam Dagan, Givat Haviva, December 1996)

The peace process brought a number of significant changes to the operation of organisations involved in coexistence work, confirming one thesis that peace and coexistence are inextricably linked:

> Our work has demonstrated the power to advance the peace process in two essential ways: first, by strengthening the efforts of Israelis, Jewish and Arab, to provide tolerance, pluralism and civility in discourse and to demonstrate that Jews and Arabs can coexist in peace and equality. And second by using that experience to help build bridges between Israelis and Palestinians in support of peace enhancing efforts across the 'Greenline'.
>
> (NIF Annual Report, 1995)

At this level, organisations such as the NIF began providing grants to organisation for the purpose of facilitating dialogues between Israelis and Palestinians and transferring skills to strengthen democracy within Palestinian society.

> The Oslo Accord between the PLO and Israel began a process that could be the turning point for Israel and the Middle East. However, declarations and agreements are a necessary but not a sufficient base for lasting peace. Special efforts are needed to prepare Israelis and Palestinians for the challenges that lie ahead.
>
> (NIF Annual Report, 1995)

Organisations were reluctant to provide an assessment of the success or achievements of such ventures, the prevailing view being that activity equalled success. As political conditions on the ground changed, so did the level of interest in such work, especially on the Palestinian side, and the impact of closures reinforced efforts on all sides to sustain contact. The new relationship between coexistence and peace was, however, viewed with a degree of scepticism amongst certain elements of the Israeli peace camp:

> Coexistence organisations are not grassroots organisations[23] ... They are not actually calling upon people to take part in anything ... They are selling a course ... so it's like asking me whether or not the university can serve as a catalyst to the peace process.
>
> (Interview with Hermann, March 1997)

> They (*coexistence groups*) didn't run a demonstration, they didn't intervene, they didn't get involved. On the contrary, they were managing a business...They don't influence policy...I have a million dollars and I want to spend it in improving the quality of nursery education in the Arab sector in Israel...is that progressive, is that humanitarian, has it anything to do with the peace movement? No. Is it solving the national problem? No.
>
> (Interview with Kaminer, November 1996)

So while peace activists agreed that there was overlapping membership between those involved in peace demonstrations and coexistence work (Hall-Cathalla, 1990), the overriding sentiment was that coexistence groups did not directly contribute to peace efforts and that their work did not have the imprint of Oslo. Yet they have been most active in developing activities across the 'Green line' since Madrid (1991) which contrasts with the 'hibernation of peace organisations'. Some coexistence activists argued that this proves the value of their past activity beyond that of the peace movement which has sought to link the conflict between Palestinians in the Occupied Territories with Palestinians inside Israel.

A number of other important changes occurred after Oslo. For example, the fracturing of internal unity between secular (pro-Oslo) and religious (anti-Oslo) Jews reached a peak following the assassination of Rabin (November 1995). The words of the trial judge in the case of Yigal Amir – the assassin of Rabin – warned: 'The fact that such a wild growth could sprout from within our midst requires us to examine which parts of Israel's education system failed to...impart the foundations of democracy...to the younger generation' (quoted in NIF's Annual Report, 1995). Coexistence organisations such as the NIF began to develop programmes 'to open new channels for dialogue among Israelis polarised by the peace process and break new ground in education for democracy'. The Unit for Coexistence and Democracy also refocused activities:

> Until a year ago, the unit had been dedicated to the conflict between Arabs and Jews...Since or almost since the assassination of our late Prime Minister, Yizhak Rabin, Israeli society has been dangerously split between religious and non religious, so at the moment I am dealing with that...
>
> (Interview with Dr Shul Paz, November 1996)

At the same time, the peace process provided the Israeli Arab community with an initial sense of optimism that their demands for equality would be met by the Labour/Meretz government.[24] But the growing uneasiness amongst Israeli Jews towards the peace process, and the increased levels of intolerance towards Arabs as a result of political violence rendered their hopes groundless. The election of a Likud government on the platform of 'Bibi: Good for the Jews' provided final evidence that the peace process was not going to bring additional benefits. As Al-Haj remarked (interview, March 1997), the peace process placed the Israeli Arab community in double periphery: they were placed at the margins of Israeli society and at the margins of the Palestinian struggle. The following extract indicates some of the new difficulties associated with this predicament at the level of coexistence work:

> We realised that the seminars between Palestinians from the West Bank and Gaza and Israelis were easier to conduct than seminars between Palestinians and Jews inside Israel. Why? The national identity conflict is the central issue inside Israel. With Palestinians from the West Bank and Gaza their identity is undisputed – they are Palestinians and Israeli Jews viewed them as Palestinians.
>
> (Interview at Neve Shalom, November 1996)

The peace movement in Israel

The Israeli peace movement emanates from the political fall out which emerged after the Six Day War. The initial reaction amongst Israelis to the victory produced two raw emotions, 'joy' and 'hope' (Bar On, 1996: 26) – 'joy' at having captured 'the land of our Fathers' and 'hope' that the Arab–Israeli conflict could be nearing resolution. Feelings of hope rested on the belief that Israel was now in a position to trade 'land for peace' with the Arab world. Yet the prospect of trading for peace was restrained by expressions of joy at maintaining a Jewish presence on land. The Six Day War drew two internal battle lines between Israelis favouring the expansion and settlement of land on the new territories and those who believed they should be traded in an attempt to secure peace. Significantly, this conflicting dynamic still dominates the Israeli political scene and the peace movement remains at the forefront of the 'land for peace' agenda.

The significance of the peace movement during the early period of the occupation was its preparedness as part of the mainstream to admit that 'the clash between the Jewish and Arab people of Palestine was at 'the very heart of the conflict' (interview with Kaminer, November 1996). This contrasts with the view expressed by Golda Meir in 1967 when it was suggested that the greatest problem facing the Israeli position in continuing to occupy the territories was 'the evolving Palestinian nation' to which she replied 'What Palestinian people? Where is there an evolving nation?' Bar On identifies the Movement for Peace and Security, established in July 1968, as the first peace movement in Israel outside the arena of party politics. Its political philosophy was based on a 'land for peace' deal and it sought to persuade the Labour government of the day to 'declare unequivocally that the state of Israel does not intend to annex territories', arguing that the territories should be 'evacuated as a result of a peace agreement based upon agreed and secure boundaries' (Bar On, 1996: 60–1). The significance of this group was its close association with members of the ruling Labour Party which had the potential to influence policy. Four characteristics define it as a peace movement:

- it managed to mobilise people outside the small circle of activists;
- it was a counter force to growing extra-parliamentary activity of the Israeli right;
- it lobbied government directly with the intention of influencing people; and
- it provided an educational and informational tool for changing public opinion. (Bar On, 1996: 63)

Research undertaken by Israeli academics (Hermann et al., 1996) provided the following working definition of peace organisations, the breadth of their activity and the principles underpinning their approach:

A peace/conflict resolution organization in the Israeli context would be any voluntary/non governmental body or group of people residing in Israel and/or the Occupied Territories, active at the relevant period of time [late 1960s to the present] which has promoted mutual recognition of national self determination as a necessary but not sufficient condition for achieving peace between Jews and Palestinians; that has sought non-violent resolution of the conflict on the political, social and cultural levels; and that has been involved with consciousness raising, dialogue, advocacy and provision

of professional services directed to assuage the injustice and grievances caused by the conflict in the social, economic, legal, religious
and cultural realms.

Hermann et al. found that the majority of grassroots peace organisations
were engaged in consciousness raising activity ranging from writing
letters to newspapers through to organising public demonstrations.
Dialogue work and advocacy activities were less frequent because of
their nature and associated time pressure. Professional services were
provided to Palestinians by less than one third of peace organisations
which the researchers examined and these included: medical, legal,
psychological, educational, economic, community and inter-organisa-
tional services. Professional groups, unlike other peace organisations,
tended to work directly with a Palestinian partner and they were not
subject to the vagaries of the political climate which sent other organisations into 'hibernation'. The Palestinian intifada witnessed an explosion
of peace groups and professional organisations. Before discussing peace
activity and the intifada, however, we consider the politics of peace.

The politics of peace

The early 1970s represented a period of 'hibernation' for peace
forces coupled with a subsequent hardening of Israeli attitudes towards
Arabs, especially after the 1973 War which left Israel feeling vulnerable and insecure. The most significant development within the
peace movement occurred following Sadat's historic visit to Jerusalem
(November 1977). In response to the reluctance of Prime Minister
Begin to agree autonomy plans for the Occupied Territories, a group
of 348 Reserve Army Officers sent him a terse letter demanding that
he 'choose the path of peace'. The officers stated that they had
'many doubts' over the government's policy of extending the boundaries of Israel 'over the achievement of peace with the Arab world'.
The officer's letter 'lit a match that ignited a huge flame' (Bar On,
1996) and it witnessed the birth of the most potent force of the
Israeli peace movement – 'Peace Now'. The newly established Peace
Now supported the Camp David process (which was rejected by
Palestinians) and requested that settlement activity in the West Bank
and Gaza should cease. Peace Now has consistently represented the
middle ground or mainstream of the Israeli peace movement and it
has become the benchmark against which other groups determine

their political platforms. Membership of Peace Now consists of activists who participate and plan activities such as demonstrations, peace vigils, lobbying and dialogue work; loyal participants who always attend demonstrations;[25] and sympathisers who either occasionally join demonstrations or sign petitions – the nature and size of this group varies in both background and according to political circumstances. In terms of its politics, Kaminer argued that 'the politics of Peace Now were far from expressing the peace sentiments of all sections of the peace movement in the country' (Kaminer, 1990: 29). This became clear during the intifada. Critics on the Left have always argued that opportunism rather than principle dictates the policy of Peace Now. Bar On, himself a leading Peace Now activist, believes that hesitancy 'tormented' the movement but its pursuit of a moderate course has resulted in its longevity which is a measure of success. Before examining the role of the peace movement through the intifada, it should be remembered that the Israeli peace movement in general, and Peace Now in particular, have taken up varying and sometimes contradictory positions. Yet these positions reflect the political realities of the moment, as one leading peace activist remarked:

> We cannot create an environment. The environment is the reality and we have to work within it. I cannot create the public agenda any more than I can do it in Peace Now. We respond to what happens...'OK we will plan and we will be ready when the right moment comes' but we don't create moments. We can't.
>
> (Interview with Janet Aviad, March 1997)

Peace activism: the Palestinian intifada

For many Israelis, the intifada provided evidence that only a political solution could resolve the conflict in the West Bank and Gaza. The intifada forced Peace Now to clarify its position 'on the critical questions like negotiations with the PLO and the Palestinian Arabs' right to establish a Palestinian state' (Kaminer, 1990: 233) and it pushed them towards directly challenging its old ally – the Labour Party. The contradictions within Peace Now surface during the intifada. Initially, it would not engage with the PLO (although it had high level political dialogue with Palestinians in the territories) and it was also supportive of the Labour Party's position which preferred the Jordanian option as a means of resolving the conflict. Yet, within years, Peace Now reversed both positions.

The intifada reactivated the peace movement and the forces of the Left, gave new life to the various groups which had previously participated in the movement and inspired the creation of new formations. The upsurge of activity created new and qualitatively different forms of protest and political activity and attracted a new generation of activists.

(Kaminer, 1990: 233)

The intifada triggered a proliferation of groups and factions within the peace movement. Some formed as a result of dissatisfaction with Peace Now's cautious posture, while others claimed they could make a unique contribution within the broader movement.

(Bar On, 1996: 220)

A crucial issue for Peace Now during the intifada related to its reaction to acts of brutality committed by the Israeli Defence Forces (IDF). That is, could it bring itself to criticise soldiers who were themselves at risk of death or serious injury? According to Kaminer (1990), it refused to condemn the actions of the IDF, preferring to take a political line which indicted politicians and military commanders for creating the circumstances under which the IDF operated. This decision, the initial failure to sanction talks with the PLO and a refusal to declare support for a Palestinian state, resulted in the growth of more militant groups which supplanted the traditional methods of the peace movement (elite political dialoguing, mass demonstrations, peace vigils and lobbying). These new actors argued that Israel must 'say yes to the intifada' and end the occupation. Kaminer (1990) has identified two groups of interest – Dai Lakibush (*End the Occupation*) and Yesh Guval (*There is a Limit*):

Dai Lakibush's main contribution to the peace movement has been its readiness to go into the streets and vent it outrage over the rising tide of cruelty and repression. Dai Lakibush has demonstrated more than any other group, repeatedly launching timely rallies and vigils against fresh acts of brutality. It has also sought to develop new forms of activity to express solidarity with the Palestinians, such as weekly educational visits to villages and refugees camps ... which has allowed many Israelis to hear first hand reports of courageous popular resistance against an occupying army composed of their own relatives and neighbours.

(Kaminer, 1990: 235)

'There is a Limit' cross the boundaries of moderate peace activities by calling on Israeli soldiers not to serve in the Occupied Territories. The grounds for refusal were that the occupation blocked the options for peace and corrupted the oath which IDF soldiers had taken to the State of Israel: 'We have taken an oath to defend the welfare and the security of the State of Israel and we are faithful to that oath. Therefore, we request that you permit us not to participate in the operations of repression and occupation in the territories' (Kidron, 1996: 131). Kaminer describes Yesh Guval's position as 'patriotic anti-militarism'. Kidron (1996) reported that nearly 200 'refuseniks' were jailed during the intifada, arguing that 'selective refusal' is 'the Israeli peace movements most original contribution to the arsenal of protest, with the general principles of civil disobedience, as forged by Ghandi and Martin Luther King, applied to that least likely of all possible settings – the army' (Kidron, 1996: 131). The high regard attached to serving in the Israeli military and the implications of refusing military rule were totally outside the confines of mainstream Israeli opinion. Peace Now argued that military service was a civic obligation and breaking the law by refusing to serve represented a rejection of the principles upon which the peace movement was based.

Both Bar On (1996) and Kaminer (1996) agreed that militant peace groups became less relevant as the intifada developed, primarily because Peace Now changed political direction. Aside from the more militant groups, there was a growth in organisations representing the mainstream such as the 'Peace Generals' or the Council for Peace and Security (April 1988) who disputed the view that the territories were essential for Israel's security. According to Hermann, this group had the most influence on the decision makers and 'they were the only ones who I know for sure sat with Rabin and Peres while starting to outline the features of the Oslo Peace Movement' (interviewed, March 1997).

The intifada also initiated a response from professional organisa-tions within Israeli society. Whilst student bodies and academics had always been active through protest activity, the 'variety of professional groups that have raised their voices against the massive repression in the territories is unprecedented' (Kaminer, 1990: 240). Professional groups sought to extend their activity, where possible, to similarly placed groups and individuals in the Occupied Territories. Kaminer quotes from a statement issued by Mental Health Workers at a conference in June 1988 which states that 'if we continue to be silent now, we will be supporting the destructive influences of continuing occupation' (quoted in Kaminer, 1990: 240). Another prominent and especially active professional group established during the intifada was the Association of Israeli and Palestinian Physicians for Human Rights which provided emergency medical assistance to both Israelis and Palestinians. Human rights monitoring was possibly one of the most widely known and successful activities to emerge from the intifada and central to this work was B'tselem. Throughout the intifada B'tselem prepared scathing reports on the human rights abuses of the Israeli Government. Viewed with great hostility by many on the Right, their work was widely used by left wing Knesset members, Palestinian and international human rights organisation and the world's media to tackle the Israeli Government.

Oslo and the Israeli peace movement: dynamics and challenge

Deliberating over the title of his book on the peace movement, Kaminer suggested that following the Madrid process an appropriate title would have been 'Noble Try' or 'Noble Failure'. The signing of the DOP, however, provided a new spirit within the peace movement. 'From any point of view, they (the DOP) bore the deep imprint of the peace movement, which was in essence a movement for Israeli-Palestinian recognition ... it is also true that most people in Israel consider the current peace process with all its limitations and complications as the crowning achievement of the Israeli peace movement' (Kaminer, 1996: 216–7). For the majority of peace campaigners, the Oslo Agreement delivered all that they had campaigned for and as a consequence, 'many Israeli peace organisations, particularly those which emerged following the outbreak of the intifada, ceased activity following the emergence of the Oslo process' (Hermann et al., 1996). The rationale behind what has been described as 'the hibernation of the peace movement' was a simple one – it had achieved *its* primary function of influencing government policy towards a resolution of the conflict based on mutual recognition of rights and a 'land for peace' deal.

> Once Oslo happened most of the people in Peace Now quite simply said that their activity was superfluous. The government is making peace anyway. Who needs to demonstrate? What are they going to demonstrate about?
>
> (Dan Leon, interviewed March 1997)

In explaining the decline of the peace movement after Oslo, Bar On (1996) identified three stages of peace activism. During the first stage, non-governmental organisations and third parties take centre stage by attempting to promote reconciliation at either the grassroots level or between key community representatives. This stage is often undertaken in opposition to government forces. The second stage occurs when official negotiations take place and the purpose of the NGOs is to create conditions and a climate for peace. Generally, this phase ends with an accord or an agreement. The final stage begins with the implementation of an agreement, 'although peace groups continue to play an important function in fostering public support for the process, the methods they employ are necessarily quite different from those used in the first and second phases, when street protests and parliamentary lobbying are the order of the day' (Bar On, 1996: 316). Bar On believes that the first phase ended before the Madrid Conference, stage two occurred between Madrid and Oslo, and the Declaration of Principles ushered in the third phase. 'With the government and a large part of the public supportive of ongoing peace efforts, the movement's role has been significantly reduced and the methods available to it limited' (Bar On, 1996: 317).

The stages automatically create new dynamics. Oslo has created a dynamic which reflects the true extent of the differences between occupied and occupier. The unity of Israeli based opposition against the occupation during the intifada has been replaced with diverging opinions on 'where to next?' Michael Warasawki (Alternative Information Centre, Jerusalem) summarises the changes as follows:

On the level of Palestinian/Israeli relations and building something which could be the basis for reconciliation, we are back to before the intifada. You see, the Palestinian uprising succeeded in bringing the Israeli population back to reality. For the first time, in perhaps thirty years, Israelis and Palestinians were relating to the same world – not necessarily to the same answers or solutions – but everyone was saying, "we have an occupation, we have an uprising" ... but Oslo pushed back the communities into speaking about different realities. Israelis, and I am speaking of peace activists, expressed anger at the Palestinian response to the peace – "why are you bitter, you should be happy, you have peace, why are you denying it, why are you demonstrating, why are you not supporting it, why do you think that it is not a good agreement? Why don't you trust us". On the other side, Palestinians were saying to Israeli peace activists, "why are you so happy, why don't you protest against your government when it imposes closures, your government is cheating us" ... You see,

Israelis are living peace and Palestinians are living occupation in a different situation.

(M. Warasawki, interviewed November 1996)

Palestinian disquiet fails to understand the nature of the Israeli peace movement which is ostensibly motivated by 'self interest' and concerned with influencing the position of the Israeli Government. Bar On's discussion on the dilemmas faced by Peace Now as a result of the IDF's response to the intifada is a typical example. There were those who believed that the peace movement had to openly criticise and challenge the activities of the IDF, arguing that to do otherwise would be giving tacit support to the brutality. The majority of activists however, preferred not to adopt this approach. The following quotation reflects the two diverging motivations of peace activism between:

> those in the movement who viewed their activities as primarily an outgrowth of Israel's self interest (in promoting the country's long term security, countering the corrupting effect of the occupation on Israeli society, and so forth), and those who were motivated by moral considerations, compassion, and solidarity with the occupied Palestinians.
>
> (Bar On, 1996: 226)

The current peace process has confirmed that the 'self interest' school of thought remains dominant. As Janet Aviad noted, the purpose of the peace movement was to show to the Israeli public that there was 'someone to talk to on the other side, there was a "Palestinian Peace Now" and that it needed to be allowed to function' (interviewed March 1997). With regard to the purpose of peace work she added, 'I don't think that it comes from the love of Abraham and Isaac and Jacob'. The increase in suicide attacks against Israel shattered the reality of peace and this made it increasingly difficult for peace groups to start protesting against the actions of their own government – 'what would we be demanding, an end to closures?' Although the election of the Likud government (May 1996) witnessed a re-birth of peace demonstrations, particularly over the issue of Hebron and the building of Jewish settlements in Arab East Jerusalem, the peace camp sidelined itself. As one activist rather candidly declared:

> We saw in the last election that the people who ostensibly supported peace, journalists, artists, the educated elite etc., were not reflecting the situation at large. Most people actually voted for, not the peace party, but the more nationalistic, more religious, more

offensive parties. So we were living an illusion. For four years it seemed that the sentiments of the pro-peace movement were shared by the whole or most of society. This was not true.

(Bat Shalom, interviewed November 1996)

The current peace process reflects the limitations of the Israeli peace movement and it emphasises the point made by Aviad that peace activity cannot create environments. Peace activity operates within a political context and the activities of the intifada are no longer applicable to the post-Oslo political environment. Peace Now, being a well structured and financed organisation, has directed attention to challenging settlement activity and developing dialogue and educational work under the heading 'Building Peace'. Other less well funded organisations drifted back into 'hibernation'. Professional groups established during the intifada and those involved in human right monitoring work continue to function but they have re-focused or downgraded activities. B'tselem, for example, continues to report extensively on human rights issues and it has also, somewhat controversially, been involved in human rights monitoring of the Palestinian Authority. The downturn in peace activity has led to a period of reflection for many organisations. Hermann believes that intifada peace groups changed the political lexicon in Israel. They supported the basic structure of the current peace process – open negotiations with the PLO – 'it put on the table certain ideas which were unspeakable at the time ... and they served as a bridge to personalities on the Palestinian side' (interviewed March 1997).

The dialogue of peace: a changing dynamic

The Oslo process has, according to Hermann, 'paralysed' dialogue work between Israelis and Palestinians because, in order to maintain contact with Palestinians, Israelis are being forced to go beyond the middle ground of Israeli politics. She describes the current situation as having moved into a 'kind of gain and lose situation':

If you gain some in the realm of co-operation with the Palestinians, you lose some in the realm of your own community.

(Interview with Hermann, March 1997)

She also identified another particularly problem in dialogue work at the grassroots level. Palestinians when engaged in dialogue activity with Israelis fail to distinguish between the peace movement and the Israeli Government.

> The dynamic is very problematic because they (Palestinians) put the blame on the peace activist as if they were part of the occupation system, and these activists do not see themselves in that way. So the situation of the 'victim' versus the 'occupier' develops in these kinds of meetings and repeats itself every time. They start by making the accusations and the Israelis become defensive. Either the peace activists say 'you are absolutely right, we are the worst on earth, it's almost like the Nazi system' or they say 'well, I am not part of it, and why do you put bombs in our buses'. The communication is immediately disrupted.
>
> (Interview with Hermann, March 1997)

A further example of the emergence of a new dialogue dynamic was reflected in a dispute between members of the editorial board of a joint Israeli/Palestine journal. An Israeli member of the board (Professor Galit Hasan-Rokem) expressed concern about the inclusion of a poem by a Palestinian poet describing the creation of the state of Israel as 'the biggest armed robbery in history' yet 'in order to honour the freedom of the poet' Hasan-Rokem agreed that it could be published. The same editorial board subsequently vetoed the publication of a poem by Hasan-Rokem on the grounds that the following lines were potentially offensive: 'A cold wind blows in the northern bank of the Seine. What is more frightening – Islam in the Heart or Islam in the Street'. In correspondence published by the journal, Professor Hasan-Rokem stated that the peace movement in Israel had always felt a deep sense of guilt over the occupation and that this guilt 'may be the reason for their (the peace movement) readiness to take formulations and reactions from Palestinians which would otherwise raise more resistance'. Two dangers, she argued, arose from such interactions. First, the tolerance reached by such a dynamic involves patronage and second, and worryingly, tolerance expressed at the expense of real equality 'may work for a while between small elitist groups. It may not be good enough preparation for a widely practised, publicly recognised peaceful interaction and co-operation between two peoples' (Hasan-Rokem, 1997: 10).

Hasan-Rokem's letter was responded to by a Palestinian member of the editorial board, Leila Dabdoub, who firstly drew a distinction between the two poems, arguing that the Palestinian work provided a political commentary which is appropriate to the journal but that

Hasan-Rokem's poem was insensitive to religion rather than politics and, as such, offensive. Dabdoub went on to state that:

> The fact that this particular line of the poem jarred with her 'sensi-tivity', is symbolic of the majority of the Israel Left and part of the peace camp. They feel uncomfortable when faced with what happened in 1948 or the 'Palestinian catastrophe'. They would like to conveniently forget it, sweep it under the rug as it were. The Palestinian-Israeli conflict for them starts in 1967. How would Prof. Hasan-Rokem respond to what happened in 1948?...Galit Hasan-Rokem and that section of the Israeli public who 'carry around their guilt' for the Israeli occupation of Palestinian land in 1967 will have to face the realities of 1948, otherwise their feelings of guilt and attempts at dialoguing and understanding will involve, to use her own words, 'patronage'. We have accepted and recognised Israel, but that does not mean we have forgotten our plight and dispossession. We are not asking to turn the clock back. We are not asking for resti-tution, not even for an admission of guilt, but we are definitely ask-ing for a recognition that indeed a wrong had been committed. Until that happens, all the efforts will remain in the realm of the condescending at best, or the hypocritical and self-serving, at worst.
>
> (Dabdoub, 1997: 11–12)

The tone and content of the above letters merely paint a picture of the changing nature of the type of interaction occurring between 'liberal and progressive forces' on each side of the conflict. Some would argue that the Palestinian position is now being more freely expressed as a result of the dynamics of the peace process and that the 'condescend-ing', 'patronising' and 'ignorant' attitudes of the Israeli Left is now being exposed. This position does not apply, however, to the entire Israeli peace camp, as Dabdoub herself notes, and particular examples of sustained interaction exist (Green, 1996; Awerbuch, 1997).

'A Palestinian peace'

A frequent criticism made of the Israeli peace movement is the absence of a Palestinian equivalent to Peace Now – 'what's the point in doing what you are doing when the other side is unwilling to talk to you even though you spearhead peace in Israel' (Hermann, interviewed March 1997). The natural implication of this argument is that the

Palestinian grassroots are not supportive of finding a peace settlement. However, as one Palestinian community activist noted, 'Palestinians were not afforded the luxury of a peace movement'. For Palestinians, peace equates with ending the occupation and peace activism translates into defying the occupation and obtaining human rights. The paralleling of grassroots activism between Israelis and Palestinians indicates a failure to understand the dynamics of the relationship between the occupied and the occupier:

> In the Israeli context, the role of these groups is much more significant in changing the public agenda than it has been on the Palestinian side because the situation is very different. Here you have an occupier and an occupied people and it's quite clear that while you are under occupation it would be a little bit out of place to start talking about resolving the conflict because it's not up to you start with. Secondly, while you are in the midst of a liberation struggle, to talk about peaceful negotiation, may cause you personal damage.
>
> (Interview with Tamar Hermann, March 1996)

This distinction between powerless and powerful, occupied and occupier cannot be underestimated when examining the interaction of Palestinian civil society with that of Israel. Hermann's comments reflect the reality that peace is not the preserve of the Palestinians – to talk of peace ignored the occupation, ignoring the occupation amounted to 'normalising the abnormal'. Palestinian organisations are therefore reluctant even to define themselves as peace groups:

> We have organisations that support the peace process but we do not have peaceniks. This is a basic distinction...Most of the organisations still have a political agenda and that, in itself, makes you a little bit hesitant to say that you are a peace organisation. Peace, for such organisations, is in the context of Palestinians getting their human rights and defying the occupation.
>
> (Interview with M. Hassassian, December 1996)

The development of Palestinian civil society therefore needs to be examined in the context of the occupation and the PLO's peace-making stance – from 'a total liberation strategy to a two state solution' as outlined in Chapter 4.

'Out administering the enemy'

In the initial aftermath of the Israeli occupation of the West Bank and Gaza, there was a belief amongst the Palestinian population that the occupation was to be short lived and as a result there was little organisational activity on a mass level. The soundings of 'land for peace' amongst elements of Israeli society seemed to give weight to this view. By the early 1970s, and taking account of the Labour Party's 'decision not to decide' on the issue of the occupation, Palestinian society began to formally mobilise to end the occupation. As one Palestinian activist said:

> It was clear to Palestinians that this attempt on the part of the Israeli military to break down the social and economic infrastructure really meant a fight for survival. That infrastructure, we all knew, was crucial for the reconstruction of Palestinian society in the future. We also knew that the Israeli military was out to possess the our land. What we didn't know was how to mobilise under occupation, when it was becoming practically impossible to move and do anything political without being subjected to arrests or attacks from the Israeli military.
>
> (Quoted in Hiltermann, 1990: 23)

The military policy carried out by the Israelis bore the hallmarks of tactics used to contain Palestinian citizens of Israel between 1948 and 1966. The key difference, however, was that political forces inside the West Bank and Gaza, supported by the PLO in the Diaspora, fought the occupation 'as a means of survival'.

In terms of resistance, Palestinian academics identify a number of phases ranging from a period of non-cooperation (1967–70) through to the negotiation phase which began at Madrid and resulted in the Oslo Agreements. The intervening periods provide critical evidence on the development and nature of grassroots activism amongst Palestinians – an activism based on non-engagement with Israel. Two phases, described as the period of 'steadfastness' and isolation', are of particular interest here.

During the period of 'steadfastness' (1970–82), the PLO began concentrating its efforts on mobilising forces against the occupation inside the occupied territories by establishing 'new organisations and, more importantly, infusing existing ones with a new ideology – to transform them in the service of nationalism' (Hiltermann, 1990: 12). At the political level, the Palestine National Front (PNF) was established to advance and capture political support for the PLO and to thwart Israeli efforts at achieving administrative autonomy through the co-option of Arab notables. The PLO's overall strategy was to create a powerbase through building institutions and political parties that would 'prepare the Occupied Territories to receive national authority'. Hence, there developed within Palestinian society a social and political infrastructure premised on 'out administering the enemy' (Ahmed quoted in Hiltermann, 1990: 12). Social organisations dealing with issues 'such as family, mosques, churches, trade unions, media institutions, sports clubs and the like' emerged in tandem with 'a *de facto* political society based on Palestinian non governmental organisations (NGOs in education, health, agriculture, human rights and labour)' (Usher, 1995: 46). Hiltermann notes that by the mid 1980s 'one can speak of the existence of a network or infrastructure of organisations that had a popular base and were able to provide the basic services lacking in the community, and also to lead the masses in times of direct confrontation with the occupier' (Hiltermann, 1990: 12). These non-governmental organisations operated at every level of civil society and represented, in the words of Usher, 'a counter-hegemonic, nationalist bloc against the occupation, "an infrastructure of resistance" that not only developed in the absence of state structures but were politically defined by that absence' (Usher, 1995: 46).

The 'isolation period' (1982–7) was influenced by the international conditions which prevailed towards the end of the 1970s and the desire on the part of 'external' elements to impose control on the Palestinians. The United States, Israel and Jordan each proposed measures aimed at controlling the growth of Palestinian nationalism. Political tensions also emerged between factions of the PLO, and these factions set about creating their own organisations and institutions in what was to become known as 'the war of the institutions'. The intifada of 1987 saved the PLO and Palestinian society from completely rupturing under internal pressures, creating a unity of purpose amongst civil society organisations against the occupation. The brutality of the Israeli response – 600 deaths and 8500 wounded in the first two years – produced a dynamic which brought about the building of a new paradigm.

The credibility gap between Palestinians and Israelis grew wider, and the likelihood of resolving the conflict seemed nil. The 'power' of the intifada, however, was at the same time working in a diametrically opposite direction...The heralding of stones and bullets, while deepening hatred and insecurity, lead to a climax of the conflict, and hence to beginning its resolution.

(Ahmed, 1994: 5–6)

The support structures built by the PLO in the early 1970s sustained the uprising, not only by providing essential services, but pushing the Israeli authorities to the point of no return: the West Bank and Gaza was ungovernable. The intifada created the basis for a new understanding in the Palestinian/Israeli conflict, an understanding born out of a realisation that the status quo could not be maintained and that the solution to the conflict could not be found through military actions.

Interlocking the intifada dynamic and Oslo

The negotiation phase (1990 to the present) witnessed a growth in the number of Palestinian organisations defining their work in terms of peace building. This activity was targeted at intra-Palestinian issues and funded by the European Union and other international donors seeking to 'create the ambience of constant and open dialogue'. Hassassian attributes the change in terminology and circumstance not only to the intifada but to key international events such as the collapse of the Soviet Union and the Gulf War which resulted in 'the triumph of democracy'. All of these factors paved the way towards creating the conditions for a change in the dynamic of Palestinian/Israeli relations which brought about the Madrid Conference. This so called 'globalisation of democracy' had a significant impact on Palestinian civil society organisations in preparing them for intra-Palestinian peace building work:

> Today we call the Palestinians and the Israelis 'partners to the conflict' and this is a change of mood, a change of lexicon, a change of attitude, a change of perception. Once that was political suicide for both parties...Now it is becoming the only pragmatic way of solving and sorting out differences.
>
> (Interview with M. Hassassian, December 1996)

Everybody today, as far as Palestinians are concerned, is trying to cater to the needs of conflict resolution programmes for the simple fact – and I am very daring to tell you – because there is money for this work. Many Palestinians and others stampeded to open what we call 'shops' – shops for conflict management. Because these shops need a secretary, a computer and a typist, they become legitimate enough to get grants to work on what they call 'civil society'.

(Interview with M. Hassassian, December 1996)

Since the signing of the DOP and following the installation of the Palestinian Authority, civil society organisations have been involved in a dual process of developing relationships with the PA while defying what it interprets as 'the new form of occupation'. Palestinian civil society has entered a new period of struggle which necessitates, possibly more than before, a commitment to prevent the 'normalisation' of relations with Israel.

The current Palestinian struggle is twofold. One, to rid ourselves of the continuing occupation and that we place in Arafat and the PNA's hands. The second is to democratise the system and state building.

(Interview with Zacharia, December 1996)

Civil society organisations have, according to Ashrawi (1995), made statehood a 'concrete reality' despite the problems over settlements, the occupation, and the final status issues 'and of course things are better in the sense that we have started the whole democratic debate, the issue of elections, preparations for institution-building and nation-building' (Ashrawi, 1995: 59). It is within this realm that organisations such as the Palestinian Centre For Democracy and Elections (1994), the Centre for Peace and Democracy (1992) and the Wiam Conflict Resolution Centre (1993) have emerged. Although informal contact is maintained with Israeli organisations, there has not been a desire on the part of these organisations to engage with Israeli groups. Whilst international donors initially (early 1990s) attempted to fund joint activities between Palestinians and Israelis, problems arose 'because the terminology is very different, the self image is different, the willingness to acknowledge what type of group you are is very different and the external limitations are obviously very different' (Hermann, interviewed March 1997). Ashrawi (1995) explains the reasons behind the lessening of contact by linking it to the new political process which emerged after Oslo:

You cannot separate the different components of the Palestinian struggle and say that you do one thing at the expense of others.

Women are now dealing with issues that have to do with Palestinian women in parliament. They are creating more awareness, particularly on the issue of elections, encouraging women to participate, whether to run or to vote, trying to establish support systems, and creating new structures at all levels. These are new challenges and concrete demands, but they do not exclude the possibility of maintaining a dialogue. Generally, we are able to address issues that were taboo before. At the same time, Palestinian women involved in dialogue organisations have come under attack because there is this backlash against 'normalisation'.

(Ashrawi, 1995: 59)

These sentiments reflect general trends at the wider societal level. Considerations over what constitutes 'normalisation' have been compounded by the Israeli government's implementation of the Oslo Agreements. The continuation of settlement activity, the ongoing security presence of the IDF, the chronic economic hardship as a result of closures and the 'ethnic cleansing' of Arab East Jerusalem, were identified as the key issues by representatives of organisations involved in peace building work. The result of these macro-political conditions directly impacts on levels of activity, or willingness to engage, with Israeli groups. For example:

I believe that Israeli imposed closures, human rights violations by the state of Israel, the socio-economic situation, the deterioration at the political level, lack of hope, lack of progress in the peace process, all impact on the situation, impact on our involvement in peace building, impact on the cycle of violence. The cycle of violence is enhanced when the political situation is deteriorating. At the checkpoint when the breadwinner is turned back home, the man – who is usually the breadwinner – will come and direct his anger at his wife. The wife will direct her anger at the children. The children will direct their anger at the children of neighbours and this is how a feud starts.

(Zougbi, interviewed March 1997)

To counter these problems, Palestinian activists suggested new forms of protest activity such as joint strike days to highlight the difficulties faced by Palestinians as a result of 'internal closures'. In general, there is a reluctance on the part of Palestinians to engage with Israeli groups for two reasons, the fear of 'normalising the abnormal' and the belief that priorities rested on building and working within Palestinian society.

I am only interested in working with Israelis who want to come and repair the damage done by their government.

(Fathai, Palestinian Centre for Peace and Democracy,
interviewed November, 1996)

The peace movement in Israel is in fact shrinking in numbers because people get highly frustrated from the unresponsiveness of the Palestinian side.

(Hermann, interviewed March 1997)

Ashrawi (1995) believes that the peace process has become 'the be-all and end-all' of relationships between Palestinians and Israelis with the result that political discourse has become fixed. Participants are 'unwilling to explore difficult issues' and move beyond the political agenda. In terms of 'normalising' relations through dialogue, Ashrawi contends that participants must have confidence in their own messages:

That does not mean I am not aware of the dangers of creating a mis-conception that disparity does not exist, that everything is normal, that we are two sides living in equal conditions trying to resolve issues on the basis of equality and justice. That is why the substance of the dialogue of any kind of joint activity has to be made clear.

(Ashrawi, 1995: 59)

People say 'how can we work with Israelis on Jerusalem'. Ninety per cent of Israelis believe that Jerusalem is the eternal capital of Israel and you are showing the world that Israel is good, that these dia-logue groups are using us to show that Israelis are good. There is logic to that, but at the same time you cannot say if you find some-one from the other side who recognises your rights "I don't want to work with you". There is no logic to that.

(Nuseibeh, interviewed November 1996)

Establishing ground rules for discussions has become a common practice with organisations involved in joint activity (The Jerusalem

Link) but it still remains a risk for participants. In view of the above, the final section reviews a programme of sponsored dialogue activity which emanates directly from the Israeli-Palestinian Interim Agreement (Oslo II – September 1995).

People to People Programme

Oslo II provided for a number of mechanisms which sought 'to establish dialogue and co-operation on the bases of equality, fairness and reciprocity' (People to People Programme, 1996). Both sides agreed to co-operate on a range of issues such as economics, tourism, education and culture. On the educational front, it was envisaged that the Israelis and Palestinians would encourage and facilitate 'exchanges in the field of education by providing appropriate conditions for direct contacts between schools and educational institutions of both sides'. In an attempt to create conditions for dialogue and relationship building, the agreement established 'The People to People Programme' in co-operation with the Kingdom of Norway. The rationale underpinning the programme was that while peace agreements could be signed by political leaders, this would not in itself lead to stability 'unless you engage the populations in some kind of reconciliation process'.

> The programme originated in the Oslo Agreements. Annex VI stated that the two governments, the PNA and the Israeli Government, would sponsor People to People projects under the Norwegian umbrella in order to deepen the roots of the peace process and push it down from the level of diplomacy to the level of people. The fact that it has been designed within the government framework is a strength. It makes it official so that it looks at the country as a whole and not volunteers, so that civil society organisations are running it alongside the government.
>
> (Janet Avaid, interviewed March 1997)

People to People is managed at both the official and NGO level. The official level consists of representatives from the Palestinian and Israeli Ministries of Foreign Affairs in association with officials from the Norwegian Embassy. Three non-governmental organisations, each representing Israel, the PNA and Norway, function at the grassroots level and form a joint planning group which considers proposals and makes recommendations to the official level for financial assistance. The financing of projects ($700,000 in 1996) is provided by the Israeli Government to the Israeli NGOs which in turn manages, evaluates and reports on progress. The Norwegian Government provided funding to the Palestinian National Authority which reallocates to the Palestinian People to People Office. The following criteria for funding projects (up to a maximum of $40,000) were established across five areas of work – youth, adult dialogue and seminars, culture, environment and media and communication:

- Projects should aim at enhancing dialogue and relations between Israelis and Palestinians;
- Projects should foster wider exposure of the two publics to the peace process through education, and encourage public discussion and involvement in the peace process;
- Projects should increase people to people exchange and have the potential to build bridges between large audiences on both sides;
- Projects should be implemented jointly by Israeli and Palestinian organisations. (People to People Programme, 1996)

The Israeli side of the project argued that the decision by then Labour Government to provide funding for dialogue activity reflected the reality of the new situation and it represented a significant contribution to peace activity. It was acknowledged that the endorsement of the Israeli Government could also be a possible source of conflict, particularly if the political situation deteriorated. For many Israeli peace activists a key factor in the deteriorating situation occurred following the election of a Likud government in May 1996 as this was the clearest sign yet that the Israeli population was not yet ready for the peace process, never mind engaging in direct activity with Palestinians. Israeli NGOs were fearful that the programme would not survive under a Likud government, although confirmation was given that the programme would continue as planned. Despite this endorsement, suspicion lurked amongst key players in the project and some felt that it provided the new government with a 'fig leaf of respectability'.

The 'fig leaf' analogy causes problems for Palestinian participants concerned about normalising relations with Israelis engaged in 'creating facts on the ground' which seek to undermine the spirit of the Oslo Agreement. Palestinian and Norwegian officials argued that projects funded through People to People should receive special treatment in relation to permits for Palestinians involved in the programme. The experience has been somewhat different.

The people who control permits are the Defence Ministry. Nobody in the Foreign Ministry has stood up and said 'OK, everybody in People to People gets through the barricades'. It hasn't happened and in fact several activities were sabotaged by not getting permits.

(Janet Avaid, interviewed March 1997)

As the macro situation deteriorated, Palestinian Ministries began withdrawing support. The reaction of the PNA to the programme is twofold. The first and the dominant view is that unless the peace process moves forward and negotiations produce tangible results, then People to People was merely sustaining or satisfying the needs of Israelis. As one observer noted, 'it serves the Israelis interests to have dialogue because they will always gain from normalisation since they hold the power'. A Palestinian Ministry of Education remarked:

You still won't see pictures of Israelis and Palestinians hugging each other around an Israeli flag. There have been several attempts at peace building work. People coming from abroad and trying to introduce joint programmes with our children and Israeli children. It won't work. The children are very honest, you know! They see the reality on the ground. You see, the facts on the ground are more compelling than the niceties of peace-building programmes.

(PNA Official, interviewed March 1997)

I cannot talk for the PNA, but my impression is that they link this programme to the political process. It is part of implementing the agreement and if the Israelis want to implement this part of the agreement then they should also implement the other parts.

(People to People spokesperson, interviewed December 1996)

The second perspective is that dialogue activity should operate independently of the peace process. The logic of this position is that 'at the end of the day, Israelis and Palestinians are bound to live together. From a humanitarian point of view, Palestinians need to get to know Israelis' (Palestinian People to People Spokesperson, interviewed December 1996). The initial round of groups expressing an interest in obtaining funding from the People to People programme in 1996 came largely from Israeli (co-existence) organisations, 'one hundred and fifteen expressions of interest were received, fifteen of which came from Palestinian groups'

(Palestinian People to People Spokesperson, interviewed December 1996). As Hermann noted:

> The People to People programme is a little bit out of place right now because there are no People to People connections. Most Palestinians are not interested in People to People connections and most Israelis are not so interested in People to People connections. We even see that most Israelis prefer to employ foreign workers from Asia, they don't even want Palestinian workers inside the 'Green Line'.

Peace building?

This chapter began by differentiating between the type of grassroots activity which existed between Palestinian citizens of Israel, Palestinians in the West Bank and Gaza, and with the Israeli coexistence and peace movement, respectively. The evidence collected suggests significant developments in the type of activities between Palestinian and Jewish citizens of the state of Israel during the early to late 1980s.

The Palestinian Israeli community has sought to assert, more fully, rights connected with developing and improving the structural issues associated with the discriminatory nature of the state. There has been a resultant shift away from engaging in dialogue activity towards intra-community development. The peace process has created a political vacuum for the Palestinian Israeli community. Their future role within the state can be assessed in two ways. The first, and most positive, scenario links the peace process with the eventual refocusing of the Israeli State's attention on the demands of this small Palestinian minority. In these circumstances, a secular Israeli state will adjust to become more relaxed about the rights of Arabs once peace is secured. The second, more widely held, view is that the peace process will harden the resolve of the Israeli State to further embed Jewishness, and the Palestinian Israeli community will receive no additional rights. The popular expression used is that the state would 'turn in on itself'.

The development of new activity at the level of relations between Jews and Palestinians from the West Bank and Gaza cannot be separated from the macro political factors which continue to dog the 'peace process'. Palestinians living in the Occupied Territories now feel less inclined to engage with Israelis, the fear of 'normalising relations' is perhaps now even more acute than it was prior to Oslo. Amongst the Palestinian NGO network there is a deep sense that 'Israel does not want peace', a fear that they are being duped. The increased levels of security force intervention through the implementation of Oslo II and the development of settlement activity makes cross community work seem contrived and irrelevant. Finally, we documented the history of the Israeli peace and coexistence movement and surprisingly, since Oslo, we noted that there has been an increase in the number of 'coexistence organisations' attempting to build new links with Palestinian groups on the West Bank and Gaza at the same time as 'hibernation' of the Israeli peace movement. The dynamics of future relations between all of the players noted in this chapter remains decidedly fixed on the macro political agenda. Peace building at the micro level is inextricably linked to the complexities of a deep and bitter conflict.

6
South Africa: Macro Political Developments

Background to the conflict

South Africa is bounded in the north by Namibia, Botswana and Zimbabwe, north-east by Mozambique and Swaziland, east by the Indian Ocean and south and west by the South Atlantic. It is an area of 1,224,691 square kilometres with a population of 41.5 million people (75.7 per cent black; 12.6 per cent white; 8.5 per cent coloured and 2.4 per cent Asian). South Africa's political transition has been described as nothing short of a 'miracle'. However, the ending of apartheid through to the first multi-racial elections in April 1994 did not come without a price. Between 1990 and April 1994, 15,000 South Africans were killed and countless thousands injured or forced to move from their homes (SA Survey, 1998).

The scale, ferocity and nature of the violence has been the subject of much academic debate and this will be examined in the context of the mechanisms put in place by political elites to quell or eliminate the violence. This chapter provides a historical outline to the momentous events of the South African 'miracle' and describes both the nature of Afrikaner nationalism and the struggle for liberation. The literature describing the early period of South African history has tended to underplay the existence of the indigenous African population, propagating the myth of 'land without a people'. Instead, as Worden notes, academics have concentrated on lauding 'the achievements of the trekkers and their descendants (Afrikaners) or on emphasising the role of the British Government and settlers' (Worden, 1995: 6). Yet 'the conquest of South Africa by people of European origin was by no means a steady or an inevitable one but marked by setbacks, uneven population movements and uncertain goals. As late as 1870, the subcontinent was

divided into a large number of polities, chiefdoms, colonies and settlements of widely differing size, power and racial composition, without
political unity or cohesion' (Worden, 1995: 5).

Towards the end of the nineteenth century, tensions which had
existed between the colonial interests of the British settlers and the
Afrikaners (Boers) resulted in the Anglo-Boer War (1899–1902). The war
completed the British conquest of the region but it created an Afrikaner
community 'whose messianic vision of rightful control of the land and
its inhabitants would lead eventually to their political ascendancy'
(McKinley, 1997: 4). Remarkably, some eight years later, 'a reconciliation on the basis of one white South African colonial 'official' nation
was achieved … when a largely independent Union of South Africa was
established' (Kellas, 1991: 126). Within this Union, the majority black
population was effectively excluded from having any political control
with white minority rule, under the pretence of democratic structures,
instituted. It also represented the beginning of the Afrikaners ascent
towards the 'rightful control' of South Africa. The defeat of the Afrikaner
by the British had 'made the Afrikaners second-class citizens of South
Africa' and they sought to radically alter that predicament. At the same
time, they were 'terrified that blacks would do what the British had
done: render them a subject minority in the land of their birth'
(McKinley, 1997: 10). Thus, two needs shaped their political philosophy – the need to win political control amongst whites and the need
to continue white domination through the political and economic
suppression of the majority black population.

A number of racially based laws followed the Act of Union (1910)
which foreshadowed the achievement of political control and complete subjugation of the black population. Blacks were excluded from
membership of the Dutch Reformed Church, white mine workers'
rights were specifically protected and legislation was enacted to keep
'undesirables' out of the country. The Native Land Act of 1913 made it
illegal for Africans to purchase or lease land outside newly designated
'Native Reserves' (comprising only 13 per cent of the land). The passage of the Land Act also demonstrated the unity of purpose forged by
British and Afrikaner interests in the new South Africa. British owned
industrial and mining industries required 'cheap black labour' while
Afrikaner farmers expressed concern that black farmers were producing
food more cheaply. The Land Act sought to crush the emergence of an
African elite and it ensured the total suppression of black economic
interests. The aim was to guarantee 'the prosperity and security of
Afrikaners, through white domination' (McKinley, 1997: 10).

This approach to 'social engineering' suggests the introduction of apartheid, some thirty five years later, was not a 'bolt out of the blue' but the culmination of a process towards the absolute and total segregation of whites and blacks. Afrikaner nationalists did not, however, merely believe in segregation for economic reasons, rather they were convinced that whites were 'at the top of the evolutionary scale ... while blacks at the bottom were primitive, less intelligent and sluggard' (Worden, 1995: 65). As Worden points out, white supremacism was embedded in 'the lengthy process of European colonialism, the subjugation of other people in territorial conquest and black enslavement' (Worden, 1995: 65). The important and crucial difference is that after the Second World War, white supremacy waned as colonies moved towards independence, whereas discrimination in South Africa became more entrenched, marking itself out for isolation (Worden, 1995: 65). The election victory of the National Party in 1948 gave the Afrikaner a golden opportunity to embed and formalise deeply held beliefs and hence, 'apartheid was born':

> The National Party retained control of government from 1948 into the 1990s and the history of South Africa in the second half of the twentieth century has been dominated by apartheid and the resistance it evoked. But apartheid has not been static or monolithic. Each decade, broadly speaking, was marked by differences in both the content and the implementation of the policy, as well as in ways of resistance.
>
> (Worden, 1995: 95)

The nature and stages of apartheid

The 1950s represented the 'heyday' of apartheid in which 'a barrage of legislation codified and extended racial discrimination' into every sphere of human activity. Table 6.1 provides a review of the major laws which constituted apartheid.

> Apartheid means 'separation'... but segregation had been a fact of South African life long before Afrikaners took power ... When the radical Afrikaner Nationalists triumphed in the 1948 elections, they created a vast legal superstructure to enforce separation. From then apartheid, governed every aspect of national life. It assigned every baby from birth to a rigid 'population group', which determined

Table 6.1 Major apartheid laws in South Africa (act number/year of enactment)

Pillars of Apartheid
Population Registration Act (30/1950)
Reservation of Separate Amenities Act (49/1953)
Group Areas Act (77/1957, as amended)
Industrial Conciliation Act (28/1956)
Extension of University Act (45/1959)
Prohibition of Improper Political Interference Act (51/1968)
Immortality Act (23/1957)
Prohibition of Mixed Marriages Act (30/1950)

Additional Related Legislation
Separate Representation of Voters Act (46/1951 and 9/1956)
Promotion of Black Self Government Act (46/1959)
Prohibition of Foreign Financing of Political Parties Act (51/1968)
Public Safety Act (3/1956)
Riotous Assemblies Act (17/1956)
Unlawful Organisations Act (34/1950)
Suppression of Communism Act (44/1950)
General Law Amendment Act (76/1962 and 37/1963)
Affected Organisations Act (31/1974)
Internal Security Amendment Act (79/1976)
Gatherings and Demonstration Act (52/1973)

Legislation Promoting 'Separate Development' in South Africa
Black Authorities Act (68/1951)
Promotion of Black Self Government Act (46/1959)
National States Citizenship Act (26/1970)
Separate Representation of Voters Amendment Act (50/1968)
Status of Transkei Act (100/1976)
Status of Boputhatswana Act (86/1977)
Status of Venda Act (107/1979)
Status of Ciskei Act (110/1981)

Source: Kriek, 1976: 64–7, adapted by Sisk, 1994: 59.

where he could live and go to school, what lavatory he could use,
and whom he could marry.

(Waldmeir, 1997: 10)

For the Afrikaner, the election of 1948 symbolised the pinnacle of a
long struggle against both the African native and the British. Afrikaner
nationalism was revived and the National Party set about creating what
Waldmeir describes as 'the myth of the monolith' – an entrenching
'white supremacy...in black minds as much as whites' (Waldmeir,
1997: 10). The following section reviews the stages of apartheid up

until its eventual and final abolition in 1992 and examines both Afrikaner psyche and the black resistance which challenged it.

As Sisk (1994) notes, and Table 6.1 indicates, the early days represented 'the more blatantly racist' dimension of National Party thinking. Every South African was registered according to the colour of their skin (Population Registration Act, 1950), mixed marriages were prohibited and the Group Areas Act (1950) made separate racial residential areas compulsory. Educational apartheid was enforced in schools, technical colleges and universities and the Separate Amenities Act (1953) enforced social segregation in all public amenities. Towards the end of the 1950s, the then Prime Minister, Verwoerd, 'turned [apartheid] into an ideology of national salvation, known as "Grand Apartheid"...And he gave it a moral dimension...Verwoerd fed them what they wanted – a moral justification for white domination' (Waldmeir, 1997: 11). Although, as Waldmeir argues, it was fatally flawed to give apartheid a conscience because morality played such a crucial role in its downfall. Verwoerd's 'grand apartheid' sought to divide South Africa into pockets of racial and ethnic homogeneous regions. Ten homeland regions or 'self governing states' were legislated for, and eventually some 3–4 million people were forced to move to the new homelands:

> Forced removals on such a massive scale were the crudest sign of state power over black lives. In most cases those relocated to homelands were consigned to barren areas far removed from employment or adequate resources. Critics of apartheid labelled such actions as tantamount to genocide.
>
> (Worden, 1995: 111)

Whilst numerous turning points and watersheds dot the political landscape of South Africa's history, the Sharpeville massacre of 1960 (69 blacks were murdered by the police) significantly changed the focus of black protest against apartheid. As Lodge noted, 'protest finally hardened into resistance...and African politicians were forced to begin thinking in terms of a revolutionary struggle' (Lodge quoted in Sisk, 1994: 71). International criticism of the South African Government began to build and the imposition of economic sanctions was called for at the United Nations. The United States and Britain, both invested heavily in South Africa industry, vetoed the move but the British Prime Minister Macmillan warned Verwoerd that 'the winds of change' were sweeping Africa and apartheid policies could no longer be supported

(Worden, 1995: 107). During the 1960s, however, the National Party viewed apartheid as 'invincible'. The economy was booming, political power was rightfully in the hands of Afrikaners – nothing would or could pressurise the government to change the course of 'grand apartheid'. Internal black resistance would be quashed and external opinion ignored. In response to hostile criticism from the Commonwealth, for example, South Africa withdrew and declared itself a Republic. Internally, the authorities introduced new security and political measures to thwart the rising tide of opposition. The African National Congress (ANC) and other black political organisations were banned, a State of Emergency was introduced and mass arrests followed black South Africans protests (strikes and stayaways) against apartheid and the Sharpeville killings. At the same time, and in response to state action, the ANC established military wings and exile units to campaign for their cause overseas without hindrance from the state. By mid-1961 both major African nationalist movements formed insurgency branches to step up the level of resistance against apartheid. The ANC formed Umkhonto we Sizwe (MK, 'Spear of the Nation') and the Pan African Congress formed Poqo (meaning 'alone' in Xhosa) (Sisk, 1994: 62). Responsibility for introducing armed action as a form of resistance was made explicitly clear by the ANC:

> The choice is not ours. It has been made by the National Government which has rejected every peaceable demand by the people for rights and freedom and answered every demand with force and yet more force.
>
> (MK Manifesto quoted in Taylor and Habib, 1997: 1)

It has been argued that 'nationalism is a parasitic movement and ideology shaped by what it opposes' (Breuilly quoted in Fine and Davis, 1990: 75), and by the late 1960s the stage had been set for the intensification of conflict based on the competing nationalisms of the black majority and white minority government.

Black resistance and the stormy years of apartheid

Black political resistance to white minority rule dates back to beyond the introduction of apartheid. Sisk (1994) noted that organised black protest predated the formation in 1914 of the National Party. For many commentators, the Act of Union (1910) provided concrete and final evidence to the African population of their inferior status within the newly created state, despite British 'rhetoric before and during the (Anglo-Boer) war about the injustices of Boer "native policy"' (Worden, 1995: 31). One response to the creation of the all white state was the establishment of the South African Native National Council SANNC (renamed the African National Congress in 1923) in 1912. Initially, the SANNC campaigned for black political and economic rights based on what McKinley (1997) describes as 'the politics of incorporation' and 'non-violence'. This particular stance grew out of a membership drawn from 'the newly emergent black petty bourgeoisie as well as the traditional chiefs' (McKinley, 1997: 6). The SANNC sought to persuade the 'civilised British' that the 'educated propertied and "civilised" Africans could be incorporated into the mainstream of South African society' (McKinley, 1997: 6).

The cautious and conservative approach of the early African protest movement persisted until the late 1930s when new political forces emerged representing unionised and urban interests. By 1940, radical elements began to change the direction of the ANC. The dual process of urbanisation and unionisation and the increasingly repressive nature of the white state against the African population, created conditions which favoured a radical departure from the unsuccessful methods of appealing to white liberal virtues. A political ideology stressing the importance of 'African leadership and self determination' emerged. The ANC Youth League (established in 1943) stressed 'the need to "go down to the masses" and it favoured the use of direct action such as boycotts, strikes and trade union mobilisation' (Worden, 1995: 86). The Youth League argued that Africans were by right 'the only people entitled to rule South Africa' (Gerhart in Worden, 1995: 86) and that white rule needed to be replaced with a multi-racial and democratic system of government.

The introduction of apartheid fundamentally altered the direction of African resistance against the white government. The ANC Youth League led the charge through the production of a Programme of Action (1949) which 'marked a decisive break with the conciliatory policies of previous decades'. Ending segregation and obtaining 'national freedom' were the expressed views of the League but the new government was determined to institutionalise apartheid. At the same time, black African organisations attempted to counter the policies of apartheid through popular protest. A range of tactics such as boycotts, stayaways, strikes and civil disobedience dominated the resistance scene of the 1950s. Significantly, apartheid unified both the 'popular and middle classes'. Class knew no boundaries under apartheid, race and colour were the determinants of status and well being. The early view of many of those leading and organising protest campaigns was that apartheid was a 'temporary aberration' which would be swept away in the wake of popular support for African nationalism' (Worden, 1995: 100). Sharp ideological divisions emerged within the ANC on the possible direction of the resistance movement. Some ANC activists argued that a resistance campaign should link up with other organisations opposing apartheid including radical white groups, while the Africanists rejected 'association with all non-African associations ranging in political terms from the moderate Liberal Party to the Communist Party' (Worden, 1995: 104). In essence, one strand promoted multi-racialism while the other argued that it undermined radical African nationalism (McKinley, 1997: 19). The ANC's Freedom Charter of 1955 endorsed the view of creating a unified front encompassing all anti-apartheid forces including white organisations such as the South African Communist Party. Charterism became the main driving force behind fighting apartheid and it signified two important developments in the ANC's political and economic programme. According to McKinley, 'it codified the ANC's commitment to an accommodationist strategic approach to national liberation' and it confirmed that the ANC was 'seeking a prominent role in governing the country' (McKinley, 1997: 21).

The heightened tensions between the apartheid state and black resistance continued through the 1960s and early 1970s. As with Sharpeville, the Soweto uprising of June 1976 represented another key milestone which was to push 'people power' to the fore of the liberation struggle provoking the state security apparatus into devising methods aimed at 'winning the hearts and minds of the black masses'. The Soweto uprising, born out of street protests organised by school-children, precipitated a change of events that would eventually bring South Africa to a position of 'mutually hurting stalemate':

> The police reacted vigorously and a riot ensued, spreading rapidly through Soweto and then to townships throughout the land. This expression of outrage hardened local resistance and world rejection, and forced a bewildered and defiant government onto the defensive ... For a decade and more, the government would wrestle with two conundrums: how to concede black political participation without

imperilling the interests of the white minority, and how to maintain control while relaxing it.

(Lawerence in Friedman and Atkinson, 1994: 2)

These two conundrums dominated the premiership of P.W. Botha (1978–89). Understanding the 'road to peace' in South Africa requires an examination of Botha's attempts at reforming apartheid during the turbulent decade of 1980s:

If Botha was a reluctant revolutionary – an unwilling, unwitting, sometimes almost unconscious one – he was a revolutionary, nonetheless. His strength, in arms and repression, gave the Afrikaner state the confidence to risk political compromise. His reforms prepared the Afrikaner mind for change. In the end, he took the Afrikaner nation beyond the Rubicon, without even noticing that he had crossed it. He charted the track that de Klerk would follow, to the new South Africa.

(Waldmeir, 1997: 40)

The beginning of the 1980s saw the National Party move into 'the ideology of survival' rather than 'the ideology of orthodoxy' (Moodie, 1980). The fundamental contradictions between 'a political policy of territorial segregation and racial disentanglement ... and the needs of a modernising and rapidly industrialising economy' produced 'a paradox of interdependence'. The prosperity of white South Africa was interlocked with the black population. 'While the political aims of territorial segregation sought to consign black South Africans to independent self-governing states, the economy demanded their labour in 'white' urban areas' (Sisk, 1994: 57). Botha's reforms of 1982 represented 'the first decisive break with the concept of a white nation' through the extension of trade union rights to blacks. The so called 'petty' apartheid laws in the social sphere were also relaxed (Spence, 1994: 2). The most significant reform involved the creation of a new 'tricameral' Constitution and a new parliament (Sisk, 1994: 45). The new parliament which was restricted to whites, coloureds and Indians excluded the majority black population. This limited reform enraged conservative elements within the National Party who broke away to form the Conservative Party and 'it proved a moment of equal or greater truth for blacks, enraged by their continued exclusion. For P.W. Botha, the consequences could hardly have been worse: whites were divided by it and blacks united against it' (Sisk, 1994: 45). In addition to constitutional reform, Botha also sought to develop a 'hearts and minds' strategy to win over black support through the provision of socio-economic development – in reality, he attempted to undermine groups and communities aligned to the ANC. Yet the reforms produced a backlash unprecedented in the history of the South African resistance movement:

> The events of 1984–1988, when the spiral of discontent reached an apex, were decisive in the struggle against the system of apartheid. The era saw the most widespread and intense uprising in the cycle of revolt and repression.
>
> (Sisk, 1994: 63)

The creation of the United Democratic Front (UDF) in August 1983, a loose alliance of some six hundred community, trade union and church groups, provided the focal point of resistance to apartheid, based on the principles of non-collaboration and 'ungovernability'. The UDF did not openly align itself to any one political movement but 'it was obvious from its inception that (it) reflected the same strategic approach as the ANC' (McKinley, 1997: 60). Charterism determined its political outlook and 'such an approach was reflected in the make up of the UDF, whose ranks included organisations ranging from the all-white, all-female and decidedly upper middle class of Black Sash (a national, liberal advocacy group), to radical and predominately working-class organisations such as the Tumahole Youth Congress (a civic group based in the Free State Province)' (McKinley, 1997: 60).

At the turn of the 1990s, both the ANC and the National Party Government had reached the point of 'a mutually hurting stalemate' (Welsh in Spence, 1994). The high point of the liberation struggle had been reached through campaigns of the early and mid-1980s. South Africa had been rendered 'ungovernable'. The heavy handed response of the government to black resistance, the constant state of emergency and the impact of international economic sanctions began to take their toll and both sides realised that a joint solution was the only way out. Elements within the National Party began to recognise the economic, political and ideological contradictions of apartheid – no change was not an option. Mandela, meanwhile, realised the value of black resistance and the impact that economic sanctions were having, but neither could be sustained indefinitely.

De Klerk recognised that South Africa was approaching 'an absolute impasse' and that apartheid was incapable of reform – it had to be jettisoned. Nelson Mandela from his prison in Cape Town, expressed alarm at 'the civil strife and ruin into which the country was now sliding'... In short, what had happened was one of those rare moments in history when powerful antagonists mutually recognise that their conflict is stalemated and can only be continued at unacceptable cost.

(Welsh in Spence, 1994: 22)

The peace process

President De Klerk' s February 1990 speech during which he unbanned the ANC and other anti-apartheid organisations and pledged to release Nelson Mandela ushered in a new phase of the conflict in South Africa. The historic decision signalled a willingness on the part of the South African Government (SAG) to negotiate directly with the ANC. The process of democratisation was under way. Between February 1990 and April 1994 South Africa roller-coastered between the highs of political agreements to the lows of countless massacres and levels of violence unprecedented in a land already scorched by bloodshed. Yet De Klerk and Mandela, whose personal relations fell apart during the years of negotiation, 'were bound together in 'antagonistic co-operation' which obliged them to keep negotiating – even if the process were punctuated by breakdowns or troubled by mutual accusations of treachery and bad faith' (Welsh in Spence, 1994: 23). Indeed, within a matter of weeks, senior ANC officials, once hounded and exiled by the apartheid state, would enter into a series of 'talks about talks' with the South African Government.

The first full scale bilateral meeting was convened at the Groote Schuur mansion in Cape Town on 2 May 1990 (Sisk, 1994: 90–3). Mandela, in a press interview after the two day meeting, described the talks as 'the realisation of a dream' (Argus, 1990). Groote Schuur signified the government's intentions to accept the demands of the ANC's Harare Declaration (August 1989) which committed the government to release all political prisoners, allow the return of exiles under conditions of immunity, amend security legislation and lift the State of Emergency. The ANC, for its part, agreed that it would not take up arms during the negotiating process, although it refused to give up the right to use violence. As a follow up to Groote Schuur some six months later, both sides further agreed to the Pretoria Minute (7 August 1990) which reiterated the parties commitment to 'promote and expedite the normalisation and stabilisation of the situation in line with the spirit of mutual trust obtaining among leaders involved' (Sisk, 1994: 93–8).

Significantly, the ANC unilaterally suspended the armed struggle 'in the interests of moving as speedily as possible towards a negotiated peaceful political settlement'. This decision, according to McKinley, caused consternation amongst the ANC rank and file, especially in the face of rising levels of indiscriminate violence which many ANC activists believed was being orchestrated by the state.

Violence was to dominate and frustrate South Africa's transition particularly since, 'the nature of the political violence was transformed from a primarily overt conflict between the regime and the forces of liberation, to a more entangled fight among a wide variety of players with disparate motives, tactics and objectives' (Sisk, 1994: 115). The primary battle of the transition was fought between supporters of Chief Buthelezi's IFP and the ANC. The portrayal of this conflict as 'black on black' violence, however, underplays a key dynamic – the role played by the apartheid state in stoking up 'inter-tribal rivalries' (Sisk, 1994: 117). Whilst much has been written about the conflict in the KwaZulu Natal region between the ANC and the IFP (Jeffers, 1997a,b), the escalation of this 'conflict' across South Africa, particularly in the Johannesburg region, after the onset of negotiations, raised serious concerns about the rationale driving it. One seemingly logical explanation, espoused by the ANC, international mediators and the Goldstone Commission, was that the violence was being orchestrated as a 'beyond the table tool' by elements within the state to ensure that 'blacks fought blacks'. In terms of explanations for the 'transitional violence', Sisk (1994) argued that all parties were, to a lesser or greater extent, culpable through either direct participation or through fomenting violence in order to: (i) halt or reverse the process; (ii) prevent marginalisation; and (iii) destabilise the opponent.

The incidence and ferocity of political violence during the transition became so intense that the ANC was forced, as a result of grassroots pressure, to withdraw from the negotiations on two occasions. Yet on the other hand, the violence led to imaginative initiatives such as the establishment of the National Peace Accord in September 1991, which attempted to manage the violence at the national, regional and local levels through the collective engagement of the political parties, church leaders, business representatives and civil society organisations. Speaking in December 1990, Nelson Mandela drew a clear distinction between those attempting to 'spoil' the process with those attempting to cement a new future:

> The aims of those planning and directing this scourge of destruction are very clearly to destroy the prospects of peace and derail our

march to freedom...The government's aim is to reform apartheid out of existence while carrying over into the future accumulated privileges and advantages of white monopoly on power. The ANC, on the other hand, seeks to attain the total eradication of apartheid and overcome as quickly as possible its ravages on our people. These basic distinctions account for the different direction in which we are pulling.

(Mandela quoted in Sisk, 1994: 97)

Mandela's analysis of the 'different directions' reflected the nature of the initial power dynamic which existed during the early phase of the negotiations stage – a dynamic which favoured the incumbent administration. Between 1990 and the early part of the 1992, the National Party believed it could determine the shape and eventual outcome of the transitional process. De Klerk thought that the National Party could create a powerful, anti-ANC alliance, using the IFP, in particular to cement factional divisions amongst the black population, which would result in a permanent power sharing administration. Indeed, De Klerk dispelled all suggestions that the government was negotiating black majority rule as 'a lie' he said. 'The National Party has said repeatedly that we reject it...We stand for power sharing and not for simple, typical majority rule. We are not sell outs of anyone. We are going to make it safer for our descendants and for the descendants of all South Africa' (Sparks, 1997: 128).

The National Party subsequently argued that the negotiations on the future of South Africa should be decided by a convention of all existing political organisations. This would, in effect, produce an anti-ANC alliance enabling the follow-through to power sharing. The political reality, however, of what the ANC would accept was sharply different. For a start, it flatly rejected the legitimacy of the party convention idea, arguing that the non-white parties were 'puppets of the state'. The transitional process needed, it argued, to be built on integrity which could only be achieved through a mandate from the people. The ANC wanted an immediate election to decide the composition of the negotiating forum. By the end of 1990, a clear stalemate existed which was only broken when the ANC agreed to convene an 'all party congress' to negotiate the route to a constituent assembly:

This offered the basis for a compromise. First there would be the multiparty convention the National Party was calling for, to negotiate an interim constitution under which one-person, one-vote elections would be held for a constituent assembly such as the one the

ANC wanted, which then would negotiate the final constitution for a new South Africa.

(Sparks, 1997: 129)

The Convention for a Democratic South Africa (CODESA) convened for the first time on the 20 December 1991 and was attended by 238 delegates representing 19 parties. This was described by Sparks as the 'broadest cross section of the country's leaders' with the notable exception of IFP, Chief Buthelezi. CODESA established a range of working groups to deal with central aspects of the transitional process as follows: principles and structures of a new constitution; the creation of a climate conducive to peaceful political participation; the form of transitional or interim government and the future path of the transition; the constitutional future of the four homelands that had accepted minimal independence; and the implementation of the agreements. It was agreed that each working group would report back to the full conference (CODESA II) within six months. In the intervening period, the National Party lost a by-election to the Conservative Party which forced De Klerk into holding a Whites Only Referendum. White South Africa was being asked to decide on whether or not the National Party should continue in negotiations with the ANC. De Klerk received a resounding endorsement, 68 per cent of voters voted to continue with the 'peace process'. Bolstered by such massive support for his position, De Klerk opted to play for time with CODESA. Mattes (1994) noted that:

The government appears to have concluded, on the basis of polling data, that it was in its interests to prolong the transition process as long as possible in the hope of reducing popular support for the ANC through attrition... In fact, several CODESA participants claimed that the National Party counselled its allies prior to the May deadlock to stall the proceedings because the government needed six more months to run an election campaign in black areas as well as to retain control of the South African Broadcasting Corporation during this critical period.

(Mattes in Reynolds, 1994: 42)

The decision by the National Party to 'play hard ball' in the CODESA II negotiations (May 1992) proved disastrous with the pendulum of power fundamentally shifting. That is, the National Party's belligerent stance that it could continue to veto the wish of the majority produced a grassroots response which clearly marked out the parameters of power within the new South Africa. The Boipantong massacre of 17 June, during which 49 people were killed, further cemented the resolve of the ANC to flex its muscle and it officially withdrew from further negotiations with the government. A strategy of 'rolling mass action' consisting of targeted strikes, boycotts, stayaways and occupations was adopted to further indicate to the National Party that the 'sands were shifting'. Part of the ANC's 'muscle flexing' involved an attempt to bring down the 'homeland region of Ciskei' in early September. The march on 'Ciskei' left 28 dead and it resulted in the official resumption of negotiations. Significantly however, throughout the mass protest campaign and the continuing violence, secret lines of communication continued between the National Party and the ANC. Towards the end of the month both parties agreed to issuing 'The Record of Understanding' which was a culmination of a 'war of letters' between the National Party's Rolf Meyer and the ANC's Cyril Ramaphosa. In explaining the new dynamic, Sisk and Sparks noted:

> The Bisho massacre, compared to the tragedy at Boipantong, reveals an important aspect of the violence nexus. Violence tends to polarise and impede negotiation when a single party is clearly culpable, but when parties are deemed by observers – especially the international community – equally culpable, incidents of violence reinforce pressures to negotiate.
>
> (Sisk, 1994: 219)

> Once again, South Africa's black and white leaders had to stare into the bays in order to recognise their mutual dependency. If violence went out of control, both would be losers. As Frederik van Zyl Slabbert, the former white opposition leader put it, they were like two squabbling drunks. They could threaten one another with much shouting and finger wagging, but neither could land a knock-out blow and in the end, they had to lean on one another to stay upright.
>
> (Sparks, 1997: 152)

The Record of Understanding, which committed both parties to interim power-sharing arrangements, permanently signalled that neither violence nor 'political spoilers' would detract the ANC and the

National Party from implementing new structures for South Africa. The Record of Understanding included the following commitments:

- an elected constituent assembly would also serve as an interim parliament;
- the constituent assembly would draft a constitution and decisions would be taken by 'special majorities';
- the constituent assembly would be bound by principles agreed to by a reconstituted CODESA;
- the constituent assembly would have 'deadlock-breaking mechanisms'; and
- an interim Government of National Unity would be constituted, which would have a 'national and regional government' and would be empowered by an interim constitution. (Sisk, 1994: 219)

Following a period of intense negotiations between the National Party and the ANC, the Multiparty Negotiation Process (MNP) was convened on 1 April 1993 with the aim of advancing decisions made through the Record of Understanding (see Sisk, 1994, Chapter 6). The MNP faced two tasks – to draft an interim constitution, including constitutional principles that would bind the future constitution making body and, to 'level the playing fields' for a future election. The multiplicity of actors at the MNP, constituting almost '100%' of the future electorate' reflected the dynamics of a process which was nearing a close. The announcement in July 1993 of the election date for 27 April 1994 gave further impetus to the process which suffered a setback following the assassination of Chris Hani, possibly the most popular ANC member after Mandela. Media predictions of an all-out backlash within the townships after Hani's death proved largely unfounded. Unlike in the past, the violence spurred the negotiating parties closer towards agreement. At breakneck speed, the ANC and the government, relying heavily on the 'sufficient consensus' rule developed at CODESA, enacted a draft constitution for ratification to parliament in November. In early December, the Transitional Executive Council (TEC) was given statutory form to 'level the playing fields' and make preparations for 'freedom day'. Television pictures of lines of people waiting patiently to vote in South Africa's first ever democratic election beamed across the globe, revealing that at last, political apartheid was dead.

> We, the people of South Africa, recognise the injustices of the past; honour those who suffered for justice and freedom in our land; respect those who have worked to build and develop our country;

and believe that South Africa belongs to all who live in it, united in our diversity.

(Preamble to South Africa's Constitution, 1996)

Post-apartheid South Africa

Prior to any examination of peace building activity in the new South Africa, we need to place in context the priorities facing the Government of National Unity. The scale of the problems cannot be understated. The levels of poverty and the disparities in wealth between whites and blacks are stark. Runaway crime statistics of 30 murders per day which currently dominate international perceptions of South Africa have created a culture of crime paranoia within white communities. Yet the outbreak of criminal activity cannot be disassociated from the damage that apartheid has inflicted on communities living a 'hand to mouth existence' in townships and squatter camps. Writing on the second anniversary of the new democracy, Interfund, an international aid organisation, noted that whilst the transition from apartheid to democracy was a watershed of momentous proportions, the problems facing the country remain stark:

> But with celebration comes a realisation that South Africa's democracy can only be sustained if there is adequate economic growth, if the most glaring inequities of apartheid are redressed, and if remaining political tensions can be resolved.
>
> (Interfund, 1996: 9)

In addition, the political horse trading which brought about the establishment of new democratic structures did not disappear after the elections. Whilst the Government of National Unity was installed, disputes and acrimonious debates continued to dominate relations between the two key partners of government, the ANC and the National Party with the latter withdrawing from government in July 1996. This decision in itself symbolises how rapidly events changed in the new political system. Most significantly perhaps, the fall in the levels of political violence after April 1994, except in the KwaZulu Natal, and the failure of extreme right wing groups to thwart political progress created conditions for the entrenchment of the democratic process.

The adoption of the South African Constitution represents the high point of the post-apartheid process. The Quaker Peace Centre in Cape Town (Annual Report, 1996) noted that the drafting of the constitution was 'the largest public participation programme ever carried out by government' in this country and the document 'represents the collective wisdom of the South African people and emerges from a process of general agreement'. Core components of the constitution aimed at offering protection to all citizens and which attempt to embed a 'culture of human rights' have been operationalised through the creation of a number of state authorities including: the Office of Public Protector (an office to ensure democratic and ethical practices in the public services); the Human Rights Commission; the Commission for Gender Equality; the Electoral Commission; the Independent Broadcasting Authority; the Cultural Commission and the Office of Auditor General. In addition, the Constitution incorporates a Bill of Rights guaranteeing:

- socio-economic rights, including the rights to housing, health care, a healthy environment, social security, fresh water and land;
- equality, human dignity, life and freedom and security of the person;
- freedom from slavery, servitude or forced labour;
- privacy;
- freedom;
- freedom of religion and opinion;
- freedom of expression and assembly, demonstration, picket, strike and petition;
- free political choice;
- citizenship, freedom of movement and residence;
- choice of own trade, occupation and profession;
- fair labour practices;
- access to courts and just administrative action;
- access to information held by the state.

Although particular areas of the constitution were hotly contested, such as the education clause, the overall framework of both the constitution and the Bill of Rights is 'infused with a strong commitment to human rights and democracy' (Interfund, 1996: 9). In addition to delivery of these structures, the successful outcome of local government elections in all 9 provinces by 1996, especially in Natal, symbolises further that democratic politics have taken root. Interfund, however, identified a number of fault lines in the new dispensation. The continuation of political violence, although on a reduced scale, in KwaZulu Natal has directly impacted on the release of development funds to the region. However, a new peace process, initiated shortly before the local government elections of June 1996, appears to be holding as a result of what Johnson (1997) described as a general war wariness, the introduction of democratic governance and a recognition that investment will not flow to the region if violence continues. Chapter 7 examines the developments at the NGO/community level from the height of apartheid to the present and discusses the contribution made by grassroots activity to peace building.

7
South Africa: Micro Grassroots Activity

Introduction

The Soweto riots of 1976 and the violent response by the state authorities cast the South African conflict further into the 'political spotlight' and created a unique platform for the ANC to internationalise the wrong doings of the apartheid state. The political capital acquired by the liberation movement after Soweto resulted in an avalanche of foreign aid primarily directed towards creating 'alternative' forms of government. The mid to late 1980s witnessed a proliferation of civil society organisations which, coupled with the imposition of economic sanctions, played a contributory role in creating the 'stalemate' of the late 1980s which led to the collapse of apartheid.

> By the eighties (and particularly from September 1994), it was clear to ever socio-political analyst that South Africa was experiencing a revolution in the making. Part of the revolutionary strategy included the strategy of ungovernability and the development of alternative structures, such as street committees, civic associations, people's courts, mass mobilisation and mass action. Indeed, a total alternative society developed alongside the existing apartheid South Africa.
> (De Kock, 1993: 7–9)

The civil society base upon which South Africa's transition to democracy was achieved consisted of a plethora of non-governmental bodies engaged in a vast range of 'semi-governmental activity'. Yet the shift of the NGO network from an anti-apartheid force to partners in the new dispensation has not been an easy one. This chapter will contextualise the dynamics of change within these organisations through three distinct periods: (i) the turbulent decade of the 1980s; (ii) the transitional phase (1990–94); and finally, (iii) the new dispensation. More crucially, we will examine the structural mechanisms put in place by 'parties to the conflict' which sought both to ease the pain of a violent and bloody transition and to bring about a peaceful reconciliation of past differences.

The politics of peace in 1980s South Africa

The very nature of apartheid resulted in the contamination of concepts such as 'peace' or 'coexistence' and there was an almost total absence of 'neutral mediating groups, peace initiatives or movements' (Taylor and Habib, 1997: 2). As Johnson remarked, to engage with the apartheid state was akin 'to supping with the devil' (personal interview with Prof. A. Johnson, Dept. of Politics, University of Natal, October 1997). Understanding the role played by grassroots organisations requires an examination of notions of 'peace', 'coexistence' and 'liberation'. At the base level, South Africa's white community equated 'coexistence' with the underlying logic of apartheid which sought to perpetuate a belief system based on the view that 'good, secured fences make good neighbours'. Hamber usefully summarised what he termed 'a central thesis' of white attitudes to apartheid which supported their notion of coexistence:

> Apartheid was an idea, it wasn't such a bad idea and when it started to get screwed up we decided to change it...The whole world is looking at separate development, all over the world every ethnic group is going for separate development, so what the big deal...OK, it got a bit out of hand in the 1980s but we fixed it up.
> (Personal interview with Brandon Hamber, Centre for the Study of Violence and Reconciliation, October 1997)

With respect to understanding peace, the white community held a 'minimalist version' of the term which translated simply into the 'absence of war' (Taylor and Habib, 1997: 3). If the two primary threats to the whites, the ANC and communism, were contained or eliminated, peace would prevail. To talk, therefore, of a peace movement within South Africa's white community is a misnomer in two respects. Firstly, the forced policy of 'coexistence' which prohibited forms of interaction between whites and blacks, limited efforts at fostering a peace movement within the white community. And secondly, the risks associated with seeking 'peace' were too high. As Duncan remarked, 'few white voices were heard calling on the government to end apartheid and relinquish power, because relinquishing power meant black majority rule' (personal interview with Sheena Duncan, and Black Sash, October 1997).

For the black community, 'a commitment to peace and non-violence was widely interpreted to mean either acquiescence to apartheid or a denial of the legitimacy of armed struggle as a means of resistance to the apartheid regime' (Taylor and Habib, 1997: 2). Civil society organisations, especially operating under the umbrella of the United Democratic Front (UDF), fought apartheid through either mass mobilisation (organising mass protest action, stayaways, strikes) or, delivering services neglected by the apartheid authorities. The function of civil society was primarily to create a 'government in waiting' through the rejection of the apartheid state.

Within the above environment, international aid, which was successfully won through the diplomatic offices of the ANC in exile, combined to create alternative structures of governance linking 'the destruction of apartheid to the creation of a new society' (UDF discussion paper, 1985, cited by Mufson, 1990 in Taylor and Habib, 1997: 4). The language of the UDF and the ANC throughout the 1980s was 'liberation' through the policy of 'ungovernability' and 'non-collaboration' with the state or the associated 'homeland administrations'.

> We call on all sections of our people to make the apartheid system more and more unworkable and the country less and less governable. At the same time we must work endlessly to strengthen all levels of mass and underground organisation and to create the beginnings of people power.
>
>   (ANC NEC Statement, 1985)

If peace were to be conceptualised, it could not have been divorced from 'justice' – the full enfranchisement of the population – and it would have translated as 'freedom from the systematic violence generated by the political, legal and socio-economic forces of the apartheid order' (Taylor and Habib, 1997: 3).

Yet during the mid 1980s, there was a growth in the number of organisations which potentially cross-cut the divide between the apartheid state and mass movement organisations (Taylor and Habib, 1997).

Definitionally, these organisations constituted South Africa's nearest equivalent to 'peace NGOs'. Organisations, for example, identified by Taylor and Habib as closer to the apartheid state were not supporters of the state, rather they failed to define their activity in terms of a specific political outcome. They attempted 'neutrality' in a 'contaminated environment'. The Centre for Intergroup Studies (now the Centre for Conflict Resolution), the Quaker Peace Centre and the Independent Mediation Service of South Africa (IMSSA) tried to occupy the neutral ground because their work centred on 'peacekeeping', mediation and conciliation which necessitated an apolitical disposition. Taylor and Habib further classified 'peace organisations' at three levels: those which were concerned with building the future today, those advocating conflict management techniques, and those out to expose the 'facts'. The underlying dimension to these organisations was that they sought to build an 'alternative, non-racial society', creating 'miniature versions of the future South Africa within our domain' (Hanf et al., 1981, quoted in Taylor and Habib, 1997: 3). Table 7.1 categorises each organisational type with 'notions of peace'.

Table 7.1   Peace organisations in 1980s South Africa

Peace as 'absence of war'	Exposing facts	Peace with justice
Centre for Conflict Resolution	South Africa Institute for Race Relations	UDF Affiliates
Quaker Peace Centre	Centre for Policy Studies	Christian Institute
Independent Mediation Service of South Africa		South Africa Catholic Bishops Conference
		South Africa Council of Churches
		National Union of South Africa Students
		National Education Crises Centre
		National Medical and Dental Association
		Legal Resources Centre
		Black Sash
		Five Freedoms Forum
		Institute for a Democratic Alternative for South Africa

Source: adapted from Taylor and Habib, 1997.

Although a significant number of the above mentioned organisations existed prior to the 1980s, they only began to take positions on creating new alternatives in the mid decade. Whilst both the South African Council of Churches (SACC) and the South African Catholic Bishops Council (SACBC) played a role in criticising the apartheid state, the nature of the public pronouncements made against apartheid and the type of assistance offered to communities rapidly shifted as the struggle intensified between the UDF and the government. Both the SACC and the SACBC called for the establishment of a multi-racial 'peoples church'. In addition, prominent members of the clergy offered direct assistance to the anti-apartheid struggle through involvement in protest activities and participating in high level negotiations with the ANC in 1986. One leading church activist and the former Archbishop of Durban, Denis Hurley, remarked that 'justice and peace cannot flourish on a diet of theory and talk'. Attempts at 'translating all these magnificent words into action' (Hurley, 1997: 3) underscored the activities of church based groups during the 1980s. In addition, a range of organisations, similar to developments in Israel/Palestine, grew up around offering 'professional support' to South Africa's alternative health, welfare and educational sectors.

In attempting to explain this growth in 'peace activity', Habib remarked that the NGO network of the mid 1980s emerged within the 'magic moment of history' and 'if the magic moment does not exist, then the NGOs wouldn't have been successful, (personal interview with A. Habib, Dept. of Political Science, University of Durban-Westville, September 1997). Habib believed that the opportunity for NGOs was created through the shifting structural dynamic between the ANC and the UDF on the one hand, and the apartheid state on the other. The National Party knew that it could maintain the status quo but it also recognised that the costs politically and economically were too great. Similarly, the democratic movement knew that the state could continue with apartheid and repression. The central question for the ANC and UDF was whether or not the community could sustain the onslaught on state terror without turning in on itself.

The combination of these two factors constituted 'the magic moment'. Habib, therefore, cautioned against overplaying the role of the NGO 'peace' network although he believed that organisations such as IDASA and the Five Freedoms Forum played an essential role in 'sensitising' the white community to the ANC. Significantly, IDASA was established in 1986 by two Progressive Federal Members of Parliament, Alex Borraine (appointed Deputy Chairperson of the TRC and Frederik van zyl

Slabbert) who believed that parliamentary democracy had no further role to play in effecting change within South Africa.[26] Habib summarised his position thus:

> I think that NGOs are important but their importance must be located within structural constraints... To look at it any other way provides a misleading picture that 'you establish one or two NGOs and all is possible'. It's only possible if certain other things happen... In South Africa, the thing that happened was that there was a balance of power, a climate created where each side knew they could not get what they wanted and in this context, NGOs could flower and come together and what they said made sense.
> (Personal interview with Adam Habib, Dept. of Political Science, University of Durban-Westville, September 1997)

As the 1980s came to a close, the signs were that something new was on the horizon. Mandela and the ANC in exile had been signalling, through channels of communication with organisations such as IDASA, and in public, via the Harare Declaration, that they were prepared for negotiations with the government. Whilst battered from a decade of violence, South Africa's much developed civil society waited in anticipation for the arrival of the new democracy. As discussed in Chapter 6, violence was to plague the transition and it fundamentally tested the resolve of the peace and conflict resolution sector. Uniquely, and in spite of the violence, a number of mechanisms were put in place which attempted to ease the transfer of power, notably the National Peace Accord. For many of the organisations and church groups listed in Table 7.1, the transition represented the shift away from being part of 'the magic moment' to being the front-line force in a deeply divided country. Between 1990 and 1994, the NGO 'peace' network facilitated, mediated, monitored, trained and reported on the unfolding events of the transition to democracy.

'The uncertain interregnum' (February 1990–April 1994)

The National Peace Accord

South Africa's transition was meant to 'heal the country's conflicts and bring peace', but the early 1990s witnessed a spiralling of political violence to unprecedented levels, especially in the Wits/Vaal and Natal regions. De Kock argued that there were a number of 'triggers' to the violence including widespread rumours which built on fears and insecurity; the allegations of third force activity; and the use of protest activity in already heightened political climes. In an attempt to restrain the onslaught, key players such as De Klerk's government, the ANC and the IFP agreed to the establishment of unique peace making structures. These structures were incorporated into the National Peace Accord (NPA) of September 1991 which included codes of conduct for political parties and organisations, the police and South African Defence Force, and measures for socio-economic development and reconstruction. Several institutions were established at the national, regional and local levels 'specifically to allow major political actors to jointly manage the challenge of containing political violence, as well as mechanisms for dispute resolution and compliance' (Sisk, 1994: 114). Two overarching aims were agreed which sought to (i) deal effectively with the causes and phenomenon of political violence and intimidation and (ii) to facilitate socio-economic reconstruction and development (National Peace Secretariat Report, 1994).

The international community hailed the NPA a success and donor organisations and foreign governments lent their full support to it either through the provision of expertise or by way of direct financial assistance. A number of observers commented on the events surrounding the NPA signing ceremony in Johannesburg. During the week prior to the signing, South Africa witnessed a series of 'random, senseless terror attacks' which left 42 dead and 50 wounded. Perhaps more ironically, the 'conference got off to a rocky start when three hundred delegates arrived to find thousands of armed IFP supporters staging mock battles in the streets outside the venue' (Sisk, 1994: 114). In spite of the high drama and the political tensions of the period, the NPA was 'without precedent internationally. Special forums have been created to settle disputes elsewhere in the world, but nowhere has this been done on a countrywide basis, from national to local level, with the formal endorsement of government and major political parties' (Nathan, 1993: 4). Indeed, at the beginning of 1994, 263 local peace committees had been established, representing a diverse cross section of the social and political composition of South Africa. Four hundred and thirty people were employed full time at the local, regional, and national level and, in addition to the input from political parties and state institutions, more than 7,000 voluntary peace workers were engaged in peace making structures (National Peace Secretariat Report, 1994). The following section examines the role of the NPA, firstly as a mechanism for macro level peace making and secondly, at the grassroots level, through the operation and workings of the local peace committees.

The politics of the NPA

The early period of South Africa's transition involved intense political wrangling between De Klerk's government and the ANC over a host of issues including arrangements for the release of political prisoners, rights of return for those exiled and the role played by the state in fomenting political violence. A series of pacts were agreed between the ANC and the government in the run up to the signing of the National Peace Accord. These pacts (referred to in Chapter 6 on the Groote Schuur and the Pretoria Minutes) came to represent the only means by which the parties could realistically prove their commitment to a nego-tiated, peaceful and democratic settlement. Extraneous factors such as 'third force' elements within the state security apparatus and intense and localised community conflict between the ANC and IFP, often characterised by local power politics, seemed beyond the control of both Mandela and De Klerk. The NPA grew, therefore, out of a desire by the political elites to jointly manage the conflict. As Sisk notes:

> Political leaders best understand the maxim that a worse outcome must be avoided. After all, it was such a realisation that brought them to the table in the first place.
>
> (Sisk, 1994: 122)

Yet the problem for both Mandela and De Klerk was that while they had agreed on a peace path, rank and file supporters had not internalised the impact of the road ahead. Some commentators accused both Mandela and De Klerk of sending out mixed political messages which under-mined the sentiments of moving towards a new South Africa. Early in 1991, Mandela and the ANC threatened to withdraw from negotiations if the government failed to deliver on the issue of prisoners and the return of exiles. The ANC also called for a two day general strike, mass protests and a consumer boycott in support of the release of political prisoners. In a climate of increased violence, the inherent contradic-tions (perceived or otherwise) of each party's position meant that the grassroots remained fully locked within a 'zero-sum' mind set. Increased political leverage was accorded to what Friedman (1994) describes as 'mid level elites' whose natural inclinations tend towards intransigence and mobilisation:

> As has been demonstrated ... political elites can easily mobilise their
> constituencies to demonstrate their power in society but they are
> unable to demobilise them when the moment of peace arrives.
>
> (Duffy and Frensley, 1989: 5)

Shaw (1993), in an assessment of the NPA, noted that at the height
of the conflict, 'many community leaders simply did not possess the
authority to call off their followers and some who tried, paid a heavy
price. Several local leaders who openly supported the peace process
have been murdered' (Shaw, 1993: 11). This confirms Sisk's view that
'transitional pacts or agreements cannot be personalised; even political
leaders of the stature of Mandela, de Klerk, and Buthelezi could not
mobilise their constituencies. The underlying forces behind the violence were mostly beyond their control' (Sisk, 1994: 123). Nossel, who
worked on the peace structures in the Johannesburg region, explained:

> We initially assumed that if Mandela had signed, then the whole
> ANC was on board, right down to grassroots ... that just turned out
> to be a fallacy. Firstly, people didn't really know about the Accord
> and if they did know, their perception was that they had been
> completely excluded from the negotiations process that had led up
> to it ... Generally they were locked into adversarial relationships and
> they weren't ready to sit round the table with the IFP or the South
> African police.
>
> (Nossel's speech made at NCPCR Conference, 'Working it
> Out: Creating Inclusive Social Structures', May 1995)

Evaluations undertaken on the macro peace structures recognised
fully the inherent difficulties of the 'coal face' reality compared with
the political language of the key stakeholders within South African
society. Yet the significance of the National Peace Accord at the macro
level related to its attempt at reducing the level of uncertainty (managing the violence) and the extent to which the NPA institutionalised
democracy. In relation to the latter, Sisk argues that the NPA constructed interim rules of 'the new political game', explicitly identifying
a democratic state as the common aim and, as such, 'it represented
South Africa's first post-apartheid institution, albeit a nascent, transitional one' (Sisk, 1994: 124). Central to cementing democracy, the
Accord committed each of the signatories to recognise and uphold

fundamental principles such as:

- freedom of conscience and belief;
- freedom of speech and expression;
- freedom of association;
- peaceful assembly;
- freedom of movement and freedom of participation in peaceful political activity.

With respect to reducing the levels of violence, it has been argued that 'the Peace Accord did not immediately succeed because the uncertainty of transition continued to reign' (Sisk, 1994: 287). In other words, violence would only be significantly reduced following the removal of the 'most visible and enduring structural cause of violence (black disenfranchisement)' (Sisk, 1994: 116). The framers of the Peace Accord were keen to emphasise that the structures were 'transitional' in nature and that they would be superseded by democratic structures of government. Nathan writing in 1993, cautioned against viewing the NPA as a panacea for all the ills of the transition:

> The National Peace Committee is an important forum, but it is not Parliament. The principles and Codes of Conduct contained in the Accord are valuable, but they are not a constitution. Most seriously, the NPA does not have the mechanisms to enforce its decisions and deal adequately with contravention of the codes.
>
> (Nathan, 1993: 5)

Equally importantly in this respect, Taylor (personal interview, October 1997) and others (Shaw, 1993; Nathan, 1993) noted that it was necessary to pose the 'counterfactual question' when assessing the impacts. In other words, would political violence have increased without the peace committees, rather than simply stating that the structures had failed because levels of violence increased in the run up to the April 1994 elections:

> Indeed, some obvious difficulties face any attempt to measure the success of peace structures. After all, we have no way of knowing whether violence would have been worse had they not been operating. And a sympathetic view that, even though they have not halted violence altogether, they have influenced local political culture positively, is equally immune to measurement.
>
> (Shaw, 1993: 8–9)

Assessing the local peace committees

The macro political assessment of the peace structures diverts attention away from the experiences of over 200 local peace committees (LPCs) which took root throughout South Africa between 1991 and 1994. LPCs were established with the aim of bringing local parties together to 'foster co-operation' and a 'culture of tolerance'. Amongst other things, LPCs were duty bound to 'create trust and reconciliation between grassroots community leadership of relevant organisations, including the police and the defence force; settle disputes causing public violence or intimidation by negotiating with the parties concerned; eliminate conditions which may harm peace accords or peaceful relations, and agree upon rules relating to marches, rallies and public gatherings' (Odendaal and Spies, 1996: 4). The extensive range of functions and tasks set before the LPCs needs to be examined against the differing regional factors of the South African conflict. Odendaal and Spies (1996) argued, for example, that rural LPCs in the Western Cape Region became 'effective instruments of peacekeeping and peacemaking' because of 'the numerical weaknesses of the IFP and right wing parties'. The climate in the Western Cape favoured 'political accommodation':

> The two dominant political parties in the Western Cape were the National Party and the ANC, both of which had made considerable political investments in the transformation process and wanted it to succeed.
>
> (Odendaal and Spies, 1996: 6)

At the other end of the spectrum, the high levels of political violence in KwaZulu Natal, coupled with the intense local rivalry between the IFP and ANC in the region, rendered the LPCs largely ineffective. The 1993 Report of the National Peace Secretariat, recognising the acute difficulties in the region, pointed to three 'major stumbling blocks ... the political climate, shortcomings in the security and judicial systems, and in the National Peace Accord structures' (National Peace Secretariat Report, 1993: 8). The report also noted that the 'regional peace committee has been unable to establish local peace committees in a number of key areas because of political parties' tactics of laying down preconditions for the formation of committees' (National Peace Secretariat Report, 1993: 8). Whilst the 1994 National Peace Secretariat Report referred to a number of 'successful interventions through mediation' by KwaZulu Natal peace structures such as the 'establishment of ANC and IFP monitors in Bhambayi, a region averaging nine deaths a week in 1993', the general consensus remains that the NPA performed poorly due to the scale of the political violence.

The restructuring of the peace networks after 1994 in Natal signified, firstly, the need for change and, more importantly, the extent to which violence continued to pose a threat to the region. Phillip Powell of the IFP in KwaZulu Natal argued that the LPCs were 'preoccupied with form rather than content...taking minutes and notes rather than following up with action' (personal interview, October 1997). But more fundamentally, Powell argued that the LPCs had no power because the committee representation was made up of 'useful idiots' who did not represent the grassroots. 'Having useful idiots serving on those structures when they were up against hardened community leaders was pointless' (personal interview, October 1997). Powell contrasts the recently constructed peace structures with those of the NPA by stressing that 'front line commanders' are now represented on committees which means that there 'is now no gap between those talking peace and the people running the show on the ground'. The ANC, in Natal, he argues, have also adapted the same approach:

> Rather than the process being driven by some smug cleric or businessman, it is driven by the people who have clout and who actually can make agreements stick...We actually locate ourselves within a particular problem area...stay for two or three weeks and we ensure that our ANC counterparts are on their side of the wire and we deal with every crime and contingency as it happens...That sends a strong message to communities.
>
> (Personal interview with Phillip Powell, IFP, October 1997)

Powell's frank portrayal of structures old and new reveals, amongst other things and maybe inadvertently, that the IFP in Natal never engaged in NPA structures despite public pronouncements to the contrary. It should also be noted that the rationale of 'making peace work' in Natal is now more directly linked to a political contest for votes between the ANC and the IFP. As Powell himself remarked, 'politicians are looking for re-election and we need to demonstrate what we have actually achieved and violence is the greatest obstacle...Colleagues are beginning to panic as they want to be back on the "gravy train" and people are going to say, "where are the houses, where are the schools"...You see, there is now no vested interest in keeping violence alive' (personal interview with Phillip Powell, October 1997).

The LPCs operating in the Wits/Vaal region represent possibly a 'half way house' between the experiences of the Western Cape and Natal. All over South Africa some LPCs floundered and others managed to create bonds of trust between warring factions. The Independent Mediation Service for South Africa (IMSSA) which was heavily involved in facilitating peace committees in the Wits/Vaal region pointed to the achievements of the peace committee in Thokoza:

> In the PWV, IMSSA staff and panellists facilitated the establishment of 14 local peace committees... IMSSA organised a peace conference in Thokoza... which led to a temporary cessation in political violence in a community which had experienced some 300 politically related deaths in the previous 18 months. The truce lasted for a six months period during which there was not one politically inspired death in Thokoza.
>
> (IMMSA, 1997: 31)

The final Report of the National Peace Secretariat (1994) provides further qualitative evidence of the 'success' of peace structures. It also identifies eleven specific achievements of the peace structures ranging from encouraging grassroots and local level reconciliation through to co-ordinating socio-economic reconstruction and development (see Table 7.2).

As with the assessment of the Peace Accord at the macro level, Shaw (1993) argued that the benchmark used for measuring success, that is the reduction in the levels of violence, was unfair and it was impossible to assess whether or not it had been achieved. Even trying to analyse

Table 7.2 Achievements of the National Peace Secretariat structures

---

Grassroots and local level reconciliation and participation
Provision of access to government structure, parastatals, NGOs and businesses
Developing community decision-making
Socio-economic reconstruction and development
Police community relations
Peace education
Youth peace education
Empowerment through training
Democratic values and practices
Monitoring and managing public events
Elections

Source: National Peace Secretariat Report, 1994.

rates of violence points up regional variations:

> Violence has clearly waned as well as waxed since the NPA was
> signed. Nor does violence occur uniformly across the country. It is
> concentrated in specific localities on the Reef and in Natal. So it is
> conceivable that the Peace Accord has contributed to periodic declines
> in violence and localising it.
>
> (Shaw, 1993: 6)

In addition, although the Accord was supposed to pre-empt violence,
LPCs were 'often set up only as a reactive measure after substantial violence had already occurred' and the voluntary nature of the committees meant that they 'emerge only where local parties and interests
agree to establish them' (Shaw, 1993: 7). Shaw argued that their greatest impact related to the monitoring of political marches. 'Effective
monitoring is now carried out at most mass gatherings and this has
undoubtedly reduced violence levels' (Shaw, 1993: 9). For example,
Fergal Keane (a well known BBC journalist, in his book *The Bondage of
Fear*) wrote that he witnessed peace monitors on several occasions,
holding the line 'between crowds of angry youths and rows of nervous
policemen' (Keane, 1994). Sisk believed that the crucial test for the
structures occurred following the murder of South African Communist
Party activist, Chris Hani in August 1993. For Sisk, the assassination
of Hani:

> Demonstrated how perilously fragile South Africa's transition to
> democracy was, yet at the same time it reaffirmed the resilience of
> the leaders' commitment to a negotiated settlement. It also demon-
> strated an unprecedented degree of co-operation among the ANC,
> security forces, international observers, and the myriad regional and
> local peace committees established by the Peace Accord.
>
> (Sisk, 1994: 228)

With regard to the other roles identified in Table 7.2, Shaw argued
that the LPCs' socio-economic development role was slightly premature
in the face of widespread communal violence: 'for even the simple act
of rebuilding a house carries with it far reaching political implications
in conflict ridden communities'. Yet valuable lessons were learnt
through the process of attempting to reconstruct and rebuild communities in violent circumstances and the process contributed to a deeper
understanding of the links between development and conflict.

At the process level, Nossel (1993) identified a number of problem areas within LPC structures in the Wits/Vaal region such as the 'top down approach' to committee formation which initially impacted on the 'ownership of the process', the over-representation of whites on committees, and failure to include constituencies such as youth groups and the unemployed. Other commentators reflected similar concerns. Odalyi, a community worker in Cape Town, could not reconcile the fact that the LPCs were mostly made up of whites (interviewed, Cape Town, September 1997). For an overall assessment, Nossel remarked that in spite of the difficulties with process issues and representatives:

> peace committees have achieved some success in tackling disputes and effecting lasting agreements between parties. Through the committees, local leaders have managed to control rumours, report threats, and defuse crises. Peace committees have also assisted victims of violence, launched workshops on negotiation, mediation, conflict resolution and held public information campaigns on the Peace Accord. They helped build consensus on community socioeconomic reconstruction/development.
>
> (Nossel, 1993: 6–7)

Hamber, drawing both the macro and micro contexts together, believed that the main strength of the Peace Accord structures lay in the dynamic created through the interaction between different parties to the conflict – a dynamic which brought about the successful outcome of the negotiating process.

> The strength [of the NPA] is the inter-dynamic, inter-group, interorganisational nature of the process it created and the social power that comes with that. When you get a whole lot of business people, even if it is for the wrong reasons, together with politicians and other interests groups, you get some level of consensus and you have made a positive step. Managing to get everybody to say, "we are sick and tired of this, 'yes', we all have our interests, 'yes', we all want something at the end of the day, but let's stop this now and in time we can fight about our own interests" is what happened through the Peace Structures.
>
> (Interviewed October 1997)

Beginning a new South Africa (April 1994–April 1998)

It could be argued that the April 1994 elections were not so much a victory for individual political parties but for the process of negotiations which triumphed over political violence. The significant, last minute, decision by the IFP to enter the election race provided South Africa with a firmer platform to build new structures and processes. Although political violence continues in Natal today, the intensity and ferocity has significantly diminished and recent events indicate a political compromise between the ANC and the IFP. Similarly, extreme right-wing violence which had threatened to wreck the democratic process during the transition disappeared. After April 1994, South Africa was on a path to new and legitimate structures of government. Yet the euphoria and emotion of the elections masked momentarily the momentous task which lay ahead in respect of healing the wounds of apartheid, building the economy and providing reasonable living standards for the long suffering African community.

In order to address these issues, two distinct measures were introduced by the Government of National Unity (GNU), although clearly the ANC was the main driving force for change. At the level of reconciliation, the ANC had long campaigned for the establishment of a commission to deal with the injustices that apartheid had inflicted on black South Africa. As a result, a Truth and Reconciliation Commission (TRC) was established at the end of 1995. The TRC has dominated the international media's coverage of the South African transition particularly through the extensive coverage of the trials of P.W. Botha and Winnie Mandela. Within South Africa, the televised proceedings of the TRC gripped the black community and proved a distinct 'turn off' to the minority white population. In addition, despite the IFP joining the political process, considerable problems surfaced over the functioning of the TRC in Natal. The IFP refused to participate on the grounds that the conflict in Natal had not been formally resolved. In addition, they accused the Commission of political bias. The second policy plank of the GNU related to implementing the Reconstruction and Development Programme (RDP), described as 'an integrated, coherent socio-economic policy framework' which aimed, amongst other things, 'to mobilise all of our people and our country's resources towards the final eradication of apartheid and the building of a democratic, non-racial and non-sexist future'. The core programmes of the RDP were outlined by the ANC as: meeting basic needs, developing human resources, building the economy, democratising the state and society, and implementing the RDP. Its implementation has created problems between government ministries and non-governmental organisations (NGOs), given their role during apartheid of service delivery across a range of government functions.

Both the TRC and RDP represent the key macro political initiatives aimed at reconciliation and reconstruction in South Africa; 'top down' initiatives with a 'bottom up' agenda. We review the implementation of both in the context of their impact on peace building, reconciliation and reconstruction. Two caveats need to be borne in mind. Firstly, the levels of poverty within South Africa and its differential impact on the white and black population and secondly, the conflicting priorities and tasks associated with structuring a new administration in such a short period of time.

The Truth and Reconciliation Commission

The Truth and Reconciliation Commission (TRC) represented a unique and historic compromise between the African National Congress and the National Party. Throughout the period of transitional negotiations, the South African Government insisted on amnesty from prosecution for members of the government, the civil service and the security forces (the so called sunset clauses). Whilst decidedly uncomfortable with a blanket amnesty, the ANC recognised the need to keep key political forces on board. ANC negotiators steered clear of Nuremberg style war crimes trials, arguing that such an approach had the potential to tear South Africa apart. Instead, they argued that 'as complete a picture as possible of the nature, causes and extent of gross violations of human rights committed' during apartheid was required. The TRC was established to carry forward this task in the spirit of 'nation building and national reconciliation' (Promotion of National Unity and Reconciliation Act, 1995). The key areas of the Commission's remit were reflected in the establishment of a (i) Human Rights Violations, (ii) Amnesty and (iii) Reparations and Rehabilitation Committees. The overall objectives of the Commission were to:

- investigate gross human rights violations committed by all parties to the conflict, including the security forces and the liberation movement;
- identify victims and perpetrators;
- grant amnesty in the case of 'political acts' where there is full disclosure;

- recommend measures to prevent the commission of gross human rights violations in the future which will build national unity and reconciliation.

The nature of the compromise

Professor John Daniels (Head of Research at the TRC in Durban, interviewed October 1997) identified two distinct compromises in relation to the establishment of the TRC. The first compromise, he argued, restricted the time frame for investigation from March 1960 up until April 1994. This time frame ran counter to the ANC's stated position that the TRC should cover the entire period of the apartheid state. The ANC's acceptance of this had implications for the second key compromise, the adoption of a narrow definition of a 'gross human rights violation' which the legislation defined as 'the killing, abduction, torture or severe ill treatment of any person or any attempt, conspiracy, incitement, instigation, command or procurement to commit an act of killing, abduction, torture or severe ill treatment' (Promotion of National Unity and Reconciliation Act, 1995). This once again fell far short of the ANC's position which regarded the apartheid state itself as a 'crime against humanity'. It also precluded from investigation key human rights violations such as the forced removals, land confiscation, the pass laws and the concept of apartheid itself. McBride (1996) noted that the narrow legalistic definition of a human rights violation created an undeserved 'parity of suffering' between the liberation movement and the apartheid state which subsequently dominated the workings of the Commission itself. The TRC has not, in her view, been able to overcome the nature of the compromises identified by Daniels. On the contrary, genuine truth and justice have been abandoned for the sake of political expediency:

> You get a feeling from the people heading the Commission that they feel this sense of balance was important. While it may be important for compromise, it is not in the end, going to satisfy a national aspiration for a Truth Commission that really gets to the truth about our history, and that history is the history of apartheid. It is the history of oppression. It is not the history of a conflict between two equal sides.
>
> (McBride, 1996: 22)

Whilst identifying compromises, Daniels believed that the 'truth telling' and symbolic power of the TRC negated the gains by the National Party to the extent that, 'it [the TRC] has blown away that whole generation of party leadership around De Klerk', consigning them 'to the political wilderness' and it has exposed to whites the full extent of the crimes committed by the apartheid state:

> It has achieved certain political objectives that needed to be achieved if in fact you were going to be able to facilitate a reconciliation (i.e., the fracturing of National Party and the eradication of the far right)...I think also that it has humbled whites, it is now pretty difficult for them to go around saying, "we don't believe this stuff"...whether or not they want to hear it is a different matter.
> (Personal interview with Professor Daniels,
> TRC Durban, October 1997)

Taylor is less inclined to believe that the process produced 'winners and losers' at either the political or community level, rather:

> Politicians have engaged in linguistic acrobatics in order to try to do anything but avoid the reality that the negotiated settlement was a compromise. If you accept that it was a compromise, the reality is, whether you like it or not, that truth is going to be compromised and this is exactly what we have seen. The real issues have not been fully confronted by the TRC. One wonders whether or not the gap between the ideal and reality is too wide.
> (Personal interview with Rupert Taylor, Dept. of Politics,
> University of Witswatersand, October 1997)

Taylor went on to remark that 'clearly behind the scenes, there was a verbal agreement that no one at a high level would be prosecuted and this is played out in the TRC – if the process was genuine, senior people should have been accountable or at least they should come clean'. The dynamic between the 'ideal' and the 'reality' looms large in any assessment of the TRC and it is to public attitudes which we now turn.

Perceptions of the TRC

At the launch of the TRC, Archbishop Tutu declared that 'even handiness will be its watchword' (quoted in *The Guardian*, November 1997). Yet the TRC has been dogged with allegations of bias against the white population and the IFP.

If you ask me who the audience should have been, I would argue that it should have been white South Africa and yet most white South Africans turn off to what is happening.

(Personal interview with Rupert Taylor, October 1997)

In addition, critics to the Left of the ANC have argued that the TRC is fatally flawed because in its attempts at 'even-handedness' it has 'treated the oppressor and the oppressed in equal terms. So members of the liberation movement who fought against an unjust system and who fought against a system recognised as a crime against humanity have to ask for the same level of forgiveness as those people who implemented that crime against humanity' (McBride, 1996: 16). The crux of the debate within South Africa revolves around the different interpretations of 'reconciliation' rather than uncovering 'truth'. Whilst the TRC epitomised Tutu's declared view that 'truth is a prerequisite to reconciliation', the process of reconciliation has been tempered with the cold realities of post-apartheid South Africa:

The government is driving at reconciliation but it has not happened ... peaceful coexistence is much more the reality. The whole process cannot be called reconciliation.

(Interview with Peter John Pearson, Peace and Justice Commission of the Catholic Church, Cape Town, September 1997)

There is a strong perception amongst white South Africans that the TRC is partial and as Hamber remarked, whites take the view that it is best 'to let sleeping dogs lie' (personal interview with Brandon Hamber, October 1997). The 'witch-hunt' thesis has been heavily exploited by the National Party and De Klerk. For many commentators, the National Party's submission to the Commission represented a lost opportunity to embed the process of reconciliation and national unity. Although the party acknowledged that apartheid had caused immeasurable pain and suffering, it failed to accept that it committed or sanctioned gross human rights violations such as torture, murder, rape or assault. De Klerk pedalled the 'one bad apple' theory in respect of state violence, and whilst admitting that 'bad judgement' and 'over zealousness' clouded certain security force operations, the National Party would not accept responsibility for actions indicating 'evil intent'. As a result of the party's defensive and 'Pontius Pilate' approach to the TRC, it followed that the white population would not be embracing reconciliation and national unity as exemplified by the TRC.

De Klerk had an historic opportunity to embrace reconciliation but he failed and that allowed white people to say "we weren't responsible – if De Klerk didn't know what was happening, then how could we have known". De Klerk did the country such a disservice.

(Interview with Patrick Kelly, TRC, Johannesburg, October 1997)

The words of Archbishop Tutu reflect the frustration felt both by the TRC and the black community in general towards the National Party's attitude to truth and reconciliation.

I am among the many that went to this government with information about the sort of things we are now investigating. There was almost an avalanche of information. To say that you [De Klerk] do not know what was happening, I find that difficult.

(Desmond Tutu, quoted in *The Guardian*, November 1997)

De Klerk's exit as leader of the National Party has not changed the party's view towards the Commission. The election of Marthinus van Schalkwyk as the new leader, failed to stem the tide of white hostility towards the workings of the Commission:

The whole process had all the potential to achieve reconciliation. But in practice it has been conducted in a way that is not regarded as even-handed by our supporters... We are very, very sorry for what we have done to other people. I think one would feel that if you are genuine, serious and honest in doing that sort of thing, it should at least be given serious consideration for acceptance... I think then there comes a point where one would start feeling like these people are not really interested in hearing us say we are sorry. What they are really interested in is to permanently put you in a position where a collective guilt complex is created ad infinitum, and where it is used as a political instrument of revenge instead of a real honest effort to look at the past and say how can we help it.

(Marthinus van Schalkwyk, Executive Director of the
National Party, quoted in Cantilevers, 1997: 13–14)

John Kane-Berman, chief executive of the South African Institute of Race Relations (SAIRR), has used the pages of *Frontiers of Freedom* to castigate the TRC at almost every turn. The thrust of his argument is that the TRC is attempting to 'saddle whites with feelings of collective guilt unless they make some sort of confession' (Kane-Berman, 1997: 1).

For Kane-Berman, whites did more than confess when they used their ballot in the March 1992 referenda to endorse negotiations with the ANC which was 'an act of bravery and statesmanship that not many countries experience. It was the act of the Afrikaner. And it did more for reconciliation than anything the Truth Commission has done' (Kane-Berman, 1997: 2). Kane-Berman initiated through the SAIRR a competition which sought entries to a competition entitled 'Best Confession to the Truth Commission'. Aside from the sardonic nature of the competition, the entries provided a telling insight into the growth of 'new white liberalism' which draws a distinction between whites supportive of apartheid and whites with general, liberal perspectives, neither supportive nor opposed to apartheid.

These feelings of collective guilt associated with the TRC have led to stress within the white community, identified by Venter (1997). The first 'new white stress' relates to the rising levels of crime which have gripped the country and the associated threats posed to personal safety and a questioning of the benefits of the new dispensation. The second stress relates to an escalation of alienation caused by radical social changes such as the introduction of different languages and relaxed attitudes to issues such as homosexuality, abortion and marriage. Both these factors have resulted in an antagonism amongst whites to the new political system, or a view that 'blacks can't govern'. The final stress is referred to as the 'Departing Monk Syndrome' and further compounds white attitudes to the new dispensation and the workings of the TRC:

> White South Africans are being effected more than ever before by something we might call the departing monk syndrome ... A monk stricken by acedia (depression or sloth) ... will begin to feel scorn and contempt for his brothers ... and he will begin to see far-off monasteries as places more conducive to accomplishment and well being ... It's when the monk leaves though that the interesting phenomena sets in. Those he leaves behind fall into a collective melancholia. Each brother asks himself: was the departing monk right? ... Were other places better and was it wise to enhance the soul by going there?
>
> (Venter, 1997: 171)

Since 1994, emigration has reached record proportions, particularly amongst English speaking whites, and this trend has hardened white liberal attitudes towards initiatives such as the TRC, affirmative action programmes and a range of reconstruction projects. The 'departing monk syndrome' has impacted most visibly on white attitudes to the TRC – the most public face of the reconciliation process. Pearson, paradoxically, remarked that although the TRC has been the prime target for white discomfort, whites fully believe that they are engaged in the reconciliation process:

> They [whites] think that they are going through a reconciliation process in that it is a 'far move from where they were'. But the 'reconciliation' process is not costing whites anything – there is nothing that they have to do – they believe that they are reconciling because they are tolerant of the new political dispensation and in some respects they almost expect to be patted on the back.
>
> (Personal interview with Peter John Pearson, Cape Town, Peace and Justice Commission of the Catholic Church, September 1997)

White attitudes can be disaggregated further between English speakers 'who are inheritors of the tradition of liberal thought' and those 'of the Afrikaner whose roots are firmly tied to Africa' (Venter, 1997: 171). The white English speakers criticise the TRC on the grounds that it offends their liberal heritage and that it is unfair to label them with the Afrikaner. As Duncan remarked,

> you won't be able to find an English speaking white who supported apartheid, 'of course we always opposed it', and since I was involved in the anti-apartheid movement, I know very well that is simply not true, absolutely not.
>
> (Personal interview with Sheena Duncan, Black Sash, October 1997)

The popular sentiment amongst the Afrikaner is that the TRC has scapegoated them, especially at the level of middle ranking police officers, and the commonly held view remains that 'they did what they had to do in order to fight revolutionary forces'. Neither community seems prepared to fully live up to the spirit of the TRC.

There can be no doubt, however, that the TRC has had a cathartic effect on the black population and it has allowed for an outpouring of grief and raw emotion throughout the length and breadth of South Africa. Hamber (1997a) evaluated the Psychological Support Services provided by the TRC, focusing specifically on the assistance given to individuals as part of what he describes as 'individual psychological restoration'. He found that the 'individual psychological impact [of the TRC]...has been extensive' (Hamber, 1997a: 3). In a very broad sense, the TRC has confirmed what the black population had always suspected, whereas the white population is either in denial or preferring not to know the true nature of apartheid. Although widely perceived by the black population as a mechanism for truth telling, a number of criticisms have emerged. McBride (1996) makes the point that at the local level people:

> really felt they had participated. They had said what was wrong in their town. People had heard it. It had been on the TV. Newspapers have been there. The people who didn't seem to understand how it was working were the amnesty commissioners – the people sitting in judgement who constantly told the crowd to keep quiet and not to participate. They tried to turn it into a courtroom, which it wasn't, because the people had already been sentenced.
>
> (McBride, 1996: 15)

In terms of measuring the 'success or impact' of the TRC a number of views were consistently aired within the black community. At one level, the black population measured impact according to the manner in which the TRC was endorsed by the white community. Their view was that there needed to be a dual process of advancement towards the reconciliation. At this level, the TRC has failed because whites refused to engage in the process. In addition, Hamber identified six core components of reconciliation which could be linked to measuring impact. Firstly, reconciliation required a state of 'peaceful coexistence'. He suggested progress had been made at this level, evidenced by the fall in the level of political violence. Nation building was the second key component and this was linked to the use of emblems and general communal pursuits which brought South Africans together. The Rugby World Cup represented an extraordinary example of nation building which has resulted in contributing to the state of peaceful coexistence. The third component refers to the process of acknowledging wrong doings and accepting that apartheid was a mistake. Hamber believed that the TRC had 'managed to do this on some levels but not all' and this has created a deep sense of disappointment within the non-white community:

> Whites have failed to see our good neighbourliness ... If we can go a mile to meet you, you have to go two.
>
> (Personal interview with Bheki Cele, ANC, Durban, October 1997)

The fourth and fifth components of reconciliation involved redress and restitution. For Hamber, the TRC has not dealt sufficiently with either issue and although a Reparations Committee was established, delivery lagged behind the initial enthusiasm generated by the TRC. There was a great deal of disquiet amongst the non-white population, for example, regarding the payment of reparations which was being provided for by the new administration and not by the perpetuators of violence. The final and most fundamental component of reconciliation related to the social, economic and political reconstructing of South African society. In this respect, the TRC remains marginal to the overall advancement of such a task.

> People will only be satisfied when their lot is improved and if that doesn't happen then there could be a regression backwards and then anger and revenge will emerge. Whenever basic needs are met then people become more creative and responsive and, with that, tolerance will flow but people's lives need to be improved.
>
> (Personal interview with Peter John Pearson, Cape Town, Peace and Justice Commission of the Catholic Church, September 1997)

The Reconstruction and Development Programme

As the name suggests, the Reconstruction and Development Programme (RDP) seeks to advance the reconciliation process through a tailored programme of activity.

> The fanfare which accompanied the RDP's arrival signalled – misleadingly – to many resource hungry NGOs, CBOs and communities that the RDP represented a new pot of gold and a new era of partnership with government. At the same time donors began to redirect funding from NGOs to the RDP office. The financial impact of this for many NGOs and CBOs has been disastrous.
>
> (Interfund, 1996: 12)

The RDP White Paper, which formed the basis of the ANC's policy programme in 1994, reminded readers that apartheid had distorted South African society to the extent that 'our income distribution ... ranks as one of the most unequal in the world ... Throughout, a combination of lavish wealth and abject poverty characterises our society'. In terms of problem areas that needed to be addressed, the RDP noted violence, lack of housing, lack of jobs, inadequate education and health care, lack of democracy and a failing economy. Five key programmes were identified – meeting basic needs; developing human resources; building the economy; democratising the state and society; and implementing the RDP. These were underpinned by the following principles: integration and sustainability; a people-driven process; peace and security for all; nation-building; linking reconstruction and development; and democratisation.

Significantly, the RDP has had to balance the aspirations of the improvised black majority whilst ensuring minimal economic loss of privileges within the white community. Civil servants, for example, were guaranteed postings within the new administration for at least five years and as Govender noted, 'it is these same civil servants who prevented development that are now trying to implement it' (Charm Govender, Centre for Community and Labour Studies, Durban). Interfund also noted that 'old practices and mind sets persist' (Interfund, 1996: 38). As with the TRC, the nature of the negotiation process and the compromise agreed has created a certain vacuum within the black community, which by and large, cannot point to tangible improvements in well being as a result of the transition. Indeed, within months of coming to power, the framers of the RDP, conscious of the need to dampen down black expectations on what was deliverable, readjusted key targets of the programme from five to twenty five years. The RDP, for example, had 'committed government to constructing 1 million low cost homes in five years' and in 1996 'only 11,000 had been built' (Interfund, 1996: 36). And in March 1996, 'in a move which surprised most political observers Mandela abolished the post of Minister without Portfolio and closed down the office of the RDP – which until then had functioned as a co-ordinating unit within the President's office'.

> The symbolic importance of the RDP office as representative of the government's commitment to development has meant that the closure is read as a signal that the government was now giving less visibility and focus to issues concerning development and more of a focus to the business of economics.
>
> (Interfund, 1996: 36)

The following discusses the main strengths and weaknesses of the RDP in practice, recognising that 'the post-apartheid reality has been a harsh testing ground for the RDP' (Interfund, 1996: 35).

Interfund's (1996) 'balance sheet review' of the RDP argued that the programme had failed to achieve its primary 'deliverable objectives'. The readjustment of targets and the closure of the RDP Office signified that the policy was faltering. The subsequent announcement of the government's macro economic plan Growth, Employment and Redistributive Strategy (GEAR) – which emphasised, inter alia, significant reductions in public spending, created a strong belief amongst NGOs that the principles of the RDP had been abandoned. As Archbishop Denis Hurley put it:

> I was very excited by the RDP … it was very much in harmony with Catholic social teaching. On the other hand, I was profoundly disappointed by GEAR, the government's new macro-economic policy. We now seem to be jumping on the same capitalist bandwagon as everyone else.
>
> (Hurley, 1997)

This situation was complicated further by the fact that international donor aid after 1994 was largely channelled to RDP structures rather than to grassroots organisations which created a funding crises within the NGO sector.

> Whether NGOs or CBOs, which provided key services to the disadvantaged in the apartheid era will be able to survive in the post apartheid era, will depend on the release of funds within the next few months. This will necessitate an urgent review of both international and local funders' priorities, as well as some mechanism to release government funds at a quicker rate.
>
> (Independent Development Trust, survey of 128 NGOs, 1995)

Although the Interfund report painted a largely pessimistic picture regarding deliverables, it pointed to process successes such as the restructuring of RDP sub-committees within Cabinet, the creation of inter-governmental forums and the establishment of provincial and regional planning offices to co-ordinate development activity and to report back to key departments (Interfund, 1996: 35). Yet the RDP's emphasis on partnership building between sectors and policy commitments to 'maintaining a vibrant civil society' through such processes as 'democratisation' and 'state building', remain at this point in time somewhat elusive.

Cameron (1996) criticised the practice of community participation through the RDP on a number of levels. First, because the concept of community participation is vague, there have been competing claims among civics to represent the community. This, in turn, has caused long delays given the range of groups which then have to be consulted. Second, the RDP forums could become a new bureaucracy with excessive red tape involved in processing applications from communities, adding to existing delays. Third, there is evidence that infighting in local RDP forums is slowing down the process of project approval. Finally, Cameron argued 'the RDP attempts to be both a top-down programme forcing agencies to reprioritise and a people-driven process. This is a contradiction and is causing tension' (Cameron, 1996: 239). Similarly, the Community Agency for Social Enquiry (CASE) found that 'only a small number of NGOs and CBOs had been involved in government sponsored projects and even fewer had been recipients of government funding' (CASE, 1997) in spite of claims that the RDP aimed to strengthen the links between the government and the voluntary sector. As Hofmeyr explained:

> Trying to raise funds for the NGO sector in the current funding climate is rather like trying to tango in the dark. You know your partner's out there somewhere, but finding her, let alone getting any sort of dance going, is nigh impossible.
>
> (Hofmeyr, quoted in CASE, 1996: 5)

Organisations involved in peace building have, like many other NGOs, struggled to obtain funding through RDP structures. The particular difficulty regarding the peace building network is that it is reliant on transient international donor aid. As Habib noted, attitudes to providing funding to South Africa have changed, 'it is now no longer glamorous to fund South African NGOs' (interviewed November 1997). Specifically, the general reduction in political violence has reduced the perceived need for conflict resolution work. Future funding priorities for peace building organisations in post-apartheid South Africa have been subject to review. Interfund and the Joseph Rowntree Foundation commissioned CASE (1995) to 'monitor the monitors'. In assessing the reasons for reviewing conflict resolution NGOs, CASE noted that:

> Violence seemed to be ebbing away ... the political terrain is dramatically different in the post election period. The country has a Bill of Rights which outlaws discrimination ... and for many observers, the motor forces of political violence have been removed.
>
> (CASE, 1995: 3)

The CASE review revealed that funders should encourage NGOs 'to charge for their services and to become as financially viable as possible' but 'funders should also accept that impoverished communities cannot be expected to pay for mediation or arbitration services' (CASE, 1995: 18). Yet no movement has been made by government to provide financial cover to vulnerable organisations and as a result, the sector has witnessed a reduction in the number of small to medium sized peace building NGOs. Significantly, RDP documentation and practice failed to make links between development work and the potential for conflict:

> It is usually assumed that development is a solution to conflict. While this may be so in the long term, our review indicates that in the short term development often contributes to conflict rather than alleviating it.
>
> (CASE, 1995: 26)

Kraak, writing in the preface to additional work undertaken by CASE (1996) on accessing RDP funds, wondered whether or not 'the time had come to sound the alarm bells':

> South Africa has one of the largest and most active civil societies in the world ranging from small grassroots organisations, community initiatives to large professional service organisations. There is scarcely a community in the country...where there is not some form of organisation – a civic association, a sewing group, a development forum or a youth forum organisation. Government has drawn many staff for some of its ministries from the larger, leading NGOs. It would be ironic indeed if this valuable resource were allowed to whither through official neglect with its potential role in helping secure social cohesion and to accelerate development.
>
> (CASE, 1996: 1)

In concluding his analysis, Kraak reminded the government of the rationale for funding and sustaining a 'vibrant NGO/CBO' sector:

- transforming ministerial bureaucracies inherited from apartheid is necessarily protracted and NGOs and CBOs are needed to fill the gap;
- government cannot meet all social needs;
- NGOs/CBOs are close to communities and thus, critically aware of community needs;

- NGOs/CBOs programmes are often innovative and experimental and can be piloted or mainstreamed; and
- NGOs/CBOs are important components of civil society and they are active in promoting rights and interests of communities.

The future

This chapter began by discussing and placing in context apartheid notions of 'peace', 'coexistence' and 'liberation'. The transition to democracy has resulted in the development of a new vocabulary based on 'reconstruction' and 'reconciliation'. Organisations involved in what we loosely defined as 'peace activity' have had to re-focus towards the needs of the new dispensation. The readjustment has not been smooth. Foreign donors have either redirected resources to the new administration, which has been dogged by problems of delivery, or developed 'exit strategies' in the mistaken belief that the conflict in South Africa has been resolved. What is clear, however, from this chapter, is that 'peace or conflict resolution NGOs' have evolved from the periphery of the 1980s – within Habib's 'magic moment' – to becoming important players in South Africa's civil society. Yet the future role of the 'peace network' remains complicated by the competing interests of the wider civil society as it grapples to fully develop relationships with the government. As Charm Govender remarked, 'the unity of networks created by apartheid has been replaced with competition over government resources' (personal interview with Charm Govender, Centre for Community and Labour Studies, October 1997).

In terms of future priorities, CASE (1995) identified the following funding gaps based on priority action areas. Table 7.3 draws together information collected on gaps and organisations which have created niche markets for their work.

NGOs have had to adjust to a changing political environment which has meant restructuring. There has been a growth in the number of organisations which undertake training sessions with police officers as a result of the creation of Community Policing Forums. The Centre for Conflict Resolution in Cape Town and the Independent Project Trust in Durban each provide, for example, training to police officers on conflict resolution/constitutional awareness and community relations. The role of church groups has, according to Duncan, diminished since the elections. Central players in the struggle against apartheid such as

Table 7.3 Conflict resolution activities

Funding gaps	Organisation	Activity/delivery mechanisms
Rural areas	Peace and Justice Commissions of the Catholic Church The Centre for Conflict Resolution	Community Outreach Programme Community Capacity Building Training
Domestic violence	Community Dispute Resolution Trust Quaker Peace Centre People Opposing Women Abuse	Alternative Justice Centres Direct Mediation and Intervention Outreach Counselling
Rehabilitation functions surrounding the TRC	Centre for the Study of Violence and Reconciliation Church Based Activities	Trauma Clinics and Policy Research Parish Based Mini-TRCs
Transforming prisons and police	Centre for the Study of Violence and Reconciliation Centre for Conflict Resolution	Criminal Justice Department Police Training Project
Legal representation of accused in court cases	Community Dispute Resolution Trust	Alternative Justice Centres
Industrial disputes	Independent Mediation Service of South Africa	Resolving workplace disputes
Primary school conflict management training programmes	Future Links South Africa Independent Project Trust	School Based Training in CR for teachers and pupils Peace Education and Education for Democracy Training
Psychological counsellors for poor communities	Justice and Peace Commission	Community Outreach Work
Informal settle – resident–local authority conflict liaison	Community Dispute Resolution Trust	Alternative Justice Centres
Conflicts over affirmative action	IMMSA	Workplace mediation

the South African Council of Churches have either 'withdrawn into themselves' (Duncan) or taken up new concerns and challenges. The Peace and Justice Commissions of the Catholic Church have re-focused from providing educational programmes on democracy and elections to highlighting economic justice issues, particularly in rural areas.

Duncan believes that church based groups need to re-emerge to 'fill the spiritual vacuum' which the NGO sector cannot address, particularly the emotions issues released within communities through TRC hearings. Some church communities have initiated mini-TRCs at the parish level. The following is an extract of the parish bulletin from St Martin's Anglican Church in Cape Town:

Before telling you about what happened to me with respect to the TRC you need to understand where I was at in terms of reconcilia-tion...In a nutshell – nowhere. In the past I voted for the old Democratic Party...just like a lot of other white English speaking South Africans. I never actually promoted apartheid principles, but equally never did anything about trying to dismantle those wrongs. As far as the TRC was concerned, it was for 'them', not for me. I per-ceived the TRC to be a huge witch hunt and certainly felt that there was little or no reconciliation taking place...but to hear Father Trevor (*the coloured minister of the parish*) ask for forgiveness for that which he believed he *hadn't* done (during the days of apartheid) was just amazing and the response of the congregation was that we asked Father Trevor for forgiveness.

(St Martin's Anglican Church Bulletin, 1997)

The Quaker Peace Centre in Cape Town has restructured programmes to include 'a new Reconciliation and Reconstruction Programme which aims to reconcile people of different opinions, faiths and cultures, and to bring them together through intervention and mediation in order to defuse tensions that might lead to conflict'. Duncan argued that reli-gious leaders at the national level must also start addressing the govern-ment on the issue of corruption, 'they must be saying to government you must set an example if you are going to expect citizens to take honesty seriously themselves'. A vast range of projects have been initi-ated by organisations focusing on school activity (Accord, Community Dispute Resolution Trust and the Independent Project Trust in Durban, Centre for Study of Violence and Reconciliation in Johannesburg and Futurelinks South Africa in Cape Town).

The key question to be asked of this sector is whether or not it has contributed to either reconstruction or reconciliation? Evidence gathered on the implementation of the TRC and the RDP suggest that both initiatives had limited success in achieving their macro level objectives. The TRC has not 'reconciled blacks and whites' and RDP has not alleviated economic hardship and poverty. However, the processes involved with both initiatives has created positive spin off at the micro level, emphasising further that peace building involves organic growth from top to bottom of society.

As to the future for reconciliation, it is perhaps appropriate to return to dissecting the new notions of 'peace' and 'coexistence'. Clearly, apartheid remains in the minds of both white and black South Africans for a variety of different reasons which have been identified in this chapter. White South Africans, uneasy with the levels of social change and the rising levels of crime, revert back to the virtues of apartheid when confronted with present day problems. Blacks, on the other hand, remain frustrated by the economic legacies of apartheid in which tangible benefits have not yet materialised. Currently, South Africa exists in a state of 'coexistence'. There seemed to be an acknowledgement that this represents the first stage towards reconciliation. Grassroots activity is, at present, almost exclusively concerned with intra-community development, principally through building black communities. The prospects for reconciliation remain difficult to assess. For Pearson, 'it is difficult to reconcile something that had never been together' (personal interview with Father P.J. Pearson, Cape Town). Closing or reconciling the political, economic and social chasm between the black and white population is a long way off. Whites and blacks, according to Johnston, continue to 'coexist in splendid isolation of each other'.

8
Conclusions:
Towards Peace Building

Introduction

This book began by setting the context for comparing Northern Ireland, Israel and South Africa through Lederach's conceptual framework of peace building. It is therefore apposite to return to this model in drawing conclusions from the empirical analysis in the previous chapters. To recap, Lederach argued that in conflict societies there is a short-term pre-occupation with political crises (the most immediate incident attracting media attention and political commentary) and a hierarchical approach to peace building dominated by political, military and religious elites (leaders with high visibility). He described this as the 'trickle-down' approach to peace in which 'the accomplishments at the highest level will translate to, and move down through, the rest of the population' (Lederach, 1997: 45). This produced a reactive and narrow approach respectively, unlikely to result in a sustainable peace. To achieve the latter, Lederach argues for a more organic model involving a broad-based constituency characterised by participation, responsibility for, and ownership of, the process of social change viewed as a long-term goal. Typically this constituency involves middle range and grassroots leaders. The former category comprises respected sectoral (business, education, agriculture, health) actors, network (religious, academic or humanitarian) stakeholders or those most closely associated with, but not politically affiliated to, ethnic groupings to the conflict. The latter category comprises local community groups and their leaders, and non-governmental organisations. Lederach argues that:

> the middle range holds the potential for helping to establish
> a relationship and skill-based infrastructure for sustaining the

peace-building process. A *middle-out approach* [our emphasis] builds on the idea that middle-range leaders (who are often the heads of, or closely connected to, extensive networks that cut across the lines of conflict) can be cultivated to play an instrumental role in working through the conflicts.

(Lederach, 1997: 51)

Political accommodation, in itself, is therefore viewed as a necessary but insufficient condition to move conflict societies from a state of transition, through transformation, and ultimately to reconciliation. This demands social, economic, socio-psychological and spiritual changes. True reconciliation, according to Lederach, requires a willingness to acknowledge truth and the past injustices – 'to remember and change'.

This book structured the country chapters to examine parallel political and grassroots or micro activities, in pursuance of Lederach's conceptual analysis of peace building. We have charted the attempts to agree a political accommodation in each of the three countries and concurrent micro developments which underpin the various efforts to achieve a 'resolution' to the conflicts. It is therefore appropriate to reflect on three key questions in this concluding chapter:

- What is the evidence, based upon the Lederach model and drawing from the case studies undertaken, that the three countries are actively engaged in peace building or, more specifically, moving from transition to reconciliation?
- Arising from this, what might usefully be learned on a cross-country or comparative basis to assist in peace building where there are obvious deficiencies in the process?
- Finally, having applied the Lederach model as the framework for analysis, how useful is it as a generic conceptual approach when considering peace building in diverse conflict societies?

Before turning to these three questions, however, it is perhaps useful to reconsider, as we pointed out in Chapter 1, the pitfalls in generalisations across the three countries whose positions on the peace process time line are different. Giliomee, in drawing comparisons between Northern Ireland, Israel and South Africa described it in this way:

No matter how carefully cases are selected for comparative analysis, it is essential not to lose sight of the fact that the selections are only imperfectly analogous. The validity of inferences drawn from comparison will depend as much upon sensitivity to dissimilarities as upon appreciation of similarities.

(Giliomee, 1990: 22–3)

This is an important reminder of the limitations in drawing sweeping conclusions on the basis of case study research carried out in the three countries yet, at the same time, accepting that comparative lessons can be learned within specified social, economic and political parameters.

Peace building at the macro level

From the case study evidence it seems obvious that there is a qualitative difference between Northern Ireland and South Africa, their involvement in peace building, and the circumstances in Israel. Perhaps one very general distinction might be the extent to which all three countries have been able to embed peace *and* reconciliation – the core of Lederach's model. To conjoin these terms could, however, be problematic. Peace and reconciliation may be non sequiturs. Wilson, for example, argues that in considering conflicts across Europe in the 1990s, 'peace has often been premised on ethnic separation, rather than on the construction of new relationships of comity between individuals and groups'. He differentiates between 'peace' premised on the notion that 'good fences makes good neighbours' and 'reconciliation'. The latter implies that those 'who have formerly lived apart in relationships of mutual suspicion will henceforth share in constructing, and then inhabiting, a common home – building trust along the way' (Wilson, 1998: 89).

The case study material clearly illustrates that Northern Ireland and South Africa have been involved through their top leadership in high-level negotiations with an emphasis on achieving a political accommodation, cease-fires and an end to political violence (level 1 of Lederach's model). Central to this process were the first multi-racial democratic elections within South Africa in April 1994, and approving an interim/final Constitution as the framework for the 'establishment of one sovereign state, a common South African citizenship and a democratic system of government committed to achieving equality between men and women and people of all races'.[27] This was referred to in Chapter 1 by one commentator as 'black South Africans did not defeat the white regime, they negotiated it out of office' or similarly by an editorial commentary following the adoption of the permanent constitution:

> South Africa's revolution has flown on the two wings of negotiation and equality. With the final constitution the first great phase of negotiated change has been completed in an exemplary, even a miraculous, fashion. Well might President Mandela greet the event by saying that "this is our national soul, our compact together as citizens". His government now has to face the contentious and divisive issues of race and class which hinge on equality rather than negotiation. It will be a greater challenge and a more searching test of the cohesive values entrenched in the constitution than any of the episodes that marked the transition from apartheid to democracy.
>
> (*The Irish Times* editorial, 9 May 1996)

Similarly in Northern Ireland, the Frameworks Document (1995) and the Peace Forum provided the basis for multi-party talks between the political parties which culminated in the Good Friday Agreement (1998). This was an agreement whose signatories, whilst recognising the tragedies of the past and the legacy of suffering left from 30 years of violent conflict, argued for a new beginning. 'We can best honour them (those who had died or been injured, and their families) through a fresh start, in which we firmly dedicate ourselves to the achievement of reconciliation, tolerance, and mutual trust, and to the protection and vindication of the human rights of all' (The Belfast Agreement, 10 April 1998, Declaration of Support: 1).

The language and deeds of reconciliation are less evident in the Wye Agreement (1998) between the Israelis and Palestinians. Although Wye is seen as an important agreement in the pursuit of 'final status' talks, it is nonetheless a phased measure with key issues yet to be resolved (Jerusalem, refugees, borders with, and withdrawals from, the West Bank). What is clear thus far, however, is that according to Wilson's definition above, the process in Israel is about 'making peace' rather than Lederach's more constructive 'peace building' and ultimately reconciliation. This kind of thinking is best described by the Israeli Ambassador in Ireland who commented:

> This Agreement [Wye], which is based upon the principles of security and reciprocity, has reduced the dangers both to Israelis and Palestinians, as well as paving the way *for peaceful coexistence* [our emphasis]. However, it will depend on whether or not all the details

of the accord are carried out faithfully. Israel desires peace and wants the agreement to succeed ... The Palestinian side must fulfil its obligations to fight terrorism. If the threat of terror is left unchecked, the newly signed accord will not survive.

(Zvi Gabay, 1998)

Israeli critics suggested that Netanyahu could simply sit back and wait on the inevitable Hamas-led terrorist incidents to occur which would vindicate his attempts to make peace, but turn Jewish public opinion against the Agreement – a win–win strategy on his part. Hence, when a suicide car bomb, the Hamas response to Wye, exploded in a Jerusalem market (6 November 1998), killing the two Palestinian bombers and injuring 21 people, the Israeli government was quick to seize the opportunity by threatening to suspend the peace process.

This contrasts starkly with events in Northern Ireland when the worst-ever terrorist atrocity was perpetrated by the dissident group, the so-called Real IRA. On 15 August 1998 a car bomb ripped through the heart of a small rural town, Omagh, killing 29 and injuring 220 innocent men, women and children. Media reports described the incident as 'tearing a bloody hole in the peace process' (*The Guardian*, 15 August 1998). Yet the worst single atrocity in the 30 years of the Northern Ireland troubles served only to strengthen the resolve of political negotiators. They (the British Government, Unionists, Nationalists and, without precedent, Sinn Féin) denounced the bombers and insisted their actions would not derail the peace deal. As one commentator put it 'a just peace is no guarantee against terrorism, but it is the very best there is' (*The Economist*, 24 October 1998). The implementation of the Good Friday Agreement continued with a significant breakthrough coming on 18 December 1998 when six new North–South administrative bodies and 10 government departments were agreed. The comparison with Israel was described thus:

The Israeli Prime Minister's behaviour in the wake of the Jerusalem attack is in stark contrast to the way the various parties reacted to the grisly bombing at Omagh several weeks after the Good Friday peace deal was signed in Northern Ireland ... The patient process of setting up institutions which the Good Friday Agreement required, carried on regardless. In Israel, regrettably, the constituency for peace has never been as strong as in Northern Ireland. Even before Mr Netanyahu the governing parties were ultra-cautious about ceding land or accepting Palestinian rights. But under Yitzhak Rabin the

Labour Party had started a new approach. Mr Netanyahu never agreed with it, and his stubborn actions yesterday show he is determined not to change soon. Caught between the rage of the Palestinians and the intransigence of its own short-sighted government, Israel's insecurity is doomed to go on.

(Leader article, *The Guardian*, 7 November 1998)

The actions of the Israeli Government also do little to suggest 'peaceful coexistence', not to mention 'reconciliation'. The foreign minister, Ariel Sharon, wanted to bulldoze a new bypass road for Jewish settlers through cultivated Palestinian land near Hebron. Following Wye, and in anticipation of withdrawal, a number of Jewish settlers in the West Bank seized hilltops adjoining their developments and installed caravan homes with apparent Israeli army condonation. Israel also called for tenders (12 November 1998) to build 1000 homes in Har Homa, the Arab East Jerusalem contested site. Such actions are hardly those of conciliators.

Is the process organic?

Lederach has argued that the process of peace building must be organic in nature. No one level in the pyramid of actors is capable of delivering sustainable peace. Having considered activity at the macro level, what does the case-study material suggest for each of the three countries in terms of involvement by middle range leaders and non-governmental activity? In other words, what evidence is there that peace building activity is organic in Northern Ireland, Israel and South Africa?

Northern Ireland

The material uncovered in Chapter 3 suggests that grassroots activity in the Northern Ireland context is dominated by UK Government funded programmes (e.g. Education for Mutual Understanding, district councils community relations programme). Although there is a thriving NGO sector (referred to as the voluntary and community sector) in Northern Ireland, those grassroots organisations involved in peace building and conflict resolution work tend to receive funding via government sources (the Central Community Relations Unit; Community Relations Council). As a result, there is some suspicion about the motives of the UK Government as a funder and, at the same time, protagonist to the conflict. Strictly defined, therefore, few *non-governmental* organisations are engaged in peace building in Northern Ireland. The direct involvement of the European Union in funding grassroots activity has tended to 'neutralise' this process. Hence the European Special Support Programme for Peace and Reconciliation has been able to assist a variety of community based peace building work, particularly through the mechanisms of district partnerships (Hughes, Knox, Murray and Greer, 1998).

Evidence also exists of the ineffectual nature of peace movements and women's groups in Northern Ireland and the ambivalent attitude of the churches to direct involvement in peace building. The relatively few clerical peace activists, somewhat surprisingly, after 30 years of violence, see this task as, only now, important. One Catholic priest, well-known for his community-based work, wrote:

> A major task for clergy in Northern Ireland is to be leaders in the struggle for reconciliation, and its co-relative, justice. It is vital *we begin* [our emphasis] to see this work of peace-making as the most important part of our calling... But reconciliation work with groups that we may resent, or even not feel confident with, is not easy. Clergy are not statues. We are human beings with our own inadequacies, failures and fears. Reconciliation and justice work in Northern Ireland is particularly difficult.
>
> (Lennon, 1995: 104–5)

There is also little evidence of direct involvement in peace building from 'middle range' leaders. The business sector in Northern Ireland, for example, has tended to make statements supportive of political progress in the knowledge that instability damages the economy – beyond that, they have not gone. Even the expansion of the Catholic middle class, largely associated with a significant increase in participation in higher education, has not produced obvious 'middle range' communitarians prepared to tackle disparities, most notably that Catholics still experience rates of unemployment over twice as high as Protestants (Osborne, 1996). All this points to a relatively low level of 'middle range' activity which has had mixed success in peace building efforts in Northern Ireland. The vibrant voluntary/community sector directed their efforts at filling the 'democratic deficit' left by the absence of devolved government and the imposition of Direct Rule in Northern Ireland. Grassroots programmes were seen by some critics as part of a government plot to woo Unionists into a United Ireland, at best, or as means of community integration, at worst. The recent involvement by Europe in supporting grassroots activity has however created a more positive momentum for peace building.

The Good Friday Agreement makes provision for a Civic Forum which recognises the value of a more inclusive form of decision making and builds upon the success of the European programmes by widening the democratic base. The consultative Civic Forum will comprise representatives of business, trade union and voluntary sectors, and such sectors as agreed by the First Minister and Deputy First Minister. It will act as a consultative mechanism on social, economic and cultural issues (Belfast Agreement, 1998: Strand One: section 34). The Civic Forum is therefore a means of harnessing the energy and talents of civic society and engaging people in a process which seeks to broaden the parameters of participative democracy (North West Community Network, 1998). Its aim is to give a voice to those who have been excluded from decision-making in the more traditional forms of government and, in that sense, could contribute to Lederach's notion of an organic approach to peace building or, at the very least, prevent the politicians, through its challenge and oversight roles, from returning to sectarian-type.

Israel

The research in Chapter 5, given the nature of the Israeli case-study, differentiated grassroots activity into two broad categories – co-existence work between the Jewish and Palestinian citizens of Israel, and peace activity between Israelis and Palestinians living in the lands occupied after 1967. The Jewish agenda for co-existence is seen as a programme to achieve Palestinian acquiescence or as Smooha (1990) described it 'the containment of restive and dissident Arabs'. Educational encounter programmes to improve relationships excluded key questions of disadvantage and inequality suffered by Israeli Arabs and the power relationship favoured Jews in these activities. As a reaction to the lack of success with these programmes the Israeli Arab population sought to influence grassroots activity which encouraged dialogue and encounters but, importantly, provided support for an equality agenda (e.g. New Israel Fund; Centre for Jewish Arab Economic Development). The scope of this work has been limited by lack of resources and overall control exercised by the Israelis who are wary that Arab empowerment could ultimately pose a threat to the state.

The Israeli peace movement, most prominently represented by Peace Now activities (demonstrations, peace vigils, lobbying and dialogue work), tried to influence government policy towards a resolution of the conflict based upon mutual recognition of rights and a 'land for peace' deal. The Oslo Agreement was seen as the successful culmination of their efforts after which, in the majority view, their raison d'être no longer existed. This position reflects the more dominant 'self-interest' wing within the peace movement whose motivation for involvement was to promote Israel's long-term security as opposed to those whose active participation was based on the moral and human rights issues of Palestinians. Once Oslo was secured the former regarded the job as done. Although the election of Likud (May 1996) witnessed a revival of peace demonstrations against issues such as Hebron and Har Homa, it was evident the movement had been sidelined by political events. Likud's credentials as 'pro-peace' were somewhat doubtful as the peace movement faltered.

Within the occupied territories 'peace' equated to the ending of occupation and peace activism translated into defying the occupation and the fight for human rights, best captured by the comment – 'Palestinians were not afforded the luxury of a peace movement'. To achieve these goals a strong NGO network developed aimed at 'out-administering' the enemy. As Shain and Sussman noted:

> Under Israeli occupation the Palestinians developed an elaborate chain of civil society agents, including charitable associations, voluntary organisations and other NGO actors. Palestinian civil society actors have developed primarily as a form of opposition to Israeli occupation, sometimes with Israel's own blessing and short-sightedness (as in the case of Hamas). By rivalling and supplementing the limited services provided by Israeli civil administration, many NGOs evolved into a 'parallel society' that gradually undermined Israeli occupation.
>
> (Shain and Sussman, 1998: 285)

Aside from the objective of ending occupation, Longland has argued that the absence of an autonomous Palestinian government in the West Bank and Gaza Strip created the space for a range of organisations to grow which 'have shown vision, energy and effectiveness of high order in health, agriculture, education, human rights and research' (Longland, 1994: 132). This, he suggests, relieved Israel, which had a responsibility as the occupying power under the terms of the Fourth Geneva Convention, of continued development of the population. Services were provided by NGOs without imposing a burden on the Israeli exchequer. Little of the Palestinian NGO activity could therefore be described as peace building since the focus is on intra-Palestinian issues. There is also a reluctance to dialogue with Israelis as this would merely 'normalise the abnormal'. Until such times as the core political grievances of Palestinians can be 'resolved' limited motivation exists for peace building activities at grassroots level.

Overall, therefore, what NGO activity exists within Israel and the Occupied Territories is to support Jewish hegemony in the former or to resist Israeli occupation in the latter. Neither provides evidence of a genuine organic approach to peace building, nor have events at the macro level encouraged such grassroots activity to take place.

South Africa

A number of initiatives developed during the struggle against apartheid which demonstrated the effective involvement of both 'middle range' leaders and grassroots activity. The churches in particular (South African Council of Churches and the Southern Africa Bishops) played a key role, with high profile activists such as Bishop Desmond Tutu, Beyers Naude and Allan Boesak to the fore. Other key players included the Congress of South African Trade Unions, the South African National Civic Organisation, the Black Sash and the United Democratic Front. The National Peace Accord (signed in September 1991 with the slogan *Peace Now – Not Another Death Later*), for example, originated as a result of the concerns of church leaders (General Secretary of the South African Council of Churches, Dutch Reformed Church [the apartheid church] and representatives of the Jewish and Muslim communities) and business leaders who met the President to discuss the level of violence in South Africa and ways of dealing with it. From this a joint committee comprising representatives of the government, the ANC and Inkatha emerged with the task of preparing peace proposals, which, in turn, led to the signing of the National Peace Accord.

The Accord aimed to provide ways to end violence by establishing a National Peace Committee for the purposes of implementing the Accord; a National Peace Secretariat to set up and co-ordinate dispute resolution committees at local and regional level; a code of conduct for political parties and organisations; codes of conduct for the police and the South African Defence Force; measures for community-building; a commission of inquiry to investigate cases of violence and intimidation; justices of the peace and special courts. The National Peace Committee was chaired by church or business community leaders with representatives from the largest political parties and its role was to ensure political parties adhered to the code of conduct, which committed each party to respect the right of people to vote freely and without intimidation and of parties to organise freely.[28]

The regional and local peace structures, referred to initially as local conflict resolution committees and subsequently local peace committees (of which there were 125 by October 1993), were a forum which brought together representatives from political organisations, churches, trade unions, industry and business, local and tribal authorities and police and defence forces. Other civic organisations, resident committees and local government were also represented. Their role was to settle disputes at grassroots level by a process of consultation and negotiation so that violence and intimidation were avoided. Local peace committees were also involved in securing agreement for, and monitoring/stewarding peace rallies and marches. As one commentator noted:

> The Peace Accord structures were demonstrating their value, even though political violence continued and in some areas the local structures were ineffective. Even so, the wide range of participants in the committees exposed many people to participatory decision-making for the first time.
>
> (Trevor Jepson, cited by Noreen Christian, 1995)

There was a large degree of flexibility in the composition of local peace structures to suit local circumstances with the aim of achieving optimal legitimacy within communities. This extended to the inclusion in some areas of traditional leaders, tribal elders and women's groups to bring both an independence and authority to the committees. Lederach's notion of an organic approach to building peace is captured by Williams writing about the 'constructive and encouraging attempts at building peace structures in South Africa against a background of political change':

> Care must be taken that structures [peace committees] do not use up, cavalierly, this hard-won grass-roots credibility. And what is needed next is a way to weave together the two strands, national authority coming down from the top, and local credibility coming up from the grass-roots, into a strong structure that can go beyond peacemaking to peace-building.
>
> (Williams, 1993: 4)

Lederach himself refers to the National Peace Accord as emerging from the rubric of formal negotiations between top-level leaders which 'set in motion a process of transition and socio-political transformation that specifically contemplated numerous levels of activity across society' (1997: 51). What must be remembered, however, according to Shaw, is that most peace structures in South Africa were established from the top downwards and were criticised by local peace committees as being devised to make life safe for business and the establishment (Shaw, cited by Field, 1995).

The Reconstruction and Development Programme (RDP) was another key initiative which institutionalised an organic approach to peace building in South Africa. The RDP was a coherent socio-economic framework which attempted to integrate development, reconstruction, redistribution and reconciliation into a unified programme to fundamentally transform South Africa. The RDP five key programmes (meeting basic needs; developing human resources; building the economy; democratising the state and society; and implementing the RDP) were underpinned by the following principles: integration and sustainability; a people-driven process; peace and security for all; nation-building; linking reconstruction and development; and democratisation. What is clear from this is that the RDP required inclusiveness through widespread consultation and participation. The mechanisms to achieve this were provincial and regional local forums set up specifically for this task and the National Economic Development and Labour Council comprising trade unions, business, civics and government representatives. NGOs could also avail of capacity building to allow them to participate fully in the RDP.

Aside from negative evaluations of the effectiveness of the RDP, which is not the focus of attention here, there has been criticism of community participation in practice. Because the concept of community participation is vague, there have been competing claims among civics to represent the community. This, in turn, has caused long delays given the range of groups which then have to be consulted. Secondly, the RDP forums could become a new bureaucracy with excessive red tape involved in processing applications from communities, adding to existing delays. Finally, there is evidence that infighting in local RDP forums is slowing down the process of project approval. Cameron argues 'the RDP attempts to be both a top-down programme forcing agencies to reprioritise and a people-driven process. This is a contradiction and is causing tension' (Cameron, 1996: 239). This highlights, in a general sense, one of the challenges of Lederach's organic model, that of 'moving beyond a hierarchical focus' towards a broad-based approach where each level in the pyramid of actors is interdependent rather than a process dominated by one sector (top, middle range or grassroots leadership).

Notwithstanding some of the criticisms of the involvement of 'middle range' and grassroots leaders, what is clear from the analysis of micro activity is that they were instrumental in the demise of apartheid. Rupert Taylor describes it thus:

> Amongst the social forces that made for peace, for creating the 'new' South Africa, were the innovative actions of an ever increasing network of progressive movements, institutions, non-governmental organisations, and associations (which included churches, trade unions, civics, and women's groups) engaged in a 'war of position' against apartheid rule. This network of anti-apartheid organisations created an alternative space outside distorted and limited binary racial thinking, seeking to undercut the apartheid state's reification of 'race' and 'ethnicity', and promote the idea of a common society. This pushed the conflict away from a 'black'/'white' racial form towards a non-racial perspective... In South Africa, more and more people decided and chose to actively co-operate to transform society, and in so doing transform themselves.
>
> (Taylor, 1999)

The problem is, having achieved the goal of dismantling apartheid, what is their current role? This, to some extent, reflects the 'Peace Now' position in Israel which secured land-for-peace as an integral part of the political process, in the case of Israel; or Palestinian NGOs set up to challenge occupation which now feel displaced by the PNA whose power base is local social elites and PLO exile returnees (Shain and Sussman, 1998). Having achieved their stated goals civic society is in a state of flux. This has also been accompanied, in the case of South Africa, by a significant loss of resources to the sector from international donors who prefer to redirect towards assisting the new democratic state. The situation is worsened by a loss or movement of personnel from the NGO sector to government employment. This dilemma is neatly described by Diescho:

> After ushering in a new freely elected democratic government ... the *raison d'être* of the more than one thousand NGOs in South Africa is virtually no more, their primary objective, that of bringing down the apartheid state, having been achieved. It becomes impossible to

continue a fight without an enemy, even more difficult, an enemy that was resoundingly defeated.

(Diescho, 1997: 13)

Diescho sets out the future challenges for NGOs within the new political environment – constructive disagreement with the state/government, inter-sectoral work with other NGOs to tackle problems such as escalating violence and crime, and the creation of a value system (sharing, compassion, empathy and sympathy, service and the desire to empower others to help themselves) around which pockets of civil society can coalesce.

Transition–transformation–reconciliation

The above summary provides us with some insights into how organic, interdependent and inclusive the process of peace building is but, of itself, is an incomplete analysis. We now turn to the third and final stage in the Lederach model to conclude our assessment of how active the three countries are in peace building. Here Lederach argues that there is a need to move from transition, through transformation, to reconciliation in order to achieve a sustainable peace. Transition and transformation will require a concentration on socio-economic and socio-political factors (e.g. financial aid, retraining, employment, development; and demobilisation, disarmament, integrating troops, professionalisation, respectively). This, he suggests, tends to be the level of focus which is clearly necessary, but insufficient. To move beyond this requires attention to socio-psychological and spiritual issues (e.g. identity, self esteem, grief process, trauma; and healing, encounter (self and other), acknowledge, forgive, respectively). Reconciliation is therefore about rebuilding relationships. This, according to Lederach, involves 'a willingness to acknowledge truth and the pains of injustice experiences and an openness to offer and accept forgiveness. That is, to start a new relationship' (Lederach, 1996: 52). How far therefore have Northern Ireland, Israel and South Africa moved along the continuum of transition, transformation and reconciliation in their quest for lasting peace?

Northern Ireland

It is undoubtedly the case that Northern Ireland has, until recently, been located in the phases of transition and transformation. A comprehensive and improving equality and equity agenda is in place reaffirmed most recently by the terms of the Good Friday Agreement. Measures therein include a new regional strategy for Northern Ireland which tackles the problems of a divided society and social cohesion in urban, rural and border areas; a new economic development strategy; the extension and strengthening of anti-discrimination legislation and a new Targeting Social Need initiative aimed at combating unemployment and progressively eliminating the differential in unemployment rates between the two communities by targeting objective need (The Belfast Agreement 1998: Rights, Safeguards and Equality of Opportunity, section 2: 19). Set alongside these socio-economic measures the Good Friday Agreement, as outlined in Chapter 1, also made provision for the decommissioning of terrorist weapons, an accelerated programme for the release of prisoners, and a review of policing and the criminal justice system. Typically, these represent what Lederach has termed socio-political factors and locate Northern Ireland in the realms of transition–transformation.

What has moved Northern Ireland, at least in part, towards the reconciliation phase is the attention now being given to the victims of violence. In November 1997 the government set up a Commission to 'examine the feasibility of providing greater recognition for those who have become victims in the last thirty years as a consequence of events in Northern Ireland' (Victims Commission: Terms of Reference: 18). The significance of this work was further highlighted in the Good Friday Agreement which makes specific reference to 'reconciliation and victims of violence':

> The participants [to the Agreement] believe that it is essential to acknowledge and address the suffering of the victims of violence as a necessary element of reconciliation ... It is recognised that victims have the right to remember as well as to contribute to a changed society. The achievement of a peaceful and just society would be a true memorial to the victims of violence ... The participants recognise and value the work being done by many organisations to develop reconciliation and mutual understanding and respect between and within communities and traditions, in Northern Ireland and between North and South, and they see such work as having a vital role in consolidating peace and political agreement.
>
> (The Belfast Agreement, 1998; Reconciliation and
> Victims of Violence, sections 11–13: 18)

The government has followed through on the Good Friday Agreement commitment by implementing a number of recommendations arising from the Victims Commission Report (*We Will Remember Them*), referred to in Chapter 1. Aside from the establishment of a dedicated Victims

Liaison Unit within government to implement agreed measures, a Survivors of Trauma Centre has been opened, a bursary scheme (£250,000) set up to provide educational assistance to children and young adults who lost a parent in the conflict, a Memorial Fund (£1 m on a matching funds basis from overseas contribution) put in place to provide support for victims who suffer financial hardship, and additional befriending and support services (£60,000) offered. All of this amounts to a comprehensive package of support to victims of violence. Although these have been grudgingly received in some quarters as the necessary price to be paid to gain public acceptance of the more unpalatable parts of the Agreement (prisoner releases in particular), this initiative clearly deals with the socio-psychological factors in Lederach's web of reconciliation.

What is striking, however, is that the Victims Commissioner Report stopped short of recommending the equivalent of a South Africa's Truth and Reconciliation Commission for Northern Ireland arguing that 'it would only be useful, non-divisive, healing and an acceptable instrument if those who are to carry our future forward agree that it can serve such a purpose' (Bloomfield, 1998: 52). The Commissioner concluded this even in the face of forceful submissions to him from groups representing victims of "state terrorism" (e.g. Bloody Sunday, the events in Gibraltar). They argued that the revelation of the full truth of controversial events was far more important for the victims they represented than any other consideration. The Victims Commissioner concluded:

> It has to be appreciated that while some in our society are talking of amnesty and general gaol delivery, others are arguing that their sufferings can best be recognised through condign punishment visited upon the perpetrators. A clear approach to truth may demand the corollary of reconciliation. Unhappily "truth" can be used as a weapon as well as a shield. If any such device [refers to Truth Commission] were to have a place in the life of Northern Ireland, it could only be in the context of a wide-ranging political accord.
>
> (Bloomfield, 1998: 38)

This is perhaps evidence of the fact that Northern Ireland has yet to fully embrace the spiritual component of reconciliation.

Israel

Israel's location on the transition–transformation–reconciliation continuum is in stark contrast to that of Northern Ireland. Arguably Israel has not yet reached the transition process, still less moving beyond this stage. Little real attention has been paid by Israelis to socio-economic or socio-political factors, not helped by a moribund political process which lurches from crisis to crisis. The plight of Israeli Arabs, in particular those living in East Jerusalem (but not exclusively so), illustrates the major inequalities and socio-economic disparities which provide little optimism in the search for evidence of reconciliation

Jerusalem is one of the most emotive issues in the conflict between Israel and the Arabs, not least because of the significance of its holy sites such as the Dome of the Rock and al Aqsa Mosque, the Western Wall of the ancient Jewish Temple and the Church of the Holy Sepulchre for Muslims, Jews and Christians respectively. During the 1967 Arab-Israeli Six Day War the Israelis seized East Jerusalem from Jordan, expanded its boundaries to include large tracts of land that were part of the West Bank and extended Israeli laws to Greater East Jerusalem. More recently (June 1998) the Likud Government produced a plan to extend Jerusalem's boundaries to the west, seen by the Palestinians as creeping annexation of the West Bank. Netanyahu argued that the purpose of the plan was not political but to create an expanded 'umbrella municipality' with improved services which would attract more investment, tax revenue and industry. Palestinians saw the plan as a municipal ruse which was drawn up in response to a study showing that Jerusalem's Palestinian community would grow to 45 per cent of the city's population by 2020. Redrawing the boundaries would mean a demographic mix of 70 per cent Jews and 30 per cent Arabs in the new municipal area by 2020, a slight increase on the current 29 per cent, with Palestinians accounting for 180,000 of Jerusalem's 630,000 residents (*The Guardian*, 23 June 1998). Palestinian critics accused the Israelis of trying to create 'facts on the ground' in advance of final status talks and a reaffirmation of Likud and Labour's position that Jerusalem is Israel's 'eternal and indivisible capital'.

This kind of gerrymandering is only the latest example of abuse perpetrated by Israelis on the Palestinians. A B'tselem study (the Israeli human rights group) found 'that since 1967 Israeli governments, of whatever sort, had pursued policies of systematic discrimination against Jerusalem's Palestinians. The central goal was to strengthen Israeli control throughout the city' (*The Economist*, 23 November 1996). This was evidenced by Palestinian dispossession under Israeli annexation when around 35 per cent of the 17,500 acres to enlarge Jerusalem (mainly privately owned) was expropriated and turned over to Israeli ownership. The Israeli authorities then built 38,500 dwellings to establish exclusive Jewish neighbourhoods in East Jerusalem. The obvious consequence is a severe housing shortage for Palestinians, three quarters of whom live in sub-standard and overcrowded conditions. Even those who can afford to build are restricted by planning rules which have zoned large areas of the city as green space, although this appears flexible for Jewish housing projects. Israeli law defines Jerusalem's Palestinians not as citizens but as 'permanent residents of Israel'. Their status can be forfeited under Israeli law if they live outside Israel or the Occupied Territories for longer that seven years or if they take foreign citizenship.

This kind of discrimination is not confined to Jerusalem's Palestinians but is widespread for Israeli Arabs. Although Israel's Declaration of Independence promised 'complete equality of social and political rights to all inhabitants irrespective of religion, race or sex', Israeli Arabs have never achieved social and economic equality. Although they make up only a fifth of the population, Arabs account for about half of those below the poverty line in Israel. On education, health and housing and all other social indicators, they lag well behind Israeli Jews. Hashem Mahameed, an Arab member of the Knesset, points out that the income of an Arab Israeli is half that of his (*sic*) Jewish counterpart and he is twice as likely to be unemployed. His towns will be relatively deprived of hospitals, factories and infrastructure and his children are three times as likely to drop out of school (Appleyard, 1998).

> In mitigation, some Israelis argue that Israel's Arabs are an underclass trapped in a cycle of deprivation, not victims of social discrimination or purposeful neglect by the state... In absolute terms their standard of living has risen rapidly over the past half-century. But their relative deprivation is well documented. And whereas other countries have made strenuous to redress such inequalities, Israel has undertaken no serious programme of affirmative action for Arabs. On the contrary, many features of the political and legal system seem almost to have been calculated to perpetuate the Arabs' disadvantage.
>
> (*The Economist*, 25 April 1998)

Israeli Arabs find themselves in an invidious position. They are seen by fellow Palestinians in the West Bank and Gaza as having accepted the process of "Israelisation" and although they share their aspirations for an independent Palestinian state will stay in Israel hoping to become more equal citizens. They are seen by Israelis, on the other hand, as fifth columnists unwillingly to commit their loyalty unequivocally to the state and certainly not to be trusted. Because they do not serve in the army, Arabs do not qualify for many welfare benefits linked to army service. They are unwelcome in defence-related jobs which represent a big proportion of the economy. One commentator described it thus: '"Security" is used as an elastic pretext for discrimination ... It is difficult to reconcile the proposition that Arabs can never be fully trusted with the claim that they are full and equal citizens' (*The Economist*, 25 April 1998). The treatment of Israeli Arabs is a good indicator of just how serious Israelis are to move the conflict with Palestinians more generally (including the Occupied Territories) through a process of transition, transformation and reconciliation. The evidence suggests they have not begun.

South Africa

If Northern Ireland is making some progress towards reconciliation and, by comparison, Israel relatively little, the evidence from South Africa presents a mixed picture. On the one hand, there are major socio-economic disparities to be addressed by the ANC, yet simultaneously the Truth and Reconciliation Report attempts to tackle the spiritual/healing component in Lederach's model. Reference in Chapter 1 to Mandela's vision for the attainment of a democratic, non-racial, non-sexist, peaceful and prosperous South Africa could be described as an operational plan to achieve reconciliation. Therein Mandela refers to 4 core issues to be tackled:

- national reconciliation and nation unity – the need for blacks and whites to live together as equals;
- the establishment of a democratic system which ensured all citizens have an equal right and equal possibility to determine their future;
- an end to the enormous race and gender disparities in wealth, income and opportunity;
- a need to rebuild and modernise the economy and set it on a high, sustainable growth path to end poverty, unemployment and backwardness.

When this is overlaid with the Truth and Reconciliation Commission, the component parts of Lederach's web of reconciliation (socio-economic, socio-political, socio-psychological and spiritual) are comprehensively set in place.

That the strategic vision and operational plan are in existence in South Africa is laudable, the problem, however, given the scale of the task, is in its implementation. As one commentator put it: 'Four years after democracy came to South Africa, the euphoria is spent. The ANC government has brought clean water to the townships, handed out housing subsidies, laid telephone lines. But plastic-shack poverty is still widespread. A third of the workforce is out of work' (*The Economist*, 31 October 1998). The average white wage is still five times the average black one, and even allowing for differences in skills and experience, the World Bank estimates whites are paid twice as much as blacks. Tackling this level of inequality and the endemic black poverty cannot be achieved in the short-run but expectations levels were unrealistically raised in April 1994, perhaps through a combination of political naiveté and popular euphoria. As reality has dawned, so too has a sense of disillusionment. Among unskilled rural black women, for example, formal unemployment is 70 per cent and there is despair in the wider unemployed population, which is rising by 1–2 per cent per year, that they will never work legally.

The other central tenet in peace building, the Truth and Reconciliation Commission, has provoked mixed reactions. The key question is whether this approach to uncovering the truth contributed to the objective of reconciliation intended by the post-apartheid government which established it? Mary Burton, one of the TRC's commissioners, remarked:

> Sometimes, we can say with honesty and humility, the generosity of forgiveness has astonished us all. Sometimes, at least, speaking out has provided a kind of catharsis, or perhaps a safe channel for long submerged anger. The right to be heard and acknowledged, with respect and empathy, did contribute to a process of healing in many cases … Much work remains to be done, however, before reconciliation on any major scale can be achieved.
>
> (Burton, 1998: 22)

The converse position is put by Alex Duval Smith[29] when he wrote that after two and a half years of being 'lead though collective therapy, no one in the still-divided South Africa pretends that either truth or reconciliation has been achieved' (Duval Smith, 1998). Interestingly, however, the Justice Minister (Dullah Omar) said the task of reconciliation should not be institutionalised within the TRC, which was not its function. Reconciliation, he claimed, was the duty of every South African.

Whether the TRC has, or has not, contributed to healing and reconciliation may soon be eclipsed by the political ramifications of its findings. The report is expected to provoke a flood of civil and criminal claims against perpetrators who either were not granted amnesty by the TRC or who never applied for it. This includes Inkatha Freedom Party leader Chief Mangosuthu Buthelezi 'the foremost perpetrator of gross human rights violations', according to the report, and all his party members who boycotted the commission. In the interests of electoral expediency (summer 1999) the ANC is coming under pressure to grant a general amnesty so that Buthelezi and his supporters are not subjected to a series of 'Nuremberg trials' when it would be more advantageous to foster an alliance with the IFP. The major problem is that to decree a general amnesty would completely undermine everything the TRC has tried to do. The process of community healing may be superseded by the impetus to forge a political confederation.

A summary of the peace building approaches in each of the three countries is set out in Table 8.1.

Conclusions

In conclusion we make three key points. First, what can be said about the status of peace building in Northern Ireland, Israel and South Africa with the benefit of Lederach's framework of analysis presented above? This question can probably only be answered with another question which is, what kind of peace building is required – an integrated or separated peace? Therein lies some comparative ambiguities or differences. In Northern Ireland, for example, there are proponents of both approaches. Consociationalists,[30] for example, according to Taylor:

> work with and solidify intra-communal networks, rather than being concerned to promote intercommunal association. Thus, in Northern Ireland the consociational agenda has consciously sought to solidify communal division, and British policies have come to be informed by notions of equality based on segregation, as opposed to simply promoting integration.
>
> (Taylor, 1999)

Simply put, this is Wilson's (1998) 'good fences makes good neighbours' point earlier in this chapter. Hadden et al. (1998) on the other hand argue that in a divided society like Northern Ireland it is equally important to ensure that equality is not achieved at the expense of good community relations and communal sharing. Hadden, a supporter of an integrated peace, claims 'equal but separate' is a partitionist concept which will only accentuate the increasing functional and

Table 8.1 Applying Lederach's model – Northern Ireland, Israel and South Africa

Peace building phase	Northern Ireland	Israel	South Africa
– Macro level – Top level leadership – Political accommodation	– Frameworks Document – Peace Forum – Multi-Party Talks – Belfast Agreement – Implementation	– Oslo peace plan – Declaration of Principles – Elections for Palestinian Council – Likud coalition government – Wye Agreement – Final status talks	– Collapse of apartheid – Multi-racial democratic elections – Government of National Unity – Interim/final Constitution
– Organic peace building – Interdependence of different tiers – NGO activity	– Limited non-government activity in peace building – Many govt. funded pro-grammes operat-ing at grassroots – Ineffectual peace movement, women's groups; ambivalence of churches – Civic Forum in Belfast Agreement – EU Peace & Reconciliation Programme	– Co-existence work seen as a means of 'containing' Palestinians – Israeli peace movement activity primarily about self-interest – Developed networks of Palestinian NGOs to resist occupation – not for peace building purposes	– National Peace Accord and local peace committees – Community participation in Recon-struction and Development Programme
– Transition – Transformation – Reconciliation	– Release of political prisoners – Policing and criminal justice review – Strong equality agenda – Victims Commission	– The problems of Israeli Arabs (East Jerusalem and Israel) – Major political and socio-economic disparities between Israelis and Palestinians	– Truth and Reconciliation Commission – National reconciliation and national unity – Democratic system with equal rights – Race and gender dispa-rities in wealth and income opportunities – Rebuilding the economy

physical separation between the two communities in Northern Ireland. The concept of an integrated peace also finds support in the Belfast Agreement where it states 'an essential part of the reconciliation process is the promotion of a culture of tolerance at every level of society, including initiatives to facilitate and encourage integrated education and mixed housing' (Belfast Agreement, 1998; Reconciliation and Victims of Violence, section 13: 18).

The position in South Africa and Israel appears to be less complex in terms of their vision of peace building as expressed by Chazan:

> In South Africa it has been clear for many years that the political solution would lie in a democratic, multi-ethnic, multi-racial state. The question was how to overcome apartheid and achieve a fully democratic, representational, *integrationist* solution. In the Arab-Israeli situation there is no one who has seriously dealt with the conflict who does not understand that the political solution in our region is *separation*, the precise opposite of the political solution in South Africa. In the Arab-Israeli conflict we are trying to find out how to successfully disengage so that we can interact in different ways. My hunch is that Northern Ireland is somewhere in the middle, *between disengagement and integration*.
>
> (Chazan, 1998: 82; our emphasis)

Is the analysis or interpretation valid? For example, what about the position of Israeli Arabs? Here the Lederach framework, in its generic form, does not take account of the fundamental differences in approaches to peace building. Yet, whether peace building is premised on an integrated or separated strategy is crucial. The debate between peaceful co-existence or assimilation, how it entrenches existing power relationships, and their relative merits in securing reconciliation, has not been satisfactorily resolved. The Lederach model overlooks this important distinction.

The second key concluding point refers to Lederach's notion of a 'middle-out' approach, or the engagement of middle range and grass-roots leaders in sustaining the peace building process. The extent to which this is happening across the three case study countries varies, yet undoubtedly the empirical evidence in Chapters 3, 5 and 7 would endorse the value of their involvement. In South Africa and Israel the energies of civics/NGOs/church leaders etc. were centrally focused on fighting apartheid and occupation respectively. Many have prematurely scaled down their efforts (to some extent because of the withdrawal or redirection of donor funding) with the ending of apartheid, or Oslo/Wye in the case of Israeli activists. In short, they have stopped at peace-making without fully recognising the need for, and challenges of, peace building. Here Northern Ireland could provide some useful examples of how to move beyond the level of a challenge role to one of rebuilding their divided societies, in particular the active involvement of civil society in the EU Peace and Reconciliation Programmes and the soon to be established Civic Forum as part of the Belfast Agreement. These middle range and grassroots leaders have the capacity to 'transform the conflict' (Taylor, 1999) by extending the democratic process and, in so doing, challenge the ethno-national cleavages which exist.

The third and final point relates to Lederach's web of reconciliation in which he argues for attention to socio-economic, socio-political, socio-psychological and spiritual factors in a process which moves divided societies from transition, through transformation, to reconciliation. The empirical evidence from the three case studies demands some refinement of this conceptualisation. Lederach argues that the concentration of effort tends to be on the socio-economic and socio-political and suggests a need to address socio-psychological and spiritual issues if reconciliation is to be achieved. What became apparent in the three case study countries was the lack of congruence, symmetry and sequence in the approaches adopted to these factors and the possible consequences for the reconciliation process. Northern Ireland, for example, was moving forward on all fronts, if somewhat tentatively on the spiritual/healing factors and perhaps only then in a reactionary way – victims became important only as part of the political process. Israel has made little or no progress on any area of reconciliation. South Africa, on the other hand, has put much of its efforts into the socio-psychological and spiritual areas, primarily through the TRC, but despite its best efforts/intentions faces major socio-economic problems.

Herein lies a general problem in seeking reconciliation. Is it necessary to adopt a combined approach or is there a sequence to, or symmetry across, these factors which conflict societies have to prioritise (possibly due to resource constraints)? In other words, if Israel were to embark upon a process of reconciliation with the Israeli Arabs would it be best advised to engage in the process of healing, address socio-economic disparities or both simultaneously? If they cannot do both, what should be the priority? Lederach's model provides little guidance in these circumstances. This dilemma is put very succinctly by Brandon

Hamber who, in discussing the role of social transformation and reconciliation in South Africa, wrote:

> If you look at most Truth Commission processes you will see that truth, for truth's sake is a pretty pointless exercise, and counselling for counselling sake is equally a waste of time unless it is coupled with some form of social transformation. The Truth and Reconciliation Commission is going to be remembered in history as a bad exercise if the government continues in the way it is presently going – in terms of its economic line and if the gaps between the rich and poor do not narrow. If people's lives do not change then reconciliation is simply a waste of time.
>
> (Hamber, 1998: 98)

This prompted the question, is reconciliation dependent on economic and social equality or can there be some reconciliation before broad social change?

Northern Ireland, Israel and South Africa all have the potential not only to make peace but to build a sustainable peace. This must involve, at the most fundamental level, political agreement and accommodation between the parties to the conflict. As importantly, however, this study has sought to demonstrate, in line with Lederach's peace building approach, that political agreements must be underpinned by the active involvement of civil society which, by widening the traditional democratic base, can consolidate and embed peace within communities. To move beyond this to true reconciliation requires the dismantling and/or reform of the military/security organs of the conflict, a strong equality agenda to address socio-economic disparities and, importantly, a capacity to 'remember and change'.

Appendix: Lists of Interviewees

South Africa

Father P.J. Pearson, Peace & Justice Commission, Catholic Church.
Mr C. Govender, Centre for Community and Labour Studies, Durban.
Father P. Kearney, Diakonia Council Of Churches, Durban.
Mr A. de Klerk, Police Training Project, Centre for Conflict Resolution, Cape Town.
Mr S. Johnstone, Futurelinks South Africa, Cape Town.
Ms S. Barade, ANC Research Department, Cape Town.
Ms Oldyai, Centre for Dispute Resolution, Cape Town.
Professor J. Malan, ACCORD, Cape Town.
Mr J. Radcliffe, Quaker Peace Centre, Cape Town.
Mr J. McGregor, St Martin's Anglican Church, Cape Town.
Ms F. Franks, School Teacher, Cape Town.
Mr N. Andrews, Cape Town.
Mr K. Govender, ACCORD, Durban.
Dr A. Habib, University of Durban Westville, Durban.
Rev M. Vorster, Diakonia, Durban.
Mr B. Cele, ANC, Durban.
Mr P. Powell, IFP, Durban.
Prof A. Johnson, Department of Politics,University of Natal, Durban.
Prof J. Daniels, TRC, Durban.
Dr R. Taylor, Politics Department, University of Witwatersrand, Johannesburg.
Mr B. Hamber, Centre for the Study of Violence and Reconciliation, Johannesburg.
Mr R. Morris, CDRT, Johannesburg.
Mr A. Abi, Interculture South Africa, Johannesburg.
Mr P. Kelly, TRC, Johannesburg.
Mr A. Lewkane, National Economic and Development Council, Johannesburg.
Ms S. Duncan, Black Sash, Johannesburg.
Father S. O'Leary, Peace and Justice Commission, Pretoria.
Mr A. Green-Thompson, Peace and Justice Commission, Pretoria.
Delegation from Independent Mediation Service of South Africa, Johannesburg.

Mr C. Staffer, Wilgespruit Spiritual Community, Johannesburg.
Representatives from the Institute for Multi-Party Democracy, Johannesburg.

Israel/Palestine

Dr A. Ghanem, Givat Haviva, Israel.
Dr A. Haddi, Palestinian Academic Society for the Study of International Affairs (PASSIA), Al-Quds.
Dr E. Kaufman, Harry Truman Institute for the Advancement of Peace, Jerusalem.
Dr G. Baskin, Director, The Israeli/Palestine Centre for Research and Information, Jerusalem.
Dr J. Aviad, Peace Now and People to People Programme, Jerusalem.
Dr M. Darweish, Peace Education Project, The Israeli/Palestine Centre for Research and Information, Jerusalem.
Dr P. Lemish, Beit Berl College.
Dr R. Twite, The Israeli/Palestine Centre for Research and Information, Jerusalem.
Dr S. Adwan, Palestine Consultancy Group, University of Bethlehem.
Dr Shul Paz, Israeli Ministry of Education, Culture and Sports, Jerusalem.
Dr T. Hermann, Tami Steinmetz Centre for Peace Research, Tel Aviv.
Mr A. Najjor, Neve Shalom/Wahat al salam.
Mr A. Pollock, UNWRA, Gaza City.
Mr C. Zacharia, Centre for Palestine Research and Studies, Nablus.
Mr D. Leon, Palestine-Israel Journal of Politics, Economics and Culture.
Mr E. Jabbour, House of Hope, Hafia.
Mr G. Shah, Ministry of Information, Palestinian National Authority, Ramallah.
Mr H. Havassey, Independent Evaluator, Tel Aviv.
Mr M. Warschawskii, Alternative Information Centre, Jerusalem.
Mr R. Kaminer, Peace Activist.
Mr Z. Zougbi, Wiam Centre for Conflict Resolution, Bethlehem.
Mrs S. Ozacky-Lazar, Research Co-ordinator, Givat Haviva.
Ms A. Badran, Jerusalem Women's Centre, Jerusalem.
Ms I. Maoz, Van Leer Institute, Jerusalem.
Ms J. Deedes, The Centre for Jewish-Arab Economic Development, Tel Aviv.
Ms J. Montel, B'Tselem, Jerusalem.
Ms L. Daboub, Palestine-Israel Journal of Politics, Economics and Culture.

Ms L. Nusseibh, Palestinian Centre for the Study of Non-Violence, Jerusalem.

Ms M. Averbuch, Bat Shalom/Women's Group, Jerusalem.

Ms Y. Green, Israeli-Palestinian Centre for Reproachment Between People, Jerusalem/Bethlehem.

Prof G. Sheffer, University of Jerusalem.

Prof M. Hassassian, Bethlehem University.

Prof S. Smooha, University of Haifa.

Ms B. Green, New Israel Fund, Jerusalem.

Ms D. Carter, New Israel Fund, Jerusalem.

Mr Y. Goodman, Ministry of Foreign Affairs, Jerusalem.

Ms L. Enderson, FAFO, People to People Programme, Jerusalem.

Dr M. al-Haj, University of Hafia, Hafia.

Dr A. Levi, Israeli Police, Jerusalem.

Notes

1 The Comparative Context for Peace Building

1 Under the existing scheme approximately 240 prisoners have been released early. Of these, only two have had to be recalled for breaching their licences. Under these existing arrangements about half of the remaining prisoners would have been released in the next two years. At October 1998, 62 paramilitary prisoners had been released under the Agreement with the prospect of half the prisoners eligible due out by January 1999.

2 The Prime Minster made a personal pledge to the people of Northern Ireland in May 1998 in advance of the referendum on the Belfast Agreement. He pledged:

- no change in the status of Northern Ireland without the express consent of the people of Northern Ireland;
- power to take decisions returned to a Northern Ireland Assembly, with accountable North/South co-operation;
- fairness and equality guaranteed for all;
- those who use or threaten violence excluded from the Government of Northern Ireland;
- prisoners kept in unless violence is given up for good.

3 The Good Friday Agreement sets in place safeguards to ensure that all sections of the community can participate and work together successfully in the operation of the Assembly, and that all sections of the community are protected. One such measure is the arrangements to ensure key decisions are taken on a cross-community basis:

(i) either parallel consent, i.e. a majority of those members present and voting, including a majority of the unionist and nationalist designations present and voting;
(ii) or a weighted majority (60 per cent) of members present and voting, including at least 40 per cent of each of the nationalist and unionist designations present and voting.

Key decisions requiring cross-community support will be designated in advance, including the Chair of the Assembly, the First Minister and Deputy First Minister, standing orders and budget allocations. In other cases such decisions could be triggered by a petition of concern brought about by a significant minority of Assembly members (30/108). Strand One Section 5: The Belfast Agreement.

4 The West Bank is divided into three areas. Area A is entirely Palestinian-run except for security, water, exits and entrances. Area B is jointly patrolled by Palestinian and Israeli soldiers, with security, water, building permits, exits and entrances entirely controlled by Israel. Area C is completely Israeli. In Area A, with about a third of the Palestinian population in the six largest

towns, constituting between 3–5 per cent of the area of the West Bank, full administrative authority was turned over to the Palestinian Authority. In Area B, including over 400 Palestinian villages and rural areas, about 25 per cent of the West Bank's area, the Palestinians assumed administrative and police authority, but Israel retains control of security. Movement of Palestinian police from Area A to Area B requires Israeli approval. Redeployment of Israeli forces from Area B occurred prior to the Palestinian Council elections in January 1996. Sparsely settled or uninhabited Area C, constituting over two thirds of the West Bank, includes Israeli settlements and military areas; these were to remain under Israeli control until establishment of the Council when Israel was to begin a phased further deployment in six-month stages to be completed by the end of 1997 (Peretz, 1996: 104).

5 Israeli control over who and what came in to and left the territories. The Israeli Government also issues work permits exercising control over the number of Palestinian workers allowed into Israel. Negotiations to achieve a full peace settlement were due to start in May 1996 and be completed by 1999. These were to deal with the major controversial issues of Israeli settlers in the territories, Palestinian refugees, borders between Israel and the Palestinians, the status of Jerusalem, military locations and water supplies.

6 Binyamin Netanyahu defeated the Labour Party's Shimon Peres by the narrowest of margins (50.4 per cent and 49.5 per cent respectively – separated by 29,000 votes). Likud's support depends upon a wide range of religious and xenophobic groupings (National Religious Party, the Shas group of Sephardic religious Jews and the United Torah Judaism) – they hold 23 seats in the Knesset. Shimon Peres, Labour's architect of the Oslo peace process, was criticised for failing to call a snap election after Yitzhak Rabin's assassination by a right-wing extremist (Yigal Amir) in November 1995.

7 Before Wye, Area A represented 2.8 per cent, Area B 24 per cent, and Area C 72 per cent of the land area of the West Bank. Wye gave the Palestinians an additional 1 per cent from Area C, and 14.2 per cent from area B, thus putting about 18.2 per cent under Palestinian control again, with the same exclusions and provisos.

8 The report, based on two and a half years of hearings, amounts to 3,500 pages, five volumes, taken from 21,000 witness accounts and more than 7,000 amnesty applications.

9 Parliamentary elections were held on 26–8 April 1994 – the electorate was 22.7m; turn-out was 86 per cent and 19 parties stood. The African National Congress (ANC) gained 252 seats with 62.7 per cent of votes cast, the National Party (NP) 82 seats with 20.4 per cent, the Inkatha Freedom Party 43 seats with 10.5 per cent, the Freedom Front 9 seats with 2.2 per cent, the Democratic Party 7 seats with 1.7 per cent, the Pan-Africanist Congress (PAC) 5 seats with 1.2 per cent and the African Christian Democratic party 2 seats with 0.5 per cent.

Voting in South Africa is along racial lines. Most blacks (who make up 76 per cent of the overall population) support the ANC and most whites (13 per cent of the population) vote for one of the three traditionally white parties (the National Party, the Democratic Party or the Freedom Front).

The National Party Government ruled South Africa from 1948 to 1994.

The ANC now controls the government, seven of the nine provinces and most town councils even in KwaZulu Natal. The Western Cape Province is run by the National Party and KwaZulu Natal by Inkatha. South Africa has, however, a strong civil society comprising women's groups, local church bodies, street committees and parents' associations.

2   Northern Ireland: Macro Political Developments

10 The nine counties are Antrim, Down, Armagh, Londonderry, Fermanagh, Tyrone, Cavan, Monaghan and Donegal. The new six county jurisdiction was without Cavan, Monaghan and Donegal.

11 The latter is now the subject of a new judicial enquiry which will re-examine the events surrounding Bloody Sunday, taking account of new evidence presented.

12 Their results improved further in the 1997 Westminster (16.1 per cent) and local government elections (16.9 per cent) of the same year.

3   Northern Ireland: Micro Grassroots Activity

13 The Labour Government policy New Deal is aimed at helping people break the cycle of unemployment or move from welfare to work. The New Deal policy options to achieve this include short-term paid employment in the public, private and voluntary sectors or full-time education.

4   Israel/Palestine: Macro Political Developments

14 A number of different titles can be used to describe Palestinian citizens of Israel–Jewish academics use the term Israeli Arab while Palestinian academics tend to use the term Israeli Palestinians. We use both terms interchangeably.

15 Begin's Autonomy Plan, 1977; the Camp David Accords, 1978; the Reagan Peace Plan, 1982; Peres–Hussein Plan, 1987; the Shultz Initiative, 1988; the Israeli Government Peace Initiative, 1989; the Baker Proposals, 1989.

16 Hiltermann notes that the uprising started in the Jabalya refugee camp in Gaza on 9 December 1987 and it spread to the West Bank soon after.

17 UN Resolution 242, November 1967, focused on the establishment of a just and lasting peace in the Middle East. Resolution 242 requested the withdrawal of Israeli armed forces from territories occupied in the Six Day War. It also requested the recognition of the sovereignty, territorial integrity, and political independence of all states in the area and their right to live in peace within secure and recognised boundaries.

Resolution 338, October 1974, called on the parties to the conflict 'to start immediately the implementation of resolution 242 and start negotiations... under appropriate auspices aimed at establishing a just and durable peace in the Middle East'.

18 The agreement carved the West Bank and Gaza into three areas:

Area A – the six large Palestinian towns;
Area B – Palestinian rural areas; and
Area C – Israeli settlements and areas of strategic importance to Israel.

19 Taken from the South African conflict, 'batunisation' means forced segregation for political ends.

20   Internal closure refers to restrictions inside the Occupied Territories which prevent movement between Areas A, B and C. All other 'closures' refer to restricting the access of Palestinians to enter Israeli territory before the 1967 War.

5   Israel/Palestine: Micro Grassroots Activity

21   Givat Haviva, Neveh Shalom/Wahat El Salam, Beit Hafegen, Midreshet Adam, the Unit for Democracy and Coexistence and the Arab-Jewish Project in the Van Leer Institute.

22   'Promoting understanding requires overcoming both psychological barriers between the two peoples and the realities of discrimination and under-development that Israeli Arabs face' (NIF, 1995).

23   Key names in coexistence such as Givat Haviva, Neve Shalom, the Adam Institute, the Centre for Jewish-Arab Economic Development developed links with Palestinian organisations to implement a plethora of programmes aimed at sustaining the peace process.

24   For a review of the period see 'Between Peace and Equality: the Arabs in Israel in the Mid-term Labour/Meretz Government', The Institute for Peace Research, Givat Haviva, 1995.

25   N = 500 of European or American origin, and 5–6,000 respectively.

7   South Africa: Micro Grassroots Activity

26   Reported to us by Habib, October 1997.

8   Conclusions: Towards Peace Building

27   First constitutional principle contained in Schedule 4 of the 1993 Constitution of South Africa Act, which was also the foundation for the 1996 Constitution of the Republic of South Africa Act.

28   The Accord committed signatories to recognise and uphold certain fundamental principles necessary in a multi-party democracy: freedom of conscience and belief; freedom of speech and expression; freedom of association; peaceful assembly; freedom of movement; freedom of participation in peaceful political activity. It also committed the signatories to practise political tolerance and prevent their members from inciting or taking part in political violence or intimidation.

29   Alex Duval Smith, writing in an article entitled 'Healing is No Nearer for a Wounded Nation'.

30   Consociationalism is a term and concept developed by Arend Lijphart: *The Politics of Accommodation: Pluralism and Democracy in the Netherlands* (Berkeley: University Press, 1968); and *Democracy in Plural Societies: A Comparative Exploration* (New Haven: Yale University Press, 1977) which argues that 'divided (or plural or segmented) societies can attain democratic stability despite the absence of cross-cutting cleavages' (McGarry and O'Leary, 1995: 320–1). Lijphart claims that 'cultural autonomy' and 'segmental isolation' reduces contact between rival subcultures, and as a consequence the occasions for conflict.

References

Abu Zayyad, Z. (1996) 'The Real Challenge', *Palestine-Israel Journal of Politics, Economics and Culture*, 3, no. 2, pp. 35–7.

Abu-Nimer, M. (1993) *Conflict Resolution Between Arabs and Jews in Israel: a Study of Six Intervention Programmes.* Unpublished Ph.D., George Mason University, Fairfax, Virginia.

African National Congress (1985) 'The Future is within our Grasp', *Statement of the National Executive Committee of the ANC.* Lusaka: ANC.

African National Congress (1994) *The Reconstruction and Development Programme.* Cape Town: ANC.

The Agreement (1998) 'Agreement reached in the multi-party negotiations', *The Belfast Agreement.* Belfast: Northern Ireland Office.

Ahmad, E. (1971) 'Revolutionary Warfare and Counterinsurgency', in Miller, N. and Roderick, A. (eds), *National Liberation: Revolution in the Third World.* New York: Free Press.

Ahmed, H.H. (1994) 'Time for Reconciliation', *Palestine-Israel Journal of Politics, Economics and Culture*, 1, no. 1, pp. 5–8.

Akenson, D. (1970) *The Irish Education Experiment: the National System in the 19th Century.* London: Routledge and Kegan Paul.

Al-Haj, M. (1990) *Arab Education in Israel.* Tel Aviv: International Centre for Peace in the Middle East.

Al-Khatib, G. (1996) 'Israeli Settlement Policy: Its Impact on the Scope of Peace in the Region', *Palestine-Israel Journal of Politics, Economics and Culture*, 3, no. 3/4, pp. 55–9.

Al-Shafi, H. (1994) 'A Political Reading of the Declaration of Principles', *Challenges Facing Palestinian Society in the Interim Period,* Jerusalem Media & Communication Centre, pp. 13–18.

Allport, G.W. (1954) *The Nature of Prejudice.* Reading, Mass.: Addison-Wesley.

Appleyard, B. (1998) 'Divided They Stand: God's Own Country', *Sunday Times Magazine*, 3 May, pp. 42–57.

Argus Newspaper (1990) Special Supplement: Men of Destiny. Cape Town.

Arthur, P. (1987) *Government and Politics of Northern Ireland.* London: Longman, 2nd edn.

Ash, T. (1996) 'Israel Pushes Peace Process off the Agenda', *Middle East Economic Digest*, 40, no. 37, pp. 6–9.

Ash, T. (1996) 'Israel: the New Government Maps Out Future Policy', *Middle East Economic Digest*, 40, no. 27, pp. 10–12.

Ashrawi, H. (1995) 'Honorary Ambassador: an Interview', *Palestine-Israel Journal of Politics, Economics and Culture*, 2, no. 3, pp. 56–62.

Aughey, A. (1989) *Under Siege: Ulster Unionism and the Anglo-Irish Agreement.* Belfast: Blackstaff Press.

Awerbuch, M. (1997) 'Building Peace: an ABC of Peace Now – Palestinian Dialogue', *Palestine-Israel Journal of Politics, Economics and Culture*, 4, no. 2, pp. 70–81.

Bar Ilan, D. (1996) 'Palestinian Self-Rule, Israeli Security – An Interview', *Palestine-Israel Journal of Politics, Economics and Culture*, 3, no. 3/4, pp. 10–17.

Bar On, M. (1996) *In Pursuit of Peace: a History of the Israeli Peace Movement*. Washington DC: United States Institute of Peace.

Bell, P. (1995) 'Northern Ireland – the Way Forward: a UK Government View'. Paper presented at ESRC seminar, Queen's University Belfast, 19 Sept.

Ben Rafael, E. and Sharot, S. (1991) *Ethnicity, Religion and Class in Israeli Society*. Cambridge: Cambridge University Press.

Bew, P. and Patterson, H. (1985) *The British State and the Ulster Crisis: from Wilson to Thatcher*. London: Verso.

Bew, P., Gibbon, P. and Patterson, H. (1979) *The State in Northern Ireland 1921–72: Political Forces and Social Classes*. Manchester: Manchester University Press.

Birrell, D. and Wilson, C. (1993) 'Making Belfast Work: an Evaluation of an Urban Strategy', *Administration*, 41, no. 1, pp. 40–56.

Bitan, D. (1996) 'Israeli Education: a Critical Profile', *Palestine-Israel Journal of Politics, Economics and Culture*, 3, no. 1, pp. 7–14.

Blair, T. (1997) 'Talks on the Political Settlement in Northern Ireland', *Belfast Newsletter*, 13 Sept.

Bloomfield, D. (1997) *Peacemaking Strategies in Northern Ireland: Building Complementarity in Conflict Management Theory*. London: Macmillan.

Bloomfield, K. (1998) 'How Should We Remember? The Work of the Northern Ireland Victims Commission', in Brandon Hamber (ed.), *Past Imperfect: Dealing with the Past in Northern Ireland and Societies in Transition*. Derry: INCORE (Initiative on Conflict Resolution and Ethnicity).

Bloomfield, K. (1998) *We Will Remember Them*. Belfast: Stationery Office.

Buckland, P. (1981) *A History of Northern Ireland*. Dublin: Gill and Macmillan.

Burton, M. (1998) 'The South African Truth and Reconciliation Commission: Looking Back, Moving Forward – Revisiting Conflicts, Striving for Peace', in Brandon Hamber (ed.), *Past Imperfect: Dealing with the Past in Northern Ireland and Societies in Transition*. Derry: INCORE (Initiative on Conflict Resolution and Ethnicity).

Cameron, R. (1996) 'The Reconstruction and Development Programme', in Murray Faure and Jan-Erik Lane (eds), *South Africa: Designing New Political Structures*. London: Sage.

Cantilevers Magazine (1997) 'Interview with Marthinus van Schalkwyk, Executive Director of the National Party'. Durban: Cantilevers Magazine.

Cashmore, E. (1995) *Dictionary of Race and Ethnic Relations*. London: Routledge, 3rd edn.

Cassidy, F. (1996) 'The Concept of Fair Participation', in D. Magill and S. Rose (eds), *Fair Employment Law in Northern Ireland: Debates and Issues*, vol. 1: Employment Equality in Northern Ireland. Belfast: Standing Advisory Commission on Human Rights.

Central Community Relations Unit (1991) *Community Relations in Northern Ireland*. Belfast: CCRU.

Central Secretariat (1993) *Policy Appraisal and Fair Treatment Guidelines*. Belfast: Central Secretariat.

The Centre for Jewish-Arab Economic Development (1995) *Annual Report 1995*. Tel Aviv: CJAED.

Centre for Palestinian Research and Studies (1994) 'The Declaration of Principles: What's in it for the Palestinians', *Palestine-Israel Journal of Politics, Economics and Culture*, 1, pp. 39–55.

Chazan, Naomi (1998) 'The Challenges and Complexities of Mediation Initiatives', in G. Kelly (ed.), *Mediation in Practice*. Derry: INCORE (Initiative on Conflict Resolution and Ethnicity).

Clarke, L. (1998) 'Hume Hails Good Friday Deal for Achieving Unity', *Sunday Times*, 14 Nov.

Clarke, L. (1998) 'Rough Road to Reality', *Sunday Times*, 1 Feb.

Community Agency for Social Inquiry (1995). *Monitoring the Monitors: Conflict Resolution Review*. Johannesburg: CASE.

Connolly, M. and Loughlin, J. (1986) 'Reflections on the Anglo-Irish Agreement', *Government and Opposition*, 21, pp. 152–63.

Connor, W. (1990) 'Ethno-nationalism and Political Instability', in H. Giliomee and J. Gagiano (eds), *The Elusive Search for Peace: South Africa, Israel and Northern Ireland*. Cape Town: Oxford University Press.

Constitution of the Republic of South Africa (1996) *Government Gazette*, no. 17068.

Cormack, R. and Osborne, R. (1991) 'Disadvantage and Discrimination in Northern Ireland', in R. Cormack and R. Osborne (eds), *Discrimination and Public Policy in Northern Ireland*. Oxford: Clarendon Press.

Cormack, R.J., Gallagher, A.M. and Osborne, R.D. (1993) *Fair Enough? Religion and the 1991 Population Census*. Belfast: Fair Employment Commission.

Cygielman, V. (1994) 'The Road to Mutual Recognition', *Palestine-Israel Journal of Politics, Economics and Culture*, 1, no. 1, pp. 9–15.

Dabdoub, L. (1997) 'Expressing a General Consensus', *Palestine-Israel Journal of Politics, Economics and Culture*, 4, no. 2, pp. 10–12.

Darby, J. (1995) 'Conflict in Northern Ireland: a Background Essay', in S. Dunn (ed.), *Facets of the Conflict in Northern Ireland*. London: Macmillan.

Darby, J., Murray, D., Batts, D., Dunn, S., Farren, S. and Harris, J. (1977) *Education and Community In Northern Ireland: Schools Apart?* Coleraine: New University of Ulster.

Darweish, M. and Rigby, A. (1995) *Palestinians in Israel: Nationality and Citizenship*. Peace Research Report no. 35: University of Bradford, UK.

Dawn (1978) *Dawn Magazine*, nos 38–9. Dublin: Dawn Group.

De Kock, C. (1993) 'The Dynamics of Public Violence in South Africa and Possible Solutions'. *Socio-Political Monitoring and Analysis*, Pretoria: Human Science Research Council.

Department of Economic Development (1989) *Fair Employment in Northern Ireland: Code of Practice*. Belfast: Department of Economic Development.

Department of Education for Northern Ireland (1987) *Cross Community Contact Scheme*, Circular 87/47. Belfast: DENI.

Department of Finance & Personnel & H.M. Treasury (1995) *Northern Ireland Expenditure Plans & Priorities: the Government's Expenditure Plans 1995–96 to 1997–98*. Cm 2816. London: HMSO.

Department of Finance & Personnel & H.M. Treasury (1997) *Northern Ireland Expenditure Plans & Priorities: the Government's Expenditure Plans 1997–98 to 1999–2000*. Cm 3616. London: HMSO.

Department of Finance & Personnel & H.M. Treasury (1998) *Northern Ireland Expenditure Plans & Priorities: the Government's Expenditure Plans 1998–99*. Cm 3916. London: HMSO.

Diescho, J. (1997) 'Whither Civil Society in the New South Africa', *Towards Democracy – Journal of the Institute for Multi-Party Democracy*, 6, no. 1, pp. 10–15.

Duffy, G. and Frensley, N. (1989) 'Community Conflict Processes: Mobilisation and Demobilisation'.

Dunn, S. (1990) *A Short History of Education in Northern Ireland 1920–1990.* Paper prepared for the Standing Advisory Commission on Human Rights. University of Ulster: Centre for the Study of Conflict.

Dunn, S., Darby, J. and Mullan, K. (1984) *Schools Together?* Coleraine: New University of Ulster.

Duval Smith, A. (1998) 'Healing is No Nearer for a Wounded Nation', *Irish Times*, 30 Oct.

The Economist (1996) 'Living with the Occupation: East Jerusalem – to Whom does Israel Belong?', 23 Nov., pp. 46–7.

The Economist (1997a) 'Treading Carefully: Northern Ireland', 18 Oct., pp. 56–7.

The Economist (1997) 'The End of a Miracle?', 13 Dec., pp. 17–20.

The Economist (1998a) 'A Lesson from South Africa', 31 Oct., pp. 22–3.

The Economist (1998b) 'Now, for my next trip…Israel's Prime Minister is Surviving by a Policy Built on Contradiction', 25 April, pp. 47–9.

The Economist (1998c) 'One in Five Israelis: Arab Population of Israel', 25 April, pp. 14–16.

The Economist (1998d) 'Out of Work, Out of Hope', 31 Oct., p. 49.

Eurolink Supplement (1995) *Special Support Programme for Peace and Reconciliation in Northern Ireland and the Border Counties of Ireland 1995–1999.* Eurolink Supplement no. 9. Northern Ireland Centre in Europe.

European Structural Funds (1994) *Physical and Social Environment Programme (PSEP): 1994–1999.* Belfast: European Community Office.

Fine, R. and Davis, D. (1990) *Beyond Apartheid: Labour and Liberation in South Africa.* Johannesburg: Ravan Press.

Finkelstein, N.G. (1995) *Image and Reality of the Israel–Palestine Conflict.* London: Verso.

Fitzduff, M. (1996) *Beyond Violence: Conflict Resolution Processes in Northern Ireland.* Tokyo: United Nations University.

Flamhaft, Z. (1996) *Israel on the Road to Peace: Accepting the Unacceptable.* Boulder, Colo.: Westview Press.

Frazer, H. and Fitzduff, M. (1986) *Improving Community Relations.* Belfast: Community Relations Council.

Friedland, W. (1982) *Revolutionary Theory.* New Jersery: Osmun and Co.

Friedman, S. and Atkinson, D. (eds) (1994) *South African Review 7: The Small Miracle: South Africa's negotiated settlement.* Johannesburg: Ravan Press.

Gabay, Zvi (1998) 'Security Essential in Push for Peace', *Irish Times*, 9 Nov.

Gallagher, A.M. (1989) *Majority, Minority Review 1: Education and Religion in Northern Ireland.* Coleraine: Centre for the Study of Conflict.

Gallagher, A.M., Osborne, R.D. and Cormack, R.J. (1995) *Fair Shares? Employment, Unemployment and Economic Status.* Belfast: Fair Employment Commission.

Gazit, S. (1994) 'Israeli Political Understanding of the Declaration of Principles', *Challenges Facing Palestinian Society in the Interim Period*, Jerusalem Media & Communication Centre, pp. 118–23.

Gerhart, G. (1978) *Black Power in South Africa: the Evolution of an Idealogy.* Berkeley: University of California Press.

Ghanem, A. and Ozacky-Lazar, S. (1990) *Autonomy for the Arabs in Israel: an Initial Discussion*. The Institute for Arabic Studies. Manashe: Givat Haviva.

Giliomee, H. (1990) 'Introduction', in H. Giliomee and J. Gagiano (eds), *The Elusive Search for Peace: South Africa, Israel and Northern Ireland*. Cape Town: Oxford University Press.

Giliomee, H. (1982) *The Parting of the Ways: South African Politics, 1976–1982*. Cape Town: David Phillips.

Green, Y. (1996) 'The Impact of Dialogue', *Palestine-Israel Journal of Politics, Economics and Culture*, 3, nos 3/4, pp. 129–37.

Greer, J. (1976) 'Religion and Cultural Change', *Compass, The Journal of the Irish Association for Curriculum Development*, 5, no. 2, pp. 65–78.

The Guardian (1998a) 'Jerusalem's walled city: Israel is disingenuous', leading article, 23 June.

The Guardian (1998b) 'The truth is not enough', leading article, 31 Oct.

Gulati, A. et al. (1996) *Tango In the Dark: Government and Voluntary Sector Partnership in the New South Africa*. Johannesburg: Community Agency for Social Inquiry (CASE).

Hadden, T. (1997) *Possible Structures for the Development and Implementation of Policy Appraisal on Separation and Sharing (PASS) – Discussion Paper*. Belfast: Centre for International and Comparative Human Rights Law, Queen's University.

Hadden, T., Rainey, B. and McGreevy, G. (1998) *Equal but not Separate: Communal Policy Appraisal*. Belfast: Centre for International Comparative Human Rights Law.

Hain, P. (1996) 'I still feel only stillness said Mandela', *New Statesman*, 125, no. 4308, pp. 30–2.

Hall-Cathala, D. (1990) *The Peace Movement in Israel, 1967–1987*. London: Macmillan Press.

Hamber, B. (1997a) 'Truth: the Road to Reconciliation', in *Cantilevers*, First Quarter, vol. 3: 5–6.

Hamber, B. (1997b) 'The Burdens of Truth: an Evaluation of the Psychological Support Services and Initiatives undertaken by the South African Truth and Reconciliation Commission'. Paper presented at the *Third International Conference of the Ethnic Studies Network*, Derry, Northern Ireland, 26–28 June.

Hamber, B. (1998) 'The Role of Social Transformation and Reconciliation', in Brandon Hamber (ed.), *Past Imperfect: Dealing with the Past in Northern Ireland and Societies in Transition*. Derry: INCORE (Initiative on Conflict Resolution and Ethnicity).

Hansard Debate (1995) *Northern Ireland (Framework Documents)*, 22 Feb., pp. 355–70.

Harvey, B. (1997) *Report on Programme for Peace and Reconciliation*. London: Joseph Rowntree Trust.

Hasan-Rokem, G. (1997) 'Clarifying a Need', *Palestine-Israel Journal of Politics, Economics and Culture*, 4, no. 2, pp. 9–11.

Hassaassian, M. (1994) 'The PLO: from Total Liberation to Peace', *Palestine–Israel Journal of Politics, Economics and Culture*, vol. 1, no. 1, pp. 5–8.

Hassaassian, M. (1996) 'The Democratization Process in the PLO: Idealogy, Structure and Strategy'. Unpublished paper.

Hawthorne, J. (1991) *Community Relations Council – First Annual Report.* Belfast: CRC.

Hermann, T. (1996) 'Israeli Public Opinion and the Peace Process: an Interview', *Palestine-Israel Journal of Politics, Economics and Culture,* 3, no. 3/4, pp. 101–9.

Hewstone, M. and Brown, R. (eds) (1986) *Contact and Conflict in Inter-group Encounters.* Oxford: Blackwell.

Hiltermann, J.R. (1991) *Behind the Intifada.* Princeton: Princeton University Press.

Hofmeyr, J. and Buckland, P. (1992) 'Education System Change in South Africa', in R. McGregor (ed.), *Education Alternatives.* Juta: Kenwyn.

Hughes, J., Knox, C., Murray, M. and Greer, J. (1998) *Partnership Governance in Northern Ireland: the Path to Peace.* Dublin: Oak Tree Press.

Hume, J. (1997) 'Northern Ireland', article by M. Riddell. *New Statesman,* 126, no. 4352, pp. 20–2.

Hurley, D. (1997) 'Passing on the Justice Mantle', in *Challenge: Church & People,* no. 44 Oct./Nov. 1997, pp. 2–4.

Inbari, P. (1996) *The Palestinians Between Terrorism and Statehood.* Brighton: Sussex Academic Press.

Interfund (1996) Development Update: *an Interfund Briefing on Development and the Voluntary Sector in South Africa.* Johannesburg: Interfund.

Interfund (1997) *Development Update: the Politics of Resource Allocation.* Johannesburg: Interfund.

The International Institute for Strategic Studies (1995) 'South Africa – can the miracle be sustained?' *Strategic Survey 1994/95.* Oxford: Oxford University Press.

Jardine, E. (1994) *Demographic Structure in Northern Ireland and its Implications for Constitutional Preference.* Paper presented to the Statistical and Social Enquiry Society of Ireland. Belfast: Policy Planning and Research Unit.

Jeffery, A. (1997a) *The Natal Story: Sixteen Years of Conflict.* Johannesburg: South African Institute or Race Relations (SAIRR).

Jeffery, A. (1997b) 'Sixteen Years of War: at Last the Facts', in *Kwazulu Natal Briefing.* Helen Suzman Foundation, no. 6: pp. 2–10.

Jepson, T. (1995) *Negotiating for a New South Africa* (privately published); cited by Noreen Christian in "The South African Experience – Lessons for Northern Ireland". Belfast: Irish Network for Non-violent Action Training and Education (INNATE).

Johnson, A. (1997) 'Does Peace Have a Chance', in *Kwazulu Natal Briefing,* Helen Suzman Foundation, no. 8: pp. 2–7.

Kaminer, R. (1990) 'The Protest Movement in Israel', in Z. Lockman and J. Beinin (eds), *Intifada: the Palestinian Uprising Against Israeli Occupation.* London: Tauris Publishers.

Kaminer, R. (1996) *The Politics of Protest: the Israeli Peace Movement and the Palestinian Intifada.* Sussex: Sussex Academic Press.

Kane-Berman, J. (1997) *Frontiers of Freedom,* no. 2, Second Quarter, p.1.

Katz, I. and Khanov, M. (1990) 'Review of Dilemmas in Facilitating Arab-Jewish Encounters Groups in Israel', *Megamot,* 73, no. 1, pp. 29–47.

Keane, F. (1994). *The Bondage of Fear.* London: Viking.

Kellas, J.G. (1991) *The Politics of Nationalism and Ethnicity.* London: Macmillan Press.

Kidron, P. (1996) 'Selective Refusal', *Palestine-Israel Journal of Politics, Economics and Culture*, 3, no. 3/4, pp. 129–37.

Knox, C. (1994) 'Conflict Resolution at the Micro Level: Community Relations in Northern Ireland', *Journal of Conflict Resolution*, 38, no. 4, pp. 595–619.

Knox, C. (1995) 'Concept Mapping in Policy Evaluation: a Research Review of Community Relations in Northern Ireland', *Evaluation*, 1, no. 1, pp. 65–79.

Knox, C. and Connolly, M. (1988) 'Recent Political Difficulties of Local Government in Northern Ireland', *Policy and Politics*, 16, no. 2, pp. 89–97.

Knox, C. and Hughes, J. (1995) 'Cross-Community Contact: Northern Ireland and Israel – A Comparative Perspective'. *Nationalism and Ethnic Politics*, 1, no. 2, pp. 205–28.

Knox, C. and Hughes, J. (1994) 'Equality and Equity: an Emerging Government Policy in Northern Ireland', *New Community*, 20, no. 2, pp. 207–25.

Kriek, D.J. (1976) 'Political Alternatives for South Africa: the Search for a paradigm', *Politikon* 3(1): 64–7.

Landau, J. (1993) *The Arab Minority in Israel, 1967–1991*. Oxford: Clarendon Press.

Lawerence, R. (1994). 'From SOWETO to CODESA', in Friedman, S. and Atkinson, D. (eds), *South African Review 7: The Small Miracle: South Africa's negotiated settlement*. Johannesburg: Ravan Press.

Lederach, J.P. (1996) *Remember and Change*. Peace and Reconciliation Conference. Enniskillen: Fermanagh District Partnership.

Lederach, John Paul (1997) *Building Peace: Sustainable Reconciliation in Divided Societies*. Washington, DC: United States Institute of Peace.

Lennon, B. (1995) *After the Cease-fires: Catholics and the Future of Northern Ireland*. Dublin: Columba Press.

Lodge, T. (1988) 'State of Exile: the ANC of South Africa 1976–1986', in P. Frankel and P. Noam (eds), *State, Resistance and Change in South Africa*. London: Croom Helm.

Longland, T. (1994) 'Development in Conflict Situations: the Occupied Territories', *Community Development Journal*, 29, no. 2, pp. 132–40.

Luiz, J. (1996) 'The Socio-Economic Restructuring of a Post-Apartheid South Africa', *International Journal of Social Economics*, 23, no. 10, pp. 137–50.

Lustick, I. (1980) *Arabs in the Jewish State: Israel's control of a National Minority*. Austin: University of Texas Press.

Making Belfast Work (1995) *Making Belfast Work: Strategy Document*. Belfast: Department of the Environment.

Mallon, S. (1998) *Speech by Seamus Mallon MP to Labour Party Conference*, Blackpool, 30 Sept.

Malone, J. (1973) 'Schools and Community Relations', *The Northern Teacher*, 11, no. 1, pp. 14–21.

Mandela, N. (1996) 'Maskhane – let us build one another together'. Text of Nelson Mandela's address to British Parliament. *New Statesman*, 125, no. 4293, pp. 20–4.

Maoz, I. (1995) *Power Relations in Intergroup Encounters: a Case Study of Jewish–Arab Encounters in Israel*. Unpublished Paper.

Mar'i, S. (1978) *Arab Education in Israel*. New York: Syracuse University Press.

Mar'i, S. (1990) *The Palestinians in Israel: Identity in Coexistence*. Beir Ziet University Research Review, pp. 33–4.

Maoz, I. (1995) 'Power Relations in Intergroup Encounters: A Case Study of Jewish-Arab Encounters in Israel'. Unpublished paper.

Mattes, R. (1994) 'The Road to Democracy: from 2 February 1990 to 27 April 1994', in Reynolds, A. (ed.), *Election '94: The Campaigns, Results and Future Prospects*. Claremont: David Phillips.

McBride P. (1996). 'Prisoners and the Negotiating Process – the South African Experience'. *The Third Annual P.J. McGrory Lecture*, Belfast: Peile an Phobail.

McCrudden, C. (1996) *Mainstreaming Fairness? A Discussion Paper on Policy Appraisal and Fair Treatment*. Belfast: Committee on the Administration of Justice.

McCrudden, C. (1996) 'The "Merit Principle" and Fair Employment in Northern Ireland', in D. Magill and S. Rose (eds), *Fair Employment Law in Northern Ireland: Debates and Issues*, vol. 1: Employment Equality in Northern Ireland. Belfast: Standing Advisory Commission on Human Rights.

McGarry, J. and O'Leary, B. (1995) *Explaining Northern Ireland: Broken Images*. Oxford: Blackwell.

McGarry, J. and O'Leary, B. (1993) *The Politics of Ethnic Conflict Regulation*. London: Routledge.

McGill, P. (1996) *Missing the Target: a Critique of Government Policy on Targeting Social Need in Northern Ireland*. Belfast: Northern Ireland Council for Voluntary Action (NICVA).

McKinley, D. (1997) *The ANC and the Liberation Struggle: a Critical Biography*. London: Pluto Press.

Metcalf, H. (1996) in J. McVey and N. Hutson (eds), *Public Attitudes to Employment Equality*, vol. 3. Belfast: Standing Advisory Commission on Human Rights.

Milton-Edwards, B. (1996) 'Political Islam in Palestine in an Environment of Peace', *Third World Quarterly*, 17, no. 2, pp. 199–225.

Mohammad, H. (1997) 'PLO Strategy: from Total Liberation to Coexistence', *Palestine-Israel Journal of Politics, Economics and Culture*, 4, no. 2, pp. 82–9.

Moodie, T. (1980) *The Rise of Afrikanerdom: Power, Apartheid and the Afrikaner Civil Religion*. Berkeley: University of California Press.

Morgan, V. and Fraser, G. (1995) 'Women and the Northern Ireland Conflict', in S. Dunn (ed.), *Facets of the Conflict in Northern Ireland*. London: Macmillan.

Morgan, V., Dunn, S., Cairns, E. and Fraser, G. (1992) *Breaking the Mould – The Roles of Parents and Teachers in Integrated Schools in Northern Ireland*. Coleraine: University of Ulster.

Morrow, D., Birrell, D., Greer, J. and O'Keeffe, T. (1994) *The Churches and Inter-Community Relationships*. Coleraine: Centre for the Study of Conflict.

Mufson, S. (1990) 'South Africa 1990'. *Foreign Affairs*, 70(1): 120–41.

Nakhal, M. (1996) 'Closures and Borders: an Examination of Israeli Closure Policies as Unique in the World, their Implementation and Consequences', *Palestine-Israel Journal of Politics, Economics and Culture*, 3, no. 3/4, pp. 10–17.

Nathan, L. (1993) Editorial in *Track Two*, Centre for Conflict Resolution, Cape Town.

National Peace Secretariat Report (1993). Pretoria: National Peace Secretariat.

National Peace Secretariat Report (1994). Pretoria: National Peace Secretariat.

New Israel Fund (1995) *New Israel Fund Annual Report*. Washington, DC: NIF.

North West Community Network (1998) *The Civic Forum: a Position Paper* Sept. issue. Derry: North West Community Network.

Northern Ireland Council for Voluntary Action (1994) *The Implementation of Targeting Social Need*. Belfast: Northern Ireland Council for Voluntary Action (NICVA).

Northern Ireland Office (1996) *Ground Rules for Substantive All-Party Negotiations*. Cm 3232, 16 April. Belfast: Northern Ireland Office.

Northern Ireland Office (1996b) *The Prime Minster's Statement: Elective Process* (Northern Ireland), 21 March. Belfast: Northern Ireland Office.

Northern Ireland Office (1997) *The Launch of Substantive Talks 15 September*. Belfast: Northern Ireland Office.

Northern Ireland Office (1997b) *Secretary of State Praises Northern Ireland Fair Employment Laws*, 2 Sept. Belfast: Northern Ireland Office.

Northern Ireland Office (1998) *Joint Statement by British and Irish Governments and Propositions on Heads of Agreement*, 12 Jan. Belfast: Northern Ireland Office.

Nossel, S. (1993) 'Building Peace: How the Peace Committees can Heal, Engage and Empower South African Communities', in *Track Two*, Centre for Conflict Resolution, Cape Town, pp. 6–7.

Nusseibeh, S. (1990) 'A Palestinian View of the Occupied Territories', in H. Giliomee and J. Gagiano (eds), *The Elusive Search for Peace: South Africa, Israel and Northern Ireland*. Cape Town: Oxford University Press.

O'Day, A. (ed.) (1997) *Political Violence and Conflict Resolution in Northern Ireland*. Westport, Conn.: Praeger Publishers.

Odendaal, A. and Spies, C. (1996) 'Local Peace Committees in the Rural Areas of the Western Cape'. Occasional Paper, *Track Two*, Cape Town: Centre for the Study of Conflict Resolution.

O'Leary, B. (1995) 'What is Framed in the Framework Documents', *Ethnic and Racial Studies*, 18, no. 4, pp. 862–72.

O'Leary, C., Elliott, S. and Wilford, R. (1988) *The Northern Ireland Assembly 1982–1986: a Constitutional Experiment*. London: C. Hurst.

Osborne, R. (1998) 'Policy Dilemmas in Belfast', *Journal of Social Policy*, 25, no. 2, pp. 181–99.

Osborne, R., Gallagher, A., Cormack, R. and Shortall, S. (1996) 'The Implementation of the Policy Appraisal and Fair Treatment Guidelines', in E. McLaughlin and P. Quirk (eds), *Policy Aspects of Employment Equality in Northern Ireland: Employment Equality in Northern Ireland*, vol. 2. Belfast: Standing Advisory Commission on Human Rights.

Palestinian Academic Society for the Study of International Affairs (1997) *PASSIA Diary*. Jerusalem: PASSIA.

Pedder, S. (1995) 'The Joys of Normality – a Survey of South Africa', *The Economist*, 335, no. 7915, pp. 3–5.

People to People Programme (1996) Promotional literature and guidance on making an application for funding.

Peretz, D. (1996) *The Arab-Israel Dispute*. Facts on File: New York.

Pycroft, C. (1996) 'Local Partnerships and Strategic Alliances for Economic Development: the Need for Economic Development Audits', *International Review of Administrative Sciences*, 62, pp. 109–22.

Quirk, P. and McLaughlin, E. (1996) 'Targeting Social Need', in E. McLaughlin and P. Quirk (eds), *Policy Aspects of Employment Equality in Northern Ireland: Employment Equality in Northern Ireland*, vol. 2. Belfast: Standing Advisory Commission on Human Rights.

Reynolds, A. (ed.) (1995) *Election '94: The Campaigns, Results and Future Prospects.* Claremont: David Phillips.

Robson, B., Bradford, M. and Deas, I. (1994) *Relative Deprivation in Northern Ireland*, Occasional Paper no. 28. Belfast: Policy Planning and Research Unit.

Rothman, J. (1992) *From Confrontation to Co-operation: Resolving Ethnic and Regional Conflict.* London: Sage.

Rouhana, N. (1990) 'The Intifada and the Palestinians of Israel', *Journal of Palestine Studies*, 19, no. 3, pp. 68–75.

Ruane, J. and Todd, J. (1996) *The Dynamics of Conflict in Northern Ireland: Power, Conflict and Emancipation.* Cambridge: Cambridge University Press.

Said, E. (1990) 'The Question of Palestine', in Z. Lockman and J. Beinin (eds), *Intifada: the Palestinian Uprising Against Israeli Occupation.* London: Tauris Publishers.

Said, E. (1998) 'The Wye Agreement is Mean-spirited and Ineffectual. Yet Again, Arafat has Betrayed his People', *The Guardian*, 7 Nov.

Shain, Y. and Sussman, G. (1998) 'From Occupation to State-Building: Palestinian Political Society meets Palestinian Civil Society', *Government and Opposition*, 33, no. 3, pp. 275–306.

Shaw, M. (1993) 'Crying Peace Where There is None? the Functioning and Future of Local Peace Committees of the National Peace Accord', Centre for Policy Studies, Research Report no. 31, Aug. 1993. Cited by Dorita Field in *The South African Experience – Lessons for Northern Ireland.* Belfast: Irish Network for Non-violent Action Training and Education (INNATE).

Sisk, T. (1994) *Democratisation in South Africa: the Elusive Social Contract.* Princeton: Princeton University Press.

Skilbeck, M. (1973) *The Schools Cultural Studies Project: a Contribution to Peace.* Directors report. Coleraine: New University of Ulster.

Smith, A. and Robinson, A. (1996) *Education for Mutual Understanding: the Initial Statutory Years.* Coleraine: Centre for the Study of Conflict.

Smith, C.D. (1996) *Palestine and the Arab-Israeli Conflict.* New York: St. Martin's Press, 3rd edn.

Smooha, S. (1990) 'Minority Status in an Ethnic Democracy: the Status of the Arab Minority in Israel'. *Ethnic and Racial Studies*, vol. 13, no. 3: 389–413.

Smooha, S. (1992) *Arabs and Jews in Israel: Change and Continuity in Mutual Intolerance*, vol. 2. Oxford: Westview Press.

Smooha, S. (1994) 'Arab-Jewish Relations in Israel in the Peace Era', *Israel Affairs*, 1, no. 2, pp. 227–44.

Sparks, A. (1997) *Tomorrow is Another Country: the Inside Story of South Africa's Negotiated Revolution.* London: Arrow.

Spence, J.E. (ed.) (1994) *Change in South Africa.* London: Pinter Publishers.

St Martin's Anglican Church Bulletin (1997) 'A Parishioners Story on TRC'. Cape Town.

Taylor, R. and Habib, A. (1997) 'Projecting Peace in Apartheid South Africa'. Unpublished conference paper.

Taylor, R. (1999) 'Northern Ireland: Consociation or Social Transformation?', in J. McGarry (ed.), *Northern Ireland in Comparative Perspective*, forthcoming.

Thornberry, C. (1998) 'Picking up the Peaces', interview with Cedric Thornberry, Tip O'Neill Chair of Peace Studies, INCORE, *University of Ulster News*, no. 1, 1997/8.

The Times (1995) 'The Frameworks Document', 22 Feb.

Trew, K. (1989) 'Evaluating the Impact of Contact Schemes for Catholic and Protestant Children', in J. Harbison (ed.), *Growing Up in Northern Ireland*. Belfast: Stranmillis College.

Trimble, D. (1998) Speech by David Trimble MP, First Minister Designate of Northern Ireland to the Labour Party Conference, Blackpool on 30 Sept.

Twite, R. and Hermann, T. (1993) *The Arab-Israeli Negotiations: Political Positions and Conceptual Frameworks*. Tel Aviv: Papyrus Publishing House.

Usher, G. (1995) *Palestine in Crisis: the Struggle for Peace and Political Independence after Oslo*. London: Pluto Press.

Venter, L. (1997) *When Mandela Goes: the Coming of South Africa's Second Revolution*. Johannesburg: Doubleday Books.

Waldmeir, P. (1997) *Anatomy of a Miracle*. London: Penguin Books.

Welsh, D. (1994) 'Negotiating a Democratic Constitution', in Spence, J.E. (ed.), *Change in South Africa*. London: Pinter Publishers.

Whyte, J. (1983) 'How Much Discrimination Was There under the Unionist Regime 1921–68?', in T. Gallagher and J. O'Connell (eds), *Contemporary Irish Studies*. Manchester: Manchester University Press.

Williams, S. (1993) 'Building Peace Structures in South Africa', *Community Relations Journal*, no. 13, July, pp. 3–4.

Wilson, Robin (1998) 'Framing the Architecture', in *New Order? International Models of Peace and Reconciliation*. Belfast: Democratic Dialogue – Report no. 9.

Woollacott, M. (1998) 'The Agony of Doing a Deal', *The Guardian*, 24 Oct.

Worden, N. (1995) *The Making of Modern South Africa: Conquest, Segregation and Apartheid*. Oxford: Blackwell.

Index

Printed in the United Kingdom
by Lightning Source UK Ltd.
99303UKS00001B/15